COOKING WITH BAZ

SEAN DOOLEY

ALLEN&UNWIN

First published in 2009

Copyright © Sean Dooley 2009

Allen & Unwin
83 Alexander Street
Crows Nest NSW 2065
Australia
Phone: (61 2) 8425 0100
Fax: (61 2) 9906 2218
Email: info@allenandunwin.com
Web: www.allenandunwin.com

National Library of Australia
Cataloguing-in-Publication entry:
    Dooley, Sean, 1968–
    Cooking with Baz: how I got to know my father /
    Sean Dooley.
    ISBN: 978 1 74175 273 1 (pbk.)
    Dooley, Barry.
    Fathers and sons–Australia–Biography.
    Authors, Australian–Biography.
    Family–Australia.
    Parent and child–Australia.
    Cookery–Anecdotes.
    306.8742

Cover and text design by Sandy Cull, gogoGingko
Typesetting by Pauline Haas, Bluerinse Setting
Edited by Jo Jarrah
Printed and bound in Australia by Griffin Press

1 2 3 4 5 6 7 8 9 10

PRAISE FOR SEAN DOOLEY

If you write well, you really can write about anything. Never has
this truism been more effectively demonstrated than in this
delightfully quirky book … [Dooley] has turned a potentially
turgid subject into a sweet wonderland of human eccentricity.
Bruce Elder, *Sydney Morning Herald*

A funny man, and surprise, surprise, *The Big Twitch* is a
disarmingly entertaining book. An unexpected charmer.
Adelaide Advertiser

This is vivid and wickedly funny writing – an unabashed celebration
of life, of diversity, and of going all-out to realize a dream.
Good Reading Magazine

[Dooley is] engaging, funny and self-aware.
Stephen Moss, *The Guardian* (UK)

[Dooley] somehow manages to amuse and engage readers
who couldn't care less whether he does catch up with
a Buff-breasted Paradise Kingfisher.
Ian Warden, *Canberra Times*

[a] marvelously funny memoir will keep even the non-birding
reader in stitches. Prepare to laugh out loud.
Nancy Bent, *Booklist*

Sean's wry observations of everyday life provide an
entertaining distraction.
www.surfbirds.com

Sean has a lively imagination, an antipodean propensity to
exaggeration and a sense of the ridiculous clearly forged in the
twin fires of his youth where Monty Python vied for his
attention as often as Bill Oddie's *Little Black Book*.
www.fatbirder.com

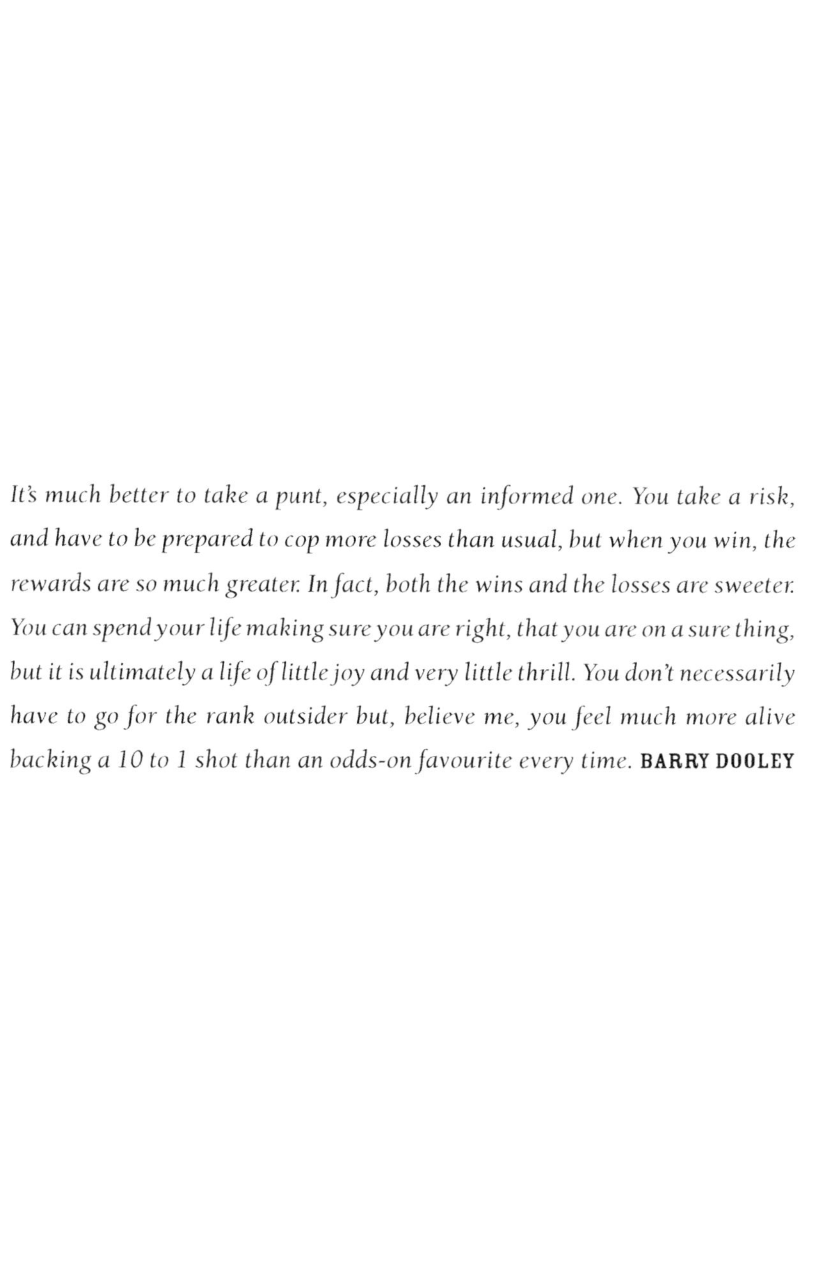

It's much better to take a punt, especially an informed one. You take a risk, and have to be prepared to cop more losses than usual, but when you win, the rewards are so much greater. In fact, both the wins and the losses are sweeter. You can spend your life making sure you are right, that you are on a sure thing, but it is ultimately a life of little joy and very little thrill. You don't necessarily have to go for the rank outsider but, believe me, you feel much more alive backing a 10 to 1 shot than an odds-on favourite every time. **BARRY DOOLEY**

CONTENTS

1

HI, DOCTOR NICK

I never thought I'd end up cooking with Baz.

It was never something that was particularly high on my agenda of things to do with my life. While I had enjoyed my father's cooking over the years, Baz and my culinary tastes had, like virtually everything in our lives, moved in different directions. He was a meat and three veg kind of bloke, particularly if you replaced one or two of the vegies with more meat. Me, well, I didn't know what kind of bloke I was; all I knew was that as I got older, a constant diet of steak and chips was not enough.

At one point in my late teens I had flirted with the notion of going vegetarian. While this phase didn't last too long, it was enough to set the plate tectonics of our relationship into a continent-size drift, particularly when one day I declared (parroting what a vegan friend had told me) that 'of all the dairy products, Dad, cheese is the biggest killer'. Baz looked at me as if I had blasphemed. He got angry on behalf of cheese and demanded to know what the hell I was on about. I didn't really know myself but stuck to my guns and gave a garbled response about high saturated fat content and cholesterol levels. As a recent survivor of bowel cancer brought on, no doubt, by a diet excessively high in animal fats and exceptionally low in fibre, I thought Baz might have been interested in such a titbit.

I was wrong. Baz's look of sheer incomprehension that his own son could believe such a thing about something as dependable and innocent as cheese said to me that my father and I were not only on a different page, we were following an entirely different cookbook. No, I never foresaw the possibility that Baz and I would ever cook together. Perhaps I could imagine stirring the gravy for him when I visited home for a roast dinner while he gave the spuds 'one last blast', and I might ask for his advice on when to turn the steak at a family barbecue, but I was sure that would be about it as far as it would go for Baz and me when it came to cooking together. But then, life is full of Vesta situations.

For those completely baffled by this last sentence, 'life is full of Vesta situations' is a line from a 1970s ad for a type of instant rice dinner. It involved boatloads of people unexpectedly dropping in on a couple in a remote lighthouse. As each visitor knocks on the door seeking shelter from the storm, the wife just smiles, pulls out a packet of Vesta and utters that memorable phrase. The woman who played the role of the philosophical housewife was the smoky-voiced comic Noelene Brown. I remember as an eight year old, thinking she was the most glamorous creature I had ever seen, and I would look forward with a salacious, yet non-sexual thrill to the moment at the end of *Blankety Blanks* when she would stage-kiss the host, Graham Kennedy. I am glad that it was a thrill of a pre-sexual kind, because it would be disturbing to me now to think that I got my rocks off watching a woman so heavily made up like a drag queen (as was the style of the time) pretending to pash a closeted gay man.

In her autobiography, Noelene comments that of all the advertising shoots she ever worked on, this was the only one where the crew didn't tuck into the food immediately after filming was over. As to the quality of the Vesta product, I can't comment. We never ate it in our house. My mother, Di, would resort to frozen hamburgers, fish fingers and packets of instant, self-saucing pasta, but somehow drew the line at Vesta. Yet, even though I never ate a Vesta dinner, the tag line from the ad will, on the odd occasion, still pop out of my mouth. I find it disturbing that the names of people I have just met slip from my grasp while slogans from TV commercials of the seventies and eighties will enter my head without any prompting. I tell you, ooh, it does get in; it really can change the colour of your day, so avagoodweekend Mr Walker ...

I put my tendency to retain TV trivia down to the fact that my seat at the family dining table was the only one that had a view of the telly in the adjacent room and I spent as much time paying attention to it as I did to the members of my family. How I came to occupy such a privileged position at the table I am not sure. Perhaps it was simply the honour of being the firstborn – where once a father would take the first son to the top of a hill and with a patriarchal sweep of the arm proclaim that 'all this land will be yours', today he gives the eldest kid control of the remote. Perhaps I had simply claimed it as *terra nullius* and my brother, who was still in the high chair, was too young to argue the toss. There never seemed to be any question of either of my parents staking their claim to it as Di was always up and down to the kitchen to either cook, dish out or clear up – a state of affairs I never paused to query – and my Dad ... well, it was an unusual event when Baz actually ate dinner with the rest of us. In those days I rarely even experienced *eating* with Baz, never mind cooking with him.

Not that my old man was some sort of corporate flyer who was always held up at the office. He was a bookie, who essentially only worked Saturdays. But until the mid eighties, when his bookmaking career finally took off, Baz worked a regular nine-to-five job. In the seventies it was for a shipping customs agent in Queen Street in Melbourne. It wasn't a badly paid job and there was never any need for Baz to put in overtime, so it meant that had he caught the first train home, Baz could have been sharing the evening meal with us every night at six. But as his regular after-work drink with the boys (which often started out as a quick one at lunchtime) would often extend late into the night, it meant that Baz would be rushing to catch the last train home. Sometimes he would manage to get on board but would fall asleep on the train and miss his station.

One night Baz woke up to find himself in a darkened carriage at Broadmeadows, on the other side of the city from where we lived at Seaford. He had slept through to the end of the line at Frankston, and kept on snoring away as the train made its way back to Melbourne and out the other side to Broady, where it was shunted for the night. Years later, when I had my first job writing for television, I penned a sketch where someone got drunk and fell asleep on the train and woke up in Perth. The sketch didn't make the cut and around this time it was suggested to me that I should base my comedy on believable situations sourced from real life. Clearly this sort of thing didn't happen to other people's fathers as often as it did to Baz and his mates.

Not that we felt terribly disadvantaged by any wayward behaviour on Baz's part; this is just what dads did as far as we knew. I'm sure Di wasn't overly impressed, however, having to scrape at least a couple of meals a week into the bin because by the time Baz got home they had dried out so much they were completely inedible. That must have been more than annoying. I do remember Mum letting Baz have it occasionally, but I don't have any lasting memory of this being an issue that caused any great tension in the house. But then, I was probably too busy watching TV to take much notice.

To be honest I don't really remember that many dinners specifically (though I can probably quote a line from almost every episode of *Get Smart* ever made), but there is one particular family meal that does stick in my mind. It was sometime in the seventies – 1975 or 1976 seems about right. I am certain, however, of the time: between 6 and 6.30 pm. I know this because I was sitting at the table eating dinner and *The Flintstones* was on. We always ate dinner when *The Flintstones* was on. I tried to make sure of it. I used to get hunger pains so bad leading up to tea time that if Mum didn't have dinner on the table by the time Fred bellowed that first 'Yabba dabba doo' I would be lying on the kitchen floor clutching my stomach, groaning and kicking the cupboards in protest. Strange behaviour really, considering I was normally a very easygoing sort of kid.

This particular night Baz was another no-show and his crumbed cutlets lay drying out on the stove. (We didn't get a microwave until the eighties so keeping a meal warm while avoiding total desiccation took all the ingenuity of the early pioneers.) Di was trying to force my brother to eat his peas. It was rare for us to have peas as Wok preferred beans. I liked peas, but as he was the fussy eater, he usually got his way. I guess when you have a child who would rather go hungry than take a mouthful of something they don't like, you serve up their favourite dishes as often as possible. Eldest child status only got you so far in my family, and I learned early that saying about the squeaky wheel getting the most oil. So we had beans instead of peas, mashed pumpkin instead of potato and crumbed cutlets, which I never really liked either, instead of good old chops.

That night the presence of peas on the plate was enough to negate Wok's pleasure at having crumbed cutlets and he was complaining, stomping and screaming as Di wrestled with him, trying to get him to eat at least one fork full of peas. My brother was not what you would call an easy child. He had been born with some kind of gastric reflux problem and had been brought into the world screaming in discomfort. His stomach problems soon settled down, but the screaming never did. Five years on he was still at it. These days he has two kids of his own and whenever they arc up he tells me with a smile, 'Now I'm getting a taste of what Mum and Dad had to put up with.'

I wasn't paying that much attention to proceedings as I was glued to the antics of Fred and Barney. From an early age I had learned to shut out most of Wok's tantrums whenever they didn't directly concern me. I think I did that with a lot of what went on in my family. I was probably a lot more fixated on my own interior world than I was with what was going on around me, but my family had a way of thrusting themselves into the deepest realms of my private universe.

I never saw the incident but I heard the yelp of pain. I looked across the table to see blood gushing out of Di's finger. Their tussle to get some peas into his mouth had escalated to the point where Wok had stabbed Di with his fork. Wok was temporarily rendered speechless as the reality of what had occurred hit him. Then all hell broke loose. Wok burst into tears about the same time Mum began crying in pain. Wok and I were bundled next door to our cousin's house (it must have been 1975 after all, as our cousins moved to North Queensland at the end of that year) while Mum drove herself to the doctor's to have her finger stitched.

Wok was inconsolable as the shame of what he had done filled him with remorse and mingled with the state of rage he had worked himself into over the injustice of having to eat peas, but I seem to remember he got out of it pretty much scot-free. Di had calmed down by the time she got back from the doctor's. Baz, when he got home (only about two hours late), hit the roof, but by then Wok had cried himself to sleep and Baz, who always had a soft spot for his youngest, calmed down and was snoring away in his armchair like Homer Simpson within minutes.

There was more than a touch of the Homers about Baz. And come to think of it, Di was a lot like Marge Simpson: she was tall, quiet, long suffering and accommodating to the point of sublimating some of her own dreams and personality for the sake of her family, all the while pouring out bucketloads of unconditional love which only too rarely got noticed. She didn't have the towering stack of blue hair though. Similarly, Baz wasn't a dumb slob like Homer, though as the years rolled on his physique and hair did start to resemble Homer's and they did share certain characteristics. While the rest of us were at church of a Sunday morning (Di was a Sunday School teacher, so Wok and I had no way out), Baz would be in his dressing gown (and/ or underwear) with his feet up watching *World of Sport* while knocking back a tinnie or three.

It wasn't just me projecting this image onto my old man. By the time *The Simpsons* had hit our screens I had moved out of home but on one occasion when I went back I brought a couple of mates from uni with me for a family birthday party. This was the first time I had mixed my two carefully separated worlds, so afterwards I was keen to know what my friends had thought of my family. One of them described a scene from *The Simpsons* where Homer tries to tell Bart about the facts of life. Homer, struggling for an apt metaphor to sum up women, hits upon the idea that they are a lot like beer. In the course of his explanation he starts drinking the beer and they cut to further down the track where a well-shickered Homer, with a sea of empties around him, is blathering on inanely to an incredibly bored Bart. 'That is you and your dad to a tee,' my friend said.

Until then I would have thought that my role in the family was nothing like Bart's – the bratty but good-hearted kid who always winds up in trouble; for that role, Wok definitely fitted the bill. I was more the Lisa Simpson, brainy do-gooder (and fun-stopper) type. But my friend had a point: Baz and I were totally different and when we did talk it was usually fairly one-way, particularly if he'd had a few. He'd be doing the talking and I'd be his reluctant audience, distracted by thoughts of how I could fake a seizure to get out of listening to the same stories over and over again.

No, Baz was a guy I never thought I would be cooking with. That's not the sort of thing we'd do. We had our own lives, different tastes and interests. Once in a blue moon I might have a drink with Baz, or go to the footy with him. But cooking? Nah, it was never going to happen.

Until one day in September 1999 I found myself sitting with Baz in the office of Dr Nick. The office was pretty much the same as that of every other doctor's I had ever been in. A central desk faced two navy blue chairs. They always seem to be blue – perhaps on graduation from medicine you get a complimentary set of surgical knives and a pair of reassuringly blue chairs. Sitting on the desk, among the patient files and pharmaceutical company notepads was the obligatory snapshot of the photogenic family – maybe all those toothy kids beaming in the photo come as part of a job lot with the chairs and the knives.

But somehow, Dr Nick's office seemed just that little bit more … well … tidy than any other doctor's office I knew. Like the man himself. Outwardly he was indistinguishable from any other specialist, but there was something particularly neat and fastidious about Dr Nick. Other doctors may have worn a similarly smart suit and tie, but you got the impression that Dr Nick would have taken that little extra time in the morning to make sure the knot in the tie was exactly proportioned and positioned, and that his crisp cuffs were protruding precisely the correct length beyond his jacket sleeves. This is by no means a complaint; these are actually traits that are welcome in a medical specialist. If you were going to have somebody fiddling about with your insides you'd prefer it to be Felix Unger rather than Oscar Madison.

Baz had actually met Oscar Madison (well, Jack Klugman, who had played him in the TV version of *The Odd Couple*), when he was out here one year for the Melbourne Cup and had placed a few bets with Baz. I think Jack's visit coincided with his appearance in a stage version of *The Odd Couple* that was touring Melbourne. Mum had bought Baz tickets and they were due to go along and see it with their best friends, my godparents, Ace and Chris.

This must have been around the time Mum was diagnosed with ovarian cancer and she was still in hospital on the scheduled night of the performance. As my Aunty Chris was down with a migraine, the theatre party ended up being Baz, Ace, Wok and me. What a night. This was in the mid eighties, when booze buses were a rarity and old habits died hard. At sixteen I was still too young to drive, so it was left to Ace to take the wheel because in comparison to Dad, Ace never appeared to get drunk. He had a remarkable capacity for handling alcohol and even though they seemed to down the same number of stubbies on the drive up and at the pub before the show, by the time we were rushing into the theatre with the late bells ringing, Ace seemed entirely sober while Baz was a staggering mess.

As we made our way up the steeply raked rows to our seats in the gods, Baz managed to lose his footing and lurched forward, only saved from toppling over the balcony by the audience member he had landed on. To make my absolute teenage mortification even deeper, Baz fell asleep within five minutes and let rip with a round of powerful snoring that really brought out the best in the acoustics of the old theatre. After one particularly voluminous snorter, Jack Klugman looked up from his onstage card game and, breaking character, glowered piercingly up at us. I don't know if he remembered Baz from his day at the races, but there was certainly no happy look of recognition on his face.

It may seem strange for someone of my generation to be referencing *The Odd Couple* but, as Baz and I sat across from Dr Nick, the theme song to that show thrust itself into my brain (actually it soon morphed into the *Get Smart* theme because I always get the two confused). Depending on Dr Nick's prognosis, my living arrangements could soon be entering distinctly *Odd Couple* territory.

I had been away on a three-month trip to Europe and had conned Baz into letting me store my stuff in Di's old painting studio. I'd only been home for about a week and my plan was to stay with Baz for just a short while until I found some new digs back in town. But while I had been away, Dad had been a bit crook. He didn't make much of it to me but his friends told me the complications from a simple haemorrhoid procedure had really knocked him low, and he never seemed to have regained the same spark. By the time I returned home he was complaining about a pain in his ribs. He said he was going to have it checked but was fairly pessimistic because Di had experienced a similar pain which turned out to be the first manifestation of the multiple myeloma that would eventually kill her. (She had made a complete recovery from the ovarian cancer and the myeloma was, we were told, totally unrelated.) I laughed and assured Dad he wouldn't have myeloma as it was such a rare disease, but he was convinced it wasn't good news. As it turned out, we were both right.

After a couple of consultations and x-rays, we found ourselves in the office of Dr Nick, the oncologist, waiting for his verdict on what was actually wrong. Whenever we were to see him in the future I always wanted to call out in Simpsons fashion, 'Hi, Doctor Nick!' but somehow he didn't seem the type that would chortle back: 'Hi, everybody!' While our Dr Nick couldn't have been more different in personality than the errant Dr Nick Riviera, he did share one thing in common with the cartoon doctor: an accent that you just couldn't place. He spoke in a rather refined way with every consonant articulated precisely, but not in the imperious manner that you sometimes get with medical people who like to give the impression that they do indeed know it all. His accent was an odd blend of Australian, English and sub-continental that had me creating a hypothetical background for him – bright young student in Sri Lanka who gets sent by rich parents or on a government scholarship to study medicine in England and then moves to Australia where he specialises in oncology and raising the smiley family that they gave him at graduation.

Any such flights of imaginary biography that were occurring during this first meeting were brought to a shattering halt by Dr Nick's simple statement: 'I am afraid I don't have good news, Barry.' He pointed to the dark spots spattered about an image of Baz's lungs. 'What we are seeing here is small cell carcinoma – a type of lung cancer.'

I looked at Baz, who was ashen but didn't seem particularly shocked. I was thinking, 'I wonder what Dad is thinking?' I was thinking, 'Not again.' I was thinking, 'God, that Dr. Nick's got incredibly tiny hands.' I was thinking all sorts of ridiculous and tumultuous thoughts at once and while I was desperately trying to take in every detail of what Dr Nick had to say, his words seemed to swirl around outside my head and it was an almost physical act to pluck them from the air and get them into my ears.

It was only when Baz finally spoke that I found I could focus. He asked whether this cancer could be related to the bowel cancer that he'd had (and beaten) in 1985.

'Oh no,' answered Dr Nick. 'This is completely unrelated. You were a smoker, yes?'

'Gave up seven years ago,' Baz replied, still managing to sound proud of the effort, in spite of Dr Nick's dismal news.

'It seems the damage had already been done. And I can assure you, Barry, that this type of cancer is most definitely caused by smoking. You'd have to be exceptionally unlucky to get this form of cancer if you were a non-smoker.'

The next half an hour or so was spent going through the generalities of the disease and what to expect. This must have been the fourth such conversation Baz would have endured in fifteen years – two for Di, two for him. It was the first time I had ever heard it from the horse's mouth, and what this well-groomed horse had to say was not hopeful. This was a particularly aggressive form of cancer that was normally not operable as it didn't tend to form big, discrete tumours that could easily be got at. Chemotherapy and even radiotherapy were treatment options, but Dr Nick was careful not to give out false hope as he reinforced that of those diagnosed with this cancer, only about five per cent were alive five years later.

This depressing statistic comes about both because of the aggressiveness of the cancer and because it is usually not detected until the more advanced stages. While it was extensive in Baz, Dr Nick had seen much worse that he had been able to treat with some success so he had already booked Baz in for chemo at the first opportunity – the following Friday. Without action, Dr Nick warned, Baz was very likely not to be alive in twelve months.

I couldn't believe how well Baz handled all this. It was more than stoic, for it wasn't like he was trying to hide any negative emotions with a show of strength; he was just taking it all in and seemingly rolling with it. I guess maybe he had already mentally prepared for it. But Baz's resilience was about to be put to the test.

'Any questions, Barry?' asked Dr Nick once he had mapped out the general battle plan for the next few months.

Baz thought for a while. 'You said I start chemo next Friday?'

'Yes, it is crucial that we get treatment underway as soon as possible. This is a very aggressive cancer,' Dr Nick reiterated.

Baz paused again. 'Can I still drink when I'm having the chemo?' I had never heard Baz ask anything so tentatively in my life.

Dr Nick was aghast at the thought, 'Oh no, Barry, you cannot drink, you are very sick.'

Baz tried another tack. 'So are you saying I can't have a drink at all?'

'Barry, drinking alcohol is the last thing someone in your situation should be doing.'

'Because of the chemo?' Baz asked again. For the first time that entire day, Dad seemed to be struggling to hold it together.

'Because you are very sick,' was Dr Nick's unwavering reply.

By now Baz was starting to look shattered. The day after Friday was Grand Final day. I knew how much he had been looking forward to the Grand Final day extravaganza at the local Sports Club where he was secretary. It was an extravaganza primarily of his own making and involved hiring a large screen TV, Baz cooking up a bit of tucker and running a book on the match. Mainly, though, it was all about drinking copious amounts of beer with his mates. It was the thought of losing this last aspect that was really distressing him. I decided, for Baz's morale, that the question needed more clarification.

'So when you say that Barry can't drink, are you saying that he can't because it will interfere with the efficacy of the chemo, that it might react badly with it? Or are you saying that drinking in general is just not a good idea for someone in Dad's position?'

Dr Nick looked uncomprehendingly back at us, trying to compute in that fastidious, efficient brain of his why we would be bothering with such a seemingly trivial question given the enormity of what he had just told us.

'But why would you want to, given how sick you are?'

Baz's shoulders ceased their droop and his eyes blazed, resurrected. 'So there's no medical reason? It's not going to affect the chemo if I have a couple of beers?'

'No, but it's not—'

Before he could finish, Baz was up shaking a bewildered Dr Nick's hand. Anyone who saw us leave the clinic that day would have thought that my father had just been given the reprieve of a lifetime. And I guess in his mind he had. Death was one thing, but the thought of not being able to have fun while still alive was clearly untenable.

We got into the car in silence. The whole death thing, I suppose. As I started up the engine, Baz turned to me and said, 'I'm glad you were there. I wouldn't have wanted to be there by myself.'

This was said and received awkwardly; although we had both been through a lot with Mum's death, neither of us was used to this sort of raw emotional honesty.

'I didn't really do much, Dad.'

'Bullshit. You got him to say I could drink on Grand Final day. I thought I was a goner.'

I started to reverse the car, more to avoid his gaze than because we needed to leave then and there. I could feel a tightness in my throat and my eyes were about to mist and I didn't want Baz to see it.

'Where to now?' I asked, looking in the rear view mirror. 'Home?'

Baz smiled slightly. 'Maybe we should stop via the club, just for one. Better tell the boys the bad news.'

2

CANCER WARD

The Sports Club was possibly the only sporting club in Australia where no sport ever actually took place. Certainly none of the members of the club had played in a sporting team in their lives. Well, not since their youth, which, judging by the size of their beer guts, was a very long time ago. Essentially it was a drinking club. At that, the boys were top of the rankings.

The club had its origins in the ashes of the old RSL club. Almost literally, for it did actually burn down, but by then it had already been abandoned, bankrupted in part through lack of members – old soldiers never die, they just get carted off to nursing homes and forgotten – but mainly because the treasurer had been embezzling the funds for years. He was caught with his hand in the till at one stage and was sent away on a bit of an enforced holiday at Her Majesty's pleasure. On being released, he came back to the RSL, tail between his legs. He was not only welcomed with open arms, but come the next AGM they voted him back into the vacant treasurer's position.

I asked Baz why on earth they would do that and he explained: 'Well, we knew he had ripped us off, but it was only a couple of grand. If we got in some other bloke that we didn't know, who knows, he might have ripped us off big time.'

The club folded soon afterwards. Baz was shattered. He loved the RSL, but not so much for the chance to get together with old comrades to remember those who had fallen in battle, because Baz never fought in a war. Unlike his father George, three of his brothers and a sister, Baz was too young to serve in World War II, and Korea finished the year before he was eligible to enlist. By the time the dreaded conscription ballots were being drawn for a tour of Vietnam, Baz was too old. His only military experience had been a stint as a national service conscript when he was eighteen. Baz was in the 'Nashos' for all of five minutes but the way he told it, he had a military career to rival General Blamey's. The truth is, he spent more time AWOL at the Seymour pub than he did attending to his duties as a gunner in the artillery, but Baz was adamant about his record – 'Nobody invaded the country on my watch!'

This stint at playing soldiers was sufficient for Baz to join every RSL club in the district. He joined as much for their traditions and mateship as for the good, cheap and readily available beer. With his local RSL closed, Baz had to drive all the way to Chelsea, a good five minutes away, if he wanted a cheap frosty one. Fortunately, around the same time the local footy club folded for want of senior players. A few junior football and cricket teams still operated out of the old footy clubrooms, but they only used the changing sheds, so Baz and his mates moved in and took over the club, reinvigorating it as an outer suburban gentlemen's drinking club.

Although he was one of the founding members of the Sports Club and had been instrumental in setting it up, it was only since Di's death that he had really put a lot of himself into the place. Never much of a joiner, through the Sports Club Baz had almost become a pillar of the community. He was always full of plans for refurbishment and extensions, and had even donated one of Di's paintings (a particular favourite of his of boats moored in a local harbour) which hung proudly above the bar. Baz had the painting covered in glass so that it wouldn't be damaged by the tobacco bushfire that raged every night in the mouths of most club members. Baz, a champion smoker for 45 years, had given up but for all the passive smoking he did every night, he may as well have kept on sucking down those cancer sticks. New extractor fans had been next on his agenda of improvements to the rooms.

The Sports Club wasn't much to look at – just a square besser block building with a flat roof and floor-to-ceiling windows on either side facing out onto the two ovals – but it had quite a cosy feel to it, particularly after Baz had got the new bar put in. There was a pool table, a parquetry dance floor in one corner should anyone decide to have a do there, and a few high, round tables, just at the right height to put your pot down and pick up the form guide whether you were sitting at one of the stools or standing. There were pubs aplenty in the district but for the members of the Sports Club, this place was theirs. And up to that point I would have said they were welcome to it. It drove me nuts having to spend more than a couple of minutes at the club. To have to hang around watching Baz and his mates get progressively drunk and boisterous was my idea of hell.

One of the most enduring myths of Australian culture is the friendliness of our pubs. It is a myth based on a certain truth, for I saw the spontaneous camaraderie Baz would engender whenever he entered a bar. As a kid, Baz dragged me into almost every pub across Victoria and as I crunched on the ice cubes in my raspberry lemonade I would look on in wonder at how many friends my dad seemed to have. He was in his element among the smoke-filled, beer-stained roar of all these men and whether he knew the blokes or not, they would soon all be laughing and joking along with Baz. But it was an intimidating kind of friendliness, one in which being loud was respected, so long as you weren't too much of a big-noter or a blowhard. My natural tendencies aren't as overtly outgoing as my father's. Some rise to the guttural roar of a bunch of blokes on the drink, but my automatic inclination is to find a quiet corner to retire to. And because I had always been with Baz, I'd never noticed that there is nothing more uncomfortable than walking into an Aussie pub where you don't know anybody. His gregariousness shielded any timidity on my part so I had always unquestioningly swallowed the notion of the friendliness of the Aussie pub.

Then I tried walking into my first bar by myself. I chose a particularly inauspicious time and place to do so – the public bar of the Cann River Hotel, one New Year's Eve right in the middle of a major confrontation between conservationists and loggers over the fate of the old-growth forests of East Gippsland. I was seventeen and had been driving through the area on a birdwatching trip (for, yes, I was a genuine birdwatcher – of the feathered kind, as I would constantly have to remind Baz when he'd snigger that he was a 'birdwatcher' himself). I was with a birding mate called Groober who was a few years older than me and had his own car. It wasn't a good car by any means, and just outside Cann River its engine seized. We were stuck for the night. We knew of a birdwatching camp that was being held on a property a few miles out of town, so while Groober dealt with the local mechanic it was decided that I would go to the pub and buy some supplies for that night's festivities. (We discovered to our horror that the festivities of the largely retirement-age birdwatching crowd included a ukulele demonstration and a few tunes on the gum leaf and then they all went to bed by nine. On New Year's Eve!)

I was fairly nervous, as this was the first time I had ever attempted to buy alcohol underage but my fear was compounded when I swung open the saloon doors – yes, they were just like the swinging doors you'd see in a typical Western, and the characters hard at it at the bar wouldn't have been out of place in a John Wayne film: loggers, log truck drivers, sawmillers and unemployed rednecks, all dressed in lumber jackets, impossibly tight Yakka work shorts and muddy Blundstone boots. Hillbilly beards were in, possessing your own teeth was not. The entire bar fell silent on my entry as all the drinkers turned suspiciously towards the newcomer. In my memory I swear the music even stopped so that all I could hear were my footsteps as I approached the bar.

'And whadda you want?' the barman spat at me.

Above his head was a large sign that read 'Fertilize the Bush – Doze in a Greenie'. I was dressed in a flannelette shirt and army trousers – exactly like the Greenie protestors they'd been battling the previous year.

I mustered up all the courage I had and, as casually as I could, said, 'A bottle of Bundy and two bottles of Coke thanks.'

At this precise moment my voice decided to break into a pubescent waver so that the word 'Bundy' was about an octave higher than the rest of the sentence. I thought I was a goner. In the eternity it took for the barman to grunt in reply, all I could think was that he was going to turn me away for being underage and all the hillbillies would laugh at the stupid, underage Greenie. Then they would beat me to death. But I guess in those parts seventeen was almost old enough to be a grandfather so he turned to the bottle shop out the back to get my bottle of rum.

The entire bar remained silent, staring at me malevolently. Suddenly Baz flashed into my mind. I could do this. I'd been with Baz in dozens of pubs like this before and he had charmed in every single one of them. So I looked around with an easygoing smile at the shaven-headed man with the long beard, bluey singlet and tatts sitting next to me at the bar and nodded:

'How's it goin', mate?' Just like Baz would have done.

The burly bloke folded his arms and said not a word. I would have settled for a 'fuck off', which would have been more convivial than the icy stare-down I was being subjected to. Thankfully the barman arrived with my booze and I got the hell out of there.

Ever since I have struggled to connect with blokes in pubs, despite years spent literally sitting at the feet of the master. I am just clearly not one of them. I never seem to get the Crocodile Dundee type extending a friendly hand, offering to buy me a drink – just the occasional hostile glance my way. I definitely get the sense that I've encroached on somebody else's sacred territory. It takes a hell of a lot before the sullen veneer of the regulars can be broken. They may indeed be the greatest bunch of characters in the world, but unless your family has lived in the district for more than two generations, you'd never know it.

At the Sports Club I had a bit more of an in than the usual outsider as I was Baz's kid, but after the initial period of grace there were more than a few awkward silences where, even with Baz present, we struggled to find much mutual ground. Even though I had sprung from this milieu I had, since my early teens, been moving steadily towards the sorts of circles where you could actually say a word like 'milieu' and not be considered a wanker. The one thing I had learned along the way – from Baz as much as anything – was that if I was to have any sort of relationship with guys like these, I had to meet them on their turf because it was a bloody long haul to get them onto mine.

The trouble was I only had a low threshold for the sort of

stuff Dad's mates were into. I could talk footy and cricket and racing for a while, but even on such safe ground the tenor of much of the conversation soon became tedious. ('Hey, Seany, out of Wayne Carey or James Hird, who do you reckon is the biggest shirt-lifter?') And then there were times when I was simply stumped for words, like when one of the blokes brought in his eldest son on his eighteenth birthday to have his first 'legal' drink. His old man proclaimed to the bar that there was double reason to celebrate, because for a birthday present he had just taken his son down to 'Irene's', the local brothel, to make a real man of him. The boy just sat there with a goofy grin, sheepish but proud of having his old man pay for him to get laid. I wasn't rushing to join the queue to shake his hand. After all, I knew where it had been.

Whenever I was visiting Baz I would do everything possible not to accompany him to the club. Usually I would just drop him off out the front, or maybe come in for a quick one so as not to be seen as stuck up, and then I would get the hell out of there before I became embroiled in one of Baz's interminable beer-soaked conversations with his mates. But that night, after we had left Dr Nick's office, I could hardly say no to Baz's request that we stop and have a drink. Baz had also suggested that we might as well eat well that night too, to 'celebrate' the diagnosis.

We dropped in on one of the local butchers, Reg. For his more discerning customers, Reg would hang an extra side of beef out the back for much longer than usual so that the steaks from it would be extra tender. Baz was the number one ticket holder. As he emerged from Reg's with two of the biggest pieces of porterhouse imaginable, Baz was like a hippie who'd found his housemates' dope stash. He unwrapped the thick slabs of bloodied meat and held them to the light to show me the quality, intoning what a great feed we'd have that night. His delight was such that you'd never have picked him for a man who'd just been told his days were numbered.

Baz looked across at me as he wrapped the steak back in its paper and commented, as he always did at such times, 'You wouldn't be dead for quids, Rupe. You wouldn't be dead for quids.'

Baz had nicknamed me Rupe when I was a toddler learning to walk. My staggering around, bumping into furniture, reminded Baz of an intellectually handicapped bloke he worked with called Rupert, whom they had christened 'Rupert the Rat'. Baz had left that job fifteen years ago and wouldn't have kept in contact with Rupert or any of the other blokes, but the name stuck, albeit shortened to Rupe. Even Baz's nicknames developed nicknames.

When we arrived at the club it was still early and aside from the barmaid, Dee, we were the only ones there. I had known Dee since primary school (in fact she was my first kiss) and when Baz told her the news her eyes filled with tears. A lot of tears would be wiped away that night, but not from the first of Baz's mates to arrive. To be honest, I failed to have the same affection for Donny that the old man still had even though Donny had nearly buggered up the building of Baz and Di's dream home. Donny was in the building trade and Baz had subcontracted him and another mate, Daggs, to build their new house on the waterfront at Patterson Lakes. Both of them were pretty good on the drink, and with Baz as their foreman, they would have cracked open their first stubby of the day by seven o'clock. In the morning. Did this affect the quality of the construction? Well, the house itself turned out fine, save for my brother's bedroom, which was so small that once his bed was in place there was no room left for my brother, let alone any other furniture. The day they came to lay the slab, Donny was too pissed to read the measurements properly and as they were pouring it the council inspector came by and pointed out that the house would be too close to the road. As the pour was half done, it was too late to start again. Donny's solution was to cut in half the length of my brother's room, so they all agreed and continued the pour as they knocked back another beer. As a consequence Wok spent his late teenage years living in a cell of Guantanamo proportions.

As soon as Donny had got his first beer from Dee he pulled up a chair at the table Baz and I were sitting at and asked, 'So, Baz, what's up?'

There was nothing prescient in this, it was how Donny greeted everyone. Baz told him his news. Donny drew back on his cigarette, thought for a while and said, 'Still, you can't help bad luck.'

'No, I suppose not,' replied a resigned Baz.

'Lung cancer, hey? I bet they're blaming the fags,' Donny said conspiratorially.

Before Baz had a chance to answer properly, Donny was off and racing: 'Yeah, they always try and say that, but it's just bullshit, you know, Baz.' And for the next ten minutes Donny launched into a tirade against the fun-stopping 'health' industry who were just trying to keep themselves in a job (as opposed to those noble, altruistic souls in the tobacco industry) to the detriment of the ordinary Aussie bloke who liked the simple, innocent pleasures of life. According to Donny the fact that his uncle who smoked a pack a day had lived to 90 counted more than every single actual medical study that proved smoking kills.

I couldn't believe it. Here in one of the darkest moments of my father's life, one of the moments when he would most need the support and understanding of those who professed to care for him, was his so-called mate spouting off his own ill-considered opinion as Baz sat there ever more grim-faced. His 'mate' was staring death in the face and all Donny could do was bang on about how unfair it was that he couldn't light up in a cinema anymore. The broken capillaries on Donny's nose and cheeks became even more pronounced as his bloated face flushed deeper red while he worked himself up into a frenzy. Ash spilled into my dad's beer as Donny jabbed his nicotine-stained fingers in Baz's direction to emphasise another spurious point.

I'd had enough. Trying to sound jokey like the rest of the blokes did, I said to him as I walked off, 'You're an idiot, Donny.' It didn't work because (a) I never spent enough time at the club to be considered one of the blokes and (b) there was too much hurt in my voice.

Donny ignored me anyway and continued on: '... and what about all the people who die of lung cancer who never smoked? What about them, Baz? Nah, they never talk about them, do they?'

I walked out the main door into the spring twilight and stood overlooking the oval. This used to be Carrum Footy Club's main ground. They wore the same colours as Fitzroy and both folded at roughly the same time – the Fitzroy Lions due to the indifference of an ever-expanding football league, the Carrum Lions due to the fact that the notion of Carrum as an individual village, an entity to be represented and fought for, had diminished as it got swallowed by the indifference of an ever-expanding suburbia so that Carrum now felt like pretty much any other suburb. The goalposts on the oval remained up because the juniors still played on a Sunday. In the half-light a couple of kids were wrestling the ball away from their dad in the goal square. Seemingly oblivious nearby was a magpie, one eye cocked towards the ground in search of worms to take back to its begging young. A middle-aged woman in a white parka walked along with an untethered lead and a plastic bag, waiting for her poodle to stop sniffing the base of the pine trees and get down to business.

All was tranquil. I tried to soak up the silence outside but was distracted by the growing growl of men filling the club for their Friday beer and bullshit session. All the regulars had rolled in – Dave the Pom, Big Terry, Stinky – but it was still Donny that was holding sway, still haranguing a hapless Baz. On any other night, Baz too would have told Donny he was an idiot, but this night he was understandably a little more reflective and, like a dingo sensing a sick lamb, Donny was in for the kill.

About a year later, Donny would die of a massive heart attack. His family was very touched that I showed up to the funeral. He had been a mate of Baz's, after all, but I couldn't help thinking as I looked at the coffin, 'Yeah, and smoking doesn't cause heart disease either, you stupid bastard.'

I turned away from the clubhouse and looked up at the first stars of the evening. Even though this was the suburbs, it was remarkable how many stars were visible compared to the inner city where I would, in normal circumstances, usually have been. But these were not normal circumstances. In fact we hadn't had normality in our family for quite a few years. Not since that horrible day late in 1993 when Di was taken to the old Peter MacCallum Cancer Hospital in Melbourne.

Peter Mac was in the process of relocating to shiny new premises on the other side of the city, and all was in utter chaos – skeletal cancer patients with translucent white skin and big, frightened eyes lay on gurneys in dilapidated corridors whose wall panels were ripped open, exposing the electrical wiring as workmen in dustcoats bustled past removing medical machinery and office furniture. It was like a scene from the fall of Stalingrad, or one from Alexander Solzhenitsyn's *Cancer Ward*, which I had read almost ten years earlier, around the time Di had her first bout of cancer. Even though, at sixteen, I was sophisticated enough (well, just) to recognise the book was a metaphor for the wider malaise of the Soviet system, the stark physical descriptions of the crumbling ward left a deep-seated impression on me, and suddenly I seemed to be right in the middle of it. I was completely overwhelmed and if it hadn't been for the fact that Mum looked the most frail and frightened of all the patients as she stared up at us, desperate for reassurance, I would have run screaming from the building.

Over the next four years there were to be more harrowing times, as well as some triumphant and joyful ones, but for full impact, that first day in the Cancer Ward was unparalleled. It all came with such a tumultuous whack. We knew Mum seemed a little unwell: she had been losing weight for much of the year and had been struggling for some time with a pain in her ribs that didn't seem to respond to any treatment. Without any of us being too conscious of it, Di just seemed to be getting weaker and weaker. Around this time, whenever I came home to stay the night and was sitting up watching telly, Di would come bursting out of her bedroom in a half-awake state of distress. She was having a recurring nightmarish feeling of being trapped. Perhaps it was her subconscious flagging the spread of the cancer through her unsuspecting body. Once she was diagnosed, those night terrors stopped. She had a real, palpable terror to deal with.

It all came to a literal breaking point one day when she was hanging out the washing. The washing basket began to slip and as she reached to halt it, her arm twisted and her humerus, the main bone of the upper arm, snapped. After she had been rushed to hospital and the arm treated, the doctors had ordered some tests to be done. They thought she must have had something like osteoporosis as bones don't just cave in like that. I remember cradling a distressed Di that night and I couldn't believe how fragile she seemed. For her generation, Di was a rather tall woman but in my arms she felt like a child. It had to be something more than osteo.

So when she and Baz gathered my brother and me around the kitchen table after they came back from the specialist, I was not entirely shocked to find out it was a form of cancer: multiple myeloma, which I had never heard of before. They explained that it was sort of related to leukaemia — a type of blood cancer that affected the white blood cells but manifested itself by eating away at the bones, hence the broken arm. Her ribs had similarly almost been eaten away.

On hearing the news, Wok burst into tears. Baz got up and awkwardly tried to comfort him, almost with a punch as much as a hug. Me, trying to be the logical strong one, desperately trying to stop the waver in my voice, pronounced, 'You beat ovarian cancer, you'll be able to beat this too.'

Mum went on to explain that myeloma was incurable. At fifty she was already too old to try a bone marrow transplant, the most effective known treatment, but even that was not a cure. The positive was that, unlike most other cancers, myeloma does not spread to the rest of the body. As long as they could control the levels of it in her blood, she could live a fairly normal life. It would get her in the end because eventually it would place too big a strain on her organs, but if the treatment went well, that could be as much as ten years away. She lasted four.

It had been less than two years since we'd buried her, and now, here we were, facing it all again. As the sky around me darkened at the Sports Club, the dog walker and the footy kids wandered home, and the magpie settled on its nest atop the pine tree. I pulled my shirt collar up to keep out the creeping cold of the evening. Strands of thought were flashing through my mind like the beams of light in a spectrum as they come out of a glass prism. But no matter how much those separate strands kept permutating, they would all eventually recombine and coagulate into that one bright, white, luminescent, overwhelming fact: cancer. For the fourth time in fifteen years our family was haunted by this spectre. I was just on the verge of starting to feel sorry for myself, of heading down the 'Why us?' path, when there was a roar from inside the club.

I turned around and through the windows I could see Baz holding court with a gathering of some of his mates. He had one arm around Donny while the other was describing the arc of some tall story or another. Everyone was in fits of laughter. I'd put the word out to some of Dad's other mates and a bunch of them had just arrived, hence the uproar. Ace, Baz's oldest mate whom he'd met at school and then been through Nashos with, was there, as was my Uncle Tarz (the husband of Dad's sister Jan), Fatty, the Spaniard and a bunch of other blokes. (To be a member of Baz's gang required only two things: you had to like beer, and you had to have an unusual nickname.) Baz was crowing and strutting and holding court, as usual. I rolled my eyes but couldn't help smiling. It was going to be a long night.

3

HOW TO COOK A STEAK

They say that what doesn't kill you only makes you stronger. We were to hear that a lot in the coming months, along with such classics as 'Oh well, it will all work out for the best,' or 'Everything happens for a reason.' While always well intentioned, platitudes like this are pretty meaningless when you think about it, especially when offered to somebody who has been diagnosed with something that is likely to kill them. They are appreciated, though, because you know the person coming out with them is fumbling for some way to show their support. They're the sorts of things you say when 'Sorry to hear you're dying' seems somehow inappropriate.

We were only into our second or third beer at the club before a mate of Baz's dropped one of those very platitudes. I'd come back in from outside and responded quietly in Dad's ear, 'More like, what doesn't kill you only leaves you horribly scarred and wounded.' Baz cracked up just as he was taking a sip and ended up snorting his beer over the well-wisher as bubbles of froth erupted from his nose.

I always liked it when I could make my dad laugh. Perhaps that was where my desire to write comedy came from initially, that desire to get the approval of a father I didn't have all that much in common with. I never really cracked him very often, which was a pity, because one of the few things he had definitely passed on to me was a love of comedy. While I had inherited his love of sport, our watching of it had always taken on a different hue so that we would often be viewing the same game through our own prisms, supporting our own teams or favourite players, analysing the action according to our own prejudices. Baz loved the flashy, spectacular players – his favourite footballer was prolific goal sneak Kevin 'Hungry' Bartlett, his favourite cricketer, Dennis Lillee. And while it was impossible for an Aussie kid in that era not to love Dennis Lillee, I always had a soft spot for leg spinner Jim Higgs, one of the lesser lights of the Chappell era of Australian cricket. The fact that he batted about as well as a frog could operate a chainsaw only made him even more appealing.

In fact it was sport that provided the impetus for the first great schism between Baz and me. From birth it was deemed that in the time honoured tradition of nearly all Melbourne families, the first son should support the same football club as the father. Baz barracked for Richmond so I was duly inducted into the Tigers clan. I was even given a Richmond footy jumper for my first birthday, an occasion noted approvingly in my baby book by Di even though she barracked for Fitzroy. (She was to have first dibs on Wok's allegiance when he was born.)

This arrangement worked well for the first four years of my life and I happily wore the yellow and black jumper with the number of Royce Hart on the back. Then one lazy Sunday afternoon at the beginning of the 1973 footy season a kid I had never seen before rode like an emissary of the devil on the footpath outside our house. I was sitting innocently in the pebble driveway on my bike, trying to get the hang of the training wheels. He was a 'big kid', all of eight or nine. He slithered up to me with a smile, holding a fistful of stickers.

'Hey, kid, what team do you go for?' asked the junior salesman.

'Tigers,' I replied proudly, and just a little scoffingly – as if anyone wouldn't barrack for the Mighty Tiges.

The pint-sized Willy Loman then produced a Richmond Football Club sticker and told me it could be mine for twenty cents. I rushed inside and begged Baz, who had his feet up watching the woodchopping on *World of Sport*, for the money. He happily obliged and I raced out and purchased the sticker and lovingly stuck it onto the crossbar of my bike. The older kid rode off happy and so was I ... for a while.

But as I sat on my bike in the driveway staring down at my new purchase, a growing horror came upon me. I was still too young to read but I could decipher a picture, and the motif that I gazed down upon looked for all the world not like a tiger, but a magpie. Apart from a love of the Tigers, Baz had instilled in me a visceral loathing of the Collingwood Football Club, whose emblem was a magpie. I was sporting the livery of the hated enemy. My beloved bike was branded with the mark of the beast.

This was not good. I fought back the rising panic and assessed my situation. After ten minutes of staring at the accursed design, I finally came to my painful decision. I marched into the lounge again to inform Baz.

'Dad, I don't barrack for the Tigers anymore, I barrack for the Magpies.'

Baz exploded off the couch like a character in a Warner Brothers cartoon, and demanded to know why, for Godsakes, why I would want to barrack for that pack of imbeciles. I told him that now I had a sticker of a magpie on my bike I had no choice. He dragged me by the scruff of the neck out to the bike and pointed at the tiger design.

'Look there's its tiger ears and there's its tiger eyes and there's its tiger bloody teeth!'

I couldn't be convinced and pointed out what I thought was the magpie's beak and eye. In fact, to this day, in my mind the sticker was black and white, not yellow and black. Despite Baz's protestations at my heresy, I would not budge. He offered to take the sticker off and buy me a new, bigger and bolder tiger sticker. I was resolute. Fate had dictated my destiny and that was to be a Magpie supporter. Oh cruel fate. Richmond was to go on to win the next two premierships and collected another in 1980 when they trounced Collingwood by a record margin. By this stage Baz had accepted my decision and took great delight in tormenting me over each of the fourteen goals the Tigers won by that day. It was probably unnecessary and ungracious on his part but I guess he was still hurting – though I suspect the real issue for Baz was not so much my betrayal but that I'd done so on such a nutty pretext. Me running around with an ice-cream container on my head for a year could have been dismissed as one of the quirks of a two year old; this, however, was concrete proof that his kid was truly weird and there was destined to be a distance between us.

But comedy was something we could always share and some of my fondest memories of feeling close to Dad as a child were when he would let us stay up to watch some seventies comedy masterpiece such as Paul Hogan or Benny Hill. Both are shows that I would prefer not to see again as I'm sure my tastes have evolved since then, and it would ruin the warm memories of sitting next to Baz long after I should have been in bed, cracking up as he cracked up at Hoges dressed as stuntman Leo Wanker copping a feel of Delvene Delaney, or Benny Hill 'accidentally' covering up the 'w' and 'o' on the women's toilets sign.

I can remember the first time I ever made Baz laugh with one of my own jokes. I was eleven and for Christmas Mum and Dad had given me a book by Bill Wannan on Australian bush customs and yarns. I looked up from reading a story about swagmen and asked, 'Dad, what does humping your bluey mean?' He explained that it meant carrying your swag, being out on the road. I then tried to deliver in as innocent a manner as possible, 'I thought it might have meant having intercourse with a red-headed lady.'

There was a long pause and then a huge splutter of incredulous laughter, almost identical to that of the beer-snorting incident in the club many years later. I still don't know whether the incredulity came about because he thought the joke was funny, or because of the fact that I was too embarrassed to use any other word but 'intercourse' in front of my dad, or because the joke had come out of the mouth of his bookish kid. But I remember being extremely surprised and just a little bit chuffed that I had made him laugh so hard.

What doesn't kill you . . . It was good to hear Baz laugh that night at the club. Along with 'You wouldn't be dead for quids', another of Baz's favourite sayings was 'We're here for a good time, not for a long time' and in this my father certainly followed through, even after the gloom of Dr Nick's prognosis. Baz had a reputation for sucking the marrow out of life, and revelled in the role of being the life of the party.

And very occasionally the death of the party. Literally. An old mate of his from Albury, Noofa Murphy, had been doing poorly. Baz made a trip up there to cheer him up. For the first time in weeks Noofa was out of bed, having a few beers, laughing and joking along with Baz. Noofa dropped off the twig the next day. Just to prove this was no isolated incident, a few years later when Baz and Di were driving around Australia they called in on our cousins in Townsville, the same cousins who had lived next door to us when I was a child. My 'Uncle' Fran had really been off his form with a chest infection. He and Baz sat up half the night drinking whiskey and swapping yarns. At one stage he had Fran up and singing songs from his shearing days. My Aunty Kay said that she hadn't seen Fran laugh so much in years. He went into hospital the next day and never came out.

When I heard, I accused Baz of being the kiss of death.

'At least they went out with a smile on their faces,' Baz replied with a smile of his own.

'Yeah, just don't turn up at my place if I'm crook, all right?' I fired back.

'Don't have to worry about that if you keep stocking that fancy foreign beer in your fridge,' Baz responded. Snap!

I often wondered who would be around to see Baz off when he teetered. It would have to be a committee of heavy hitting drinkers, I surmised – perhaps the blokes who turned up at the club the night Baz got his bad news. Drinking partners from the previous five decades, they all gathered together in what was essentially a wake-like atmosphere, but one with the guest of honour still alive and kicking. It looked like it could go on all night. For once this was a prospect that didn't bother me.

But then, much to my surprise, Baz took me aside and said quietly, 'How 'bout we head home and cook up those steaks, hey, Rupe?'

I think the adrenaline had drained from Dad's body after the first few drinks and by the time I got him home he seemed uncharacteristically tired. It may have been that those little black shadows Dr Nick had shown us on the x-ray were already taking their toll on Baz's fitness, but I suspect that he was as emotionally exhausted as he was physically.

I offered to cook the steaks and he willingly accepted. He got us a stubbie each from the beer fridge and pulled up a stool at the kitchen bench with a clear view of the stove-top, just so he could keep an eye on things. I protested that I knew how to cook a steak. He countered that these weren't just any steaks, but from Reg's special stash and as such deserved not to be messed up by some mug. Gee, thanks Dad.

Baz made sure I had the oil in the pan steaming hot, almost to the point of smoking. The only seasoning he would allow was a sprinkling of salt and pepper; anything more would have adulterated the pure flavour of the meat. The steaks were about an inch thick and after slapping them down on the pan, Baz only let me turn them once. He told me how much give they would have in them to ensure they were still rare enough on the inside. If there was one thing Baz couldn't tolerate, it was an overcooked steak. He didn't bag Di too often, even less so after she died, but on this occasion he bemoaned how, like many women, she was squeamish about having a bit of blood running through the steak and would insist on it being well-done.

'May as well have given her some cheap rubbish from the supermarket if she was going to cook the bejesus out of it,' he complained. 'When it came to steak, your mum was a fair dinkum Afghan.' This was one of Baz's regularly used sayings that had some derogatory element to them. It came from the racist view that the Afghan camel drivers who plied the hot and dusty routes servicing the Overland Telegraph line in the nineteenth century were a bunch of filthy heathens. Baz never actually had anything directly against the Afghani people (he'd never even met one) but it was a word he liked to invoke because the sound of it seemed so apt for the circumstances – the same way he would yell 'poofter' when he cut his finger or banged his shin on a tow bar. Though Baz was homophobic to a degree, he didn't say poofter to put down gays, it just sounded like such a good word at those times. And if you say it out loud in the privacy of your own company, it does sound like an expletive should – a soft sound building up to a sharp release on the 'ter'. The trouble for me was, I didn't consider myself homophobic but after spending a few days in Baz's company I would get into the habit of dropping it in moments of frustration: an utterance that didn't go down well when I was back in the city hanging out among people who might easily take offence.

When the steaks were ready I insisted that we let them rest. Baz said he didn't usually bother with this step as he was too impatient to get stuck in but he seemed impressed at my knowledge of how to handle a good piece of meat. We held out for barely a minute before we tucked into them. Baz allowed me to put on some form of mustard, but that was it. No other accompaniments. No greens. No spuds. Nothing to distract from the sanctity of the porterhouse.

And I had to admit it was indeed delicious, quite possibly the best steak I had ever eaten. Maybe it tasted better because of the emotion wrought by the day's events. For whatever reason, it was bloody good. My first meal cooking with Baz.

As we sat there eating the last of our naked slabs of seared meat, Baz said to me, 'Don't make a bad team in the kitchen, hey, Rupe?'

'I guess not.'

He paused while he removed a piece of fat from his mouth, then paused again and asked, 'What are your plans, Rupe? I suppose you'll be wanting to move out soon.'

'What do you mean? I'm going to stay here and look after you, of course. Just until you get better.'

Baz gave a half-smile, whether at my offer to stay or about the prospect of him getting better I'm not sure.

'I'll be right,' he said. 'I know you were looking to move back up to town. I don't want you to put your life on hold because of this bastard of a thing. If things get crook I can always get Aunty Joyce or Jannie to stay with me for a while,' he went on, referring to his two sisters who both lived in nearby Chelsea. Too far to go to the RSL, but close enough to come minister to the sick, apparently.

I could feel the same lump in the back of my throat that I had felt in the car after we left Dr Nick's office threatening to force its way into my mouth again, so I answered as quickly as I could before it choked me up: 'You looked after Mum when she was sick. So now I'm going to look after you, whether you like it or not.'

I think Baz was slightly taken aback at my vehemence but after a moment he broke into a smile and his great, thick, freckled Irish hand reached across and grabbed my finer, olive-skinned one.

'Thanks, Rupe. It won't be for long. Who knows, we might even just beat it.'

I was trying to think of something witty and flippant to say. I couldn't. But nothing would have got past that thickset lump and into my mouth anyway. Thankfully Baz broke the silence: 'So you better make yourself useful then, and grab us another stubbie.'

As I went to the bar fridge I wondered what the hell I had just agreed to. This was not what I had figured in my plans for the future. I'd seen Baz turn himself inside out looking after Di, and he deserved every bit as much love and care for himself, but would I be any good at looking after a dying man? Would I be able to stand spending so much time with him? I loved him but aside from our shared history, we didn't have too much in common. The trajectory of my life had been moving away from his for so many years, I could not have envisaged making such a pledge even five or six years earlier. I knew a lot had changed in that time, but living with Baz? How had it come to this?

4

LEECHES FOR WATERMELON

Michael Barry Dooley was the youngest of George and Alma Dooley's ten children. In something of a family tradition, Baz was never called by his official first name. (His oldest brother Pat was really a Francis, his sister Joyce an Evelyn, another sister whom everyone knew as Janice was actually Marina, and so on.) And I have to say, Baz was certainly never a Michael. A Mick maybe, but somehow Barry suited him to a tee.

Barry, especially when shortened to Baz, has a definite larrikin ring to it. Maybe the Barries you know aren't like that but every Baz I've been acquainted with certainly fits the bill in terms of being cheeky, loud or simply loving a laugh. Sure, I have only known a grand total of three so it's not a comprehensive sample size – although I did once sit next to Barry Humphries, which would make it four Barries, and he didn't choose to call his archetypal ocker hero 'Bazza' McKenzie for nothing, you know.

Coincidentally, when Baz first went into treatment for his lung cancer, one of the other Bazzes I knew was at the same hospital after having suffered a stroke. The father of a close friend, I had known him since I was seventeen. When his daughter brought me in to his darkened room to say g'day, he brightened up and, mustering what must have been an enormous effort, started trying to crack a gag or two. Like our Baz, he was a boisterous bloke who loved a drink and a laugh so I was deeply saddened when a couple of days later my friend rang to say her Baz hadn't pulled through. They were very close and I think she called me, as much as anything, to glean some insight into how to cope with the grief of losing a parent. Talking to her it suddenly hit me that even though the memory of Di's death was still so raw, I felt like I had very little to offer, each person's experience of grief being totally unique.

The only practical advice I could give was to make sure she read the eulogy out loud to herself as many times as possible before she had to deliver it. That way she'd hopefully have gotten out enough tears that she'd be able to hold it together on the day. She gave a great speech and the funeral was a fitting celebration of a true Baz. She told me later that my advice got her through the eulogy and that just being able to talk to someone who had been in the same situation had been incredibly helpful. I guess that's the key – we look for definitive answers where there probably are none, but just the process of opening up and sharing provides more solace than we will ever know.

So what made my Baz such a Baz? I guess genetics had something to do with it. By the time I knew him, Baz's father, George, was very frail, but my main memory of him was of a very loud man who was always shouting. Not in anger – though apparently he could let fly with the best of them – but because he was not a shy man, and when he had something to say he made sure he was always heard. Alma wasn't shy in coming forward either. In fact the entire Dooley clan seemed to be a raucous bunch and my childhood memories are of uproarious gatherings around George and Alma's kitchen table.

As the youngest, I can imagine Michael Barry had a lot of noise to overcome just to be heard, but that alone wouldn't have guaranteed that he would follow in their gregarious footsteps. I've always thought that my brother and I were both inherently shy, though we dealt with it in different ways. My natural inclination is to stay in the background but if I know people are going to be focusing their attention on me I can gather myself and put on a performance, thereby taking some control of the situation. Wok's shyness took another route, that of taciturn silence, presumably hoping that attention would soon shift elsewhere. I strongly suspect our public shyness stems from having had such an extrovert, loud father.

One of Baz's favourite games when we were very young was to assume a cockeyed 'monster' pose and chase us around the house. Even when I was squealing with supposed delight as he relentlessly lumbered after us, moaning like Frankenstein, I remember thinking that I wasn't particularly enjoying myself and wished we could play more quietly. I suspect that when you have a boisterous father you can go one of two ways – try and compete, or go into your shell. I think both Wok and I chose the latter.

From the outset, though, it seems that Baz was always destined to be a true Baz. The earliest photo I have of him, a 1941 class shot, is in some senses atypical, as Baz doesn't look particularly cheeky; in fact, he has an almost doleful air about him. But the more I look at the photo, the more he commands attention. The eye is drawn to this skinny, scruffy-haired kid wearing a black skivvy in the middle of the back row. I think it is because he is the only one who is not smiling or putting on some sort of pose for the camera. He seems remarkably self-assured for a five year old, like he doesn't have anything to prove to the camera, and it looks to me as if he is defying it, as if he has some place better to be. He seems to have a certain charisma that the other children lack, a feeling heightened by the fact that one of the kids next to him has turned away from the photographer to look directly at Baz.

Maybe my analysis is simply the result of a son looking for traces of the remarkable in his father, but there might be something to it. A few years later Baz went for a brief time to a Catholic high school. (He left, as many kids did, at the age of fifteen to join the workforce.) Baz always had extremely fond memories of that school in spite of his brief tenure – he really did love being a Catholic. Many years later in one of the first scandals of its kind to reach the courts, one of the brothers from Baz's school was charged with child molestation of former students in his care. Baz knew some of the victims, but his reaction was not one of outrage so much as lack of surprise.

'I always knew there was something off about that brother.

Always staring at the kids. But strange enough he left me alone –
wouldn't even look me in the eye,' Baz mused, touching on
something that I have read about paedophiles since – that they
single out the insecure children, those they can manipulate into
compliance with their sordid actions. I wouldn't mind betting
that this priest saw the same quality in Baz that I could see in
the 1941 photo, that of a kid who was definitely his own person,
and confident in who he was. I was just beginning to admire my
dad's strength of character when Baz ruined the whole effect by
continuing: 'Yep, he never tried to fiddle with me once. Makes me
feel left out, like I was ugly or something.' Thanks for that, Baz.

It was not long after this photograph was taken that George
moved the family to the safer climes of Yarrawonga on the Murray
River while he was away in the navy fighting the Japanese in
the Pacific. Not the entire family, as three of Baz's brothers – Pat,
Peter and Ken – had also joined up and were in the navy and an
older sister, Joan, was serving in the Women's Army, but George
felt it was better that the young ones were out of harm's way.
Today this might seem like an overreaction but as the family lived
near the beach at Chelsea, I wonder if maybe George had some
inside information on how dangerous things could have become
had a Japanese fleet made it into Port Phillip Bay. And so it was
that Baz spent the ages of five to nine living along the Murray,
where even a mini-sub would have been hard pressed to make
its way across the Barmah Choke near Echuca to attack the town.

The way Baz talked about it, this part of his childhood
was something straight out of Huck Finn (or, more appropriately,

Fatty Finn), although I suspect that Baz was more like Ginger Meggs, as Baz had both Meggsy's impish sensibility and his reddish hair and freckles. The one story Baz told of this time that really sticks in my mind was of the day he and 'Monkey' Ryan sat in the waters of the Murray River for hours on end, collecting leeches. Not with a net; instead they waited for the leeches to attach to their bodies. When a surfeit had accumulated they would pick the bloodsuckers off their shivering, blood-spattered bodies, straight into a specimen jar. Once they had filled a couple of jars they would take them to the local chemist, who in those days still used leeches to bleed patients. He would pay the boys handsomely and they would then splurge on whatever an eight year old in the bush would spend his money on.

This particular time, the local grocer had just taken delivery of some watermelon. In an era of wartime rationing, fresh fruit was scarce even in the countryside, so Baz had never seen, let alone eaten, watermelon before. He and Monkey Ryan bought as many as they could carry and took them down to the river where they feasted on this exotic treat. Baz said he gorged on so much watermelon that pretty soon he was spewing a fluorescent pink torrent into the turbid brown waters of the Murray. To his dying day, this man who could demolish a slab of beer without any ill effect to his digestive system would always blanch at the thought of eating a slice of watermelon.

After the war, a repatriated George moved his family back to Chelsea. For a brief time in the twenties, when the train line to the city was electrified and people started to build their holiday homes there, Chelsea flourished as a seaside resort. The Depression knocked the stuffing out of the holiday market and the place soon reverted to its backwater status, which was pretty much how most of the locals liked it. Baz said they used to refer to Chelsea as 'Dogpatch' after the American comic strip 'Li'l Abner' about a bunch of small-town hicks. It was the sort of place where everybody knew everyone else's business, something that could be both a great comfort and terribly oppressive.

The Depression had also seen George put out of work. He was a butcher by trade (hence, I guess, Baz's appreciation of a good steak) and the only work going at the time was with the navy, so George joined up. Ten years later this father of ten found himself in the middle of a war, boning meat in the festering Pacific sun while Kamikaze planes slammed onto the deck of his ship. They say war is 90 per cent tedium interrupted by a few insane moments of action, and to while away those languid tropical days when nothing was going on, George became the ship's SP bookmaker. He would run a book for his fellow shipmates on whatever was going. Due to communication difficulties and wartime censorship, they couldn't always be guaranteed to get a direct broadcast of the races, so George would frame a market on just about anything – the proverbial two flies up a wall or even who would be the next unlucky bastard to cop it from a Japanese pilot with a misguided sense of loyalty to an emperor he'd never met, and not enough petrol to make it back to base.

It turned out that George was a natural at the bookmaking caper and he came back from the war with a duffle bag full of cash and a determination never again to have to flense mutton that had turned rancid in the tropical heat. He also brought back a propeller tip from a Kamikaze plane that, according to family legend, had landed at my grandfather's feet after clattering onto the deck of the ship – it could just as easily have been a bit of metal off some piece of abattoir machinery, but that would not have been nearly as impressive a story for show-and-tell at primary school. With the money he had made on the ship, George was able to take out a legitimate bookie's licence and he became a regular fixture on Melbourne racetracks for the next 25 years.

It turns out that Baz had inherited something of the same entrepreneurial spirit and was never short of ways to make a quid as a youngster. On weekends he would take the train into town and stand outside the racetrack selling 'lucky' pencils to the punters. Apparently it was considered good luck to buy your pencil – used to mark down your picks in the race book – from a street urchin and Baz soon worked out that if he bought a packet of HB pencils from Coles for, say, a shilling, he could divide each pencil into three, sharpen the tips of all of them and sell each one for twopence and make a killing. Or something like that. For someone raised on decimal currency like I was, Baz's explanations of imperial coinage made as much sense as they would have if he'd used terms such as pygmies, gobstoppers and woozle-wazzles. And that was before he even got on to the topic of what they nicknamed different denominations. When I worked as a bookie's clerk for Baz I would look up in total confusion when he'd call a bet as 'a gorilla on the favourite'.

How was I to know that a monkey was $500 and a gorilla $1000 because it was twice as big as a monkey, especially when nobody was ever satisfactorily able to tell me why five hundred bucks was called a monkey in the first place?

During football season Baz would stand outside the MCG selling the Footy Records, a kind of form guide to the football. As he got older, Baz worked his way inside the G, moving to the more lucrative trade of selling food at the matches. The way Baz tells it, he spent most of his time making money on the side, like his scam with the hot dog concession. For some bizarre reason his boss counted the bread rolls but not the number of sausages sold, so Baz would offer the kids half-price hot dogs if they didn't mind eating the sausage out of a piece of (unused) toilet paper instead of a roll. Baz pocketed the entire proceeds. Another lurk he'd run on hot days at the cricket involved oranges: he'd buy a few bags which he'd keep in the ice boxes in the caterer's kitchen, then sell the frozen fruit for half of what it cost for an ice-cream – again, a nice little earner.

With so much money coming in as a teenager, I wondered why our family didn't end up millionaires – after all this was the sort of story that the Donald Trumps and Lindsay Foxes of the world told about how they got started. But over the years it dawned on me that for Baz, making money, no matter how enjoyable, really was just a means to an end and whatever he earned he spent on the good life. And for Baz a good lifestyle meant a decent feed, a bit of money for the punt and hanging out with mates, and booze – always buckets of booze.

Baz could have continued on to become another self-made mogul, but bookmaking was in his blood so, as soon as he was old enough, he started working at the track for George. Most of George's boys had stints with their old man – my Uncle Norm continued working with other bookies until he died – but it was Baz who really took to the racing game in a big way. By the time he was twenty Baz was George's chief penciller (the one who wrote down all the bets and kept a tally of what each horse was going to pay if it won). By the time Baz was 25 he was pretty much running the show, filling in for George whenever his illnesses kept him off the track. After suffering a series of minor strokes in his later years, George was no longer up to the mental rigours involved in bookmaking. It got to the point that Baz not only had to take to the stand to run the show, but he would also have to follow his father into the urinals as he had developed a habit of dropping large, rolled-up bundles of cash on the toilet floor – not a good indication of one's ability to be on top of the game when facing a mob of avaricious punters looking for any advantage.

Even today, bookmaking is about the only business that you cannot sell. No matter how much goodwill a bookmaker has built up in the business, no matter how extensive a list of clients has been accumulated, the bookie can't pass it on to anyone. So with George too ill to continue, Baz had to set out on his own if he wanted to stay in the game. There were not many equipment costs associated with bookmaking aside from the leather bookie's bags, betting books and a portable betting board for setting up at country picnic race meetings. The one thing you needed was money: collateral to cover potential losses. Back in the early seventies when Baz was getting started, the authorities demanded that potential bookmakers have at least $20 000 in their bank account before being granted a licence. This was about twice the average annual wage. Being one of ten children, Baz could expect no special treatment from George, so short of knocking over a TAB, the only way he was going to make his bank account look healthy enough was to find a silent partner.

Enter one property developer and mad punter named Danny Ryan. He was one of those businessmen that the press would euphemistically call 'a colourful racing identity'. Danny used to bet with Baz while he was running George's stand and they became drinking buddies. Like many an entrepreneurial type, Danny was attracted to the glamour of the racing industry and saw Baz as an exciting business prospect, so into Baz's account went a lazy 20K. But the partnership was not to last. The trouble was that while Danny was thinking in terms of hundreds of thousands, the reality of starting out as a bookmaker meant Baz was dealing only in hundreds. Danny soon lost interest in such small returns and moved his investment elsewhere, but Baz had been given his start and over the next twenty years he built the business up until he was finally admitted to the elite rank of rails bookmaker.

The 'rails' refer not to the fence around the racetrack separating the horses from the punters, but to the rail that divides the race club members from the hoi polloi in the public enclosure, about the only overt manifestation of a class divide in

Australia. The rails bookies are supposedly the rich ones because they have access to punters on both sides of the fence, but the reality is that they deal in big money because the clientele on the 'right' side of the fence are the ones with the big trust funds, the executive bonuses or the skill to embezzle clients' accounts that enable them to lay out the really big money.

For Baz, it was a long haul to hitch himself to these particular rails. The first decade of his career involved slogging around the Victorian countryside going to any little picnic race meeting that would have him. Not that this was an unpleasant chore – in fact for Baz, these were his favourite times in the same way that The Beatles talked of their Hamburg days before the pressure of success kicked in, when it was as much about the fun of the job as it was the material rewards. If you were inclined to really stretch the Beatles metaphor, the one who played the Paul McCartney to Baz's John Lennon was Ace. Actually, it's probably not the best analogy as although, like Lennon and McCartney, they met at school, Ace and Baz remained firm friends until the very end.

Baz and Ace were never actually that close at school. It was when they both served in Nashos that their friendship really firmed, on the back of a mutual love of going AWOL, drinking and getting on the punt. Unlike Baz, Ace was quite a sportsman and played a couple of games for Fitzroy in the VFL. (He doesn't actually appear in the *Encyclopedia of League Footballers* but Ace swears he played at least one senior game, perhaps as many as two.) He was also a gun professional sprinter, winning the Wangaratta Gift and making the semi-final of the Stawell Gift.

At one stage Baz decided to cash in on Ace's athletic ability and concocted a scam whereby Ace would run in a 400 metre race (an event he hadn't trained for – he was strictly a 100 metre runner) at the old Albert Park oval in South Melbourne. The idea was that Ace would pick a race where he knew the other runners would be taking it easy as they saved themselves for bigger meetings later in the season, and he would surprise them all by entering the longer distanced event and blitzing them with the run of a lifetime. Baz, in the meantime, would make a plunge in the betting ring, taking advantage of the long odds that Ace would attract. The plan went smoothly, with Ace busting a gut to get across the line by a nose. An excited Baz ran up to congratulate his mate only to have an exhausted Ace promptly vomit all over him. They never tried the scam again.

With Ace, his partner in crime, by his side and a rotating cast of other clerks with them, Baz would set off every Saturday morning for some far-flung corner of Victoria. Ace was the driver and guaranteed that he could get Baz anywhere in the state by ten o'clock. Not that the races started at ten – they wouldn't usually jump in the first race until around one. In fact generally the racecourse wasn't even open at ten. But the pubs were. My earliest memories of my father at work consist of standing outside a pub banging on the door at one minute past ten demanding to be let in. Between the breakneck speed that Ace would drive in order to fulfil his promise, and the fact that they would visit the same pub after the races, it was amazing that they ever made it home at all.

As a career, the bookie caper was a perfect fit for a Baz; it certainly was for this Baz. It gave him permission to be loud – to be heard in the ring and get the punters to take notice, a good bookie needs a bit of showmanship. For most of his career Baz mainly bet on interstate races, Adelaide in particular, and when things were slow he would suddenly leap onto the stand and with a great flourish flick his stack of betting tickets and bellow 'Adelaide, Adelaide, ever-lovin' Adelaide' to the milling crowd in the betting ring. For years I thought this was some particular quirk of Baz's; I had no idea it was a song from *Guys and Dolls*. One time when I was on the stand filling in for Baz I decided to try my own version, and began singing out 'Adelaide' à la the Paul Kelly song. None of the old blokes on the punt that miserable winter's day at Flemington had a clue who Paul Kelly was and my half-hearted warbling trailed off into embarrassed silence and a barrage of uncomprehending stares.

Being a bookie was an outlet not just for the extrovert in Baz, it also gave him a legitimate outlet to exercise his intelligence, something that, despite his larrikin 'I left school at fifteen' façade, Baz had in spades. And it wasn't just the rat cunning of the hustler; a bookmaker must be able to instantly calculate an enormous mass of figures under incredible pressure. The successful bookmaker has another kind of smarts in his armoury and it has very little to do with being a good judge of horseflesh. The non-racegoer (and many a punter) thinks the secret to being a successful bookie is knowing all about horses and their form, whereas in actuality, this knowledge is fairly low down on the scale. Possibly the greatest mistake a bookie can make is to assume that he can pick the winners and losers. That sort of hubris essentially reduces the bookie to the level of the mug punter, and the entire gambling industry is based upon the immutable fact that winning streaks will always end. Baz seemed to take relatively little notice of form and would leave it to the punters to decide what they wanted to back, though he did have an uncanny ability to pick a winner. It wouldn't happen too often – say, once every couple of months – that Baz would suddenly pronounce, 'You know what, boys, I've got a feeling about this filly. Let's keep her a fraction under and see how we go.' He would keep the odds on that horse below what the other bookies were offering, so that nobody would bet on it with him. It was amazing how often Baz's hunches turned out to be right on the money and the horse would get up and win.

Above all, though, it was Baz's ability as a judge of people that singled him out as a great bookie. He had a sixth sense for sniffing out when something was up. He was one of the few bookies that didn't get caught out by the Fine Cotton affair. Fine Cotton was a bit of a plodder. A plan was hatched to substitute Fine Cotton for a much better horse called Bold Personality that superficially resembled it. (Well, when I say resembled, they were both horses – that's about where the similarities ended. The two horses were actually different colours, a trifle the geniuses who devised the scheme thought they could cover up with a bottle of hair dye and a tin of white paint.) The idea was that those in the know would bet like fury with unsuspecting bookmakers who were giving inflated odds that the good horse would never have got if everybody knew it was running. The scam was soon picked up, particularly when on the way back to the mounting yard after the race the white paint on the horse's legs started to peel off, but Baz had been onto it from the start. Early on in the betting he thought something was up and told his clerks to turn the odds right down on this hitherto unknown horse that all sorts of desperados suddenly seemed too eager to bet on, declaring, 'Turn this nag down, boys, she must be a ring-in!' And Baz was spot on. In most areas of his life you wouldn't pick Baz as terribly sensitive to the ways of others, but on a racetrack there was no better judge of human behaviour.

But for Baz the truly great thing about being a bookie was that he was able to make a living out of doing the sort of thing that he would have been doing if he wasn't working – hanging out with his mates and drinking beer. Baz had what could be described as a Catholic work ethic: work hard, play harder, and if at all possible try and make your play your work. Right from the start, Baz's workers were his best mates. His hiring criteria for his bookie's clerks were not based so much on their skills as a penciller or baggie, but on how much Baz liked to have a drink with them – before, after and even during work.

I don't know of too many workplaces where the boss regularly insists you drop what you are doing and join him for a drink, but that is what happened when you worked for Baz. Once the horses had jumped out of the barrier, Baz and the other clerks would dump all the gear with the payout clerk and head for the bar. Sometimes Baz would leap off the stand, pushing past the punters who had just seconds ago been bustling around trying to place a bet so that he could get to the bar before them. These between-race tipples came after a session at the pub from ten o'clock till about half past eleven with another couple of quick pots downed at the nearest bar at the track itself. Amazingly the beer very rarely seemed to affect Baz's performance as a bookie and he remained lucid and primed for the battle against the punters all day. That is, until they jumped for the last race of the day. At this point the adrenaline must have drained from Baz's system and by the time the last winner had saluted the judge he was often a blithering mess.

This fondness for having a good time may not exactly have been the look the racing authorities were wanting for the racecourse and it may very well have impeded Baz's rise through the bookmaking ranks, but eventually Baz's success, and his willingness to take the punters on, couldn't be ignored and he was finally given his shot at the rails. With the advent in the early sixties of the state-owned off-course TAB, followed by casinos, phone betting and other technological advances, being a bookie had long stopped being the licence to print money it had been in George's day. Many bookies started to become far more timid as they took hit after hit from well-organised betting syndicates, so while Baz never became a true heavy hitter of the ring he certainly was a breath of fresh air, and the serious punter knew they could always get a bet on with him at decent odds. Baz's mantra was never back an odds-on favourite and he came alive at the scent of a battle with a punter who was willing to throw down a large wad of cash on a horse at very skinny odds.

While Baz was not an inveterate gambler, he did like to have a punt in life, a stance definitely reflected in his choice of life partner. The woman he decided he wanted to spend the rest of his life with was one of the longest shots of Baz's life. You would never have picked them as suited to each other at all, and yet it was a bet that in the end really paid off for Baz.

5

LADY DI

My mother, Diane, was an artist, and a pretty decent one at that. This is not just the blinkered view of an admiring son of a suburban housewife who dabbled in art and craft: others also thought she was genuinely talented, as evidenced by the fact that over the course of her lifetime she sold hundreds of works, so it can't just have been me who thought she was any good. She was not, however, a famous artist, so after my parents had died and I was sorting through their belongings I was confronted with the dilemma of what to do with the two hundred or so pieces that she had retained in her studio. Some were those she had only recently finished before her death, some were favourites of hers that she had kept and hung around the house (there was a rotation of around 30 paintings hanging on our walls at any one time), some were those she had simply been unable to sell. Even so, there weren't many duds among them.

If she had been well known we could have mounted a retrospective and made a mint, but she wasn't so I had to think of some other way of dealing with them as it seemed a crime that these pieces she had poured so much of her passion into should end up turfed into a skip along with old lamps that didn't work, bags of cement that had hardened during the years spent in the garage not being used for the projects they had originally been intended for, and decades worth of crappy birthday knick-knacks that really should never have been given in the first place.

So Wok and I went through everything, put a red sticker on our favourite pieces to reserve them and opened the house to relatives and friends to come in and grab their own genuine Diane Dooley original. Even then I was left with a load of paintings that I still can't bear to throw out, instead lugging them from house to house waiting for a time when I have enough wall space to hang them.

Even more problematic was what to do with the many portraits Di painted of me. Most people would get some sort of thrill out of sitting for a painting but growing up with an artist for a mum I was fodder for Di's developing technique and disliked sitting so much that in the end she had to bribe me. As a result, I had my life chronicled in oils, charcoal and pastel from the ages of four to nineteen. One girlfriend commented that she thought my mum had improved over the years because the older I got the more in proportion my head was to the rest of my body. Then she saw some photos of me as a child and realised that the oversized noggin Di had painted was unerringly accurate. I simply can't bring myself to dispose of these portraits as they are a direct connection with my mother, but it would be horrendously narcissistic and rather unnerving to have them hanging around the house.

When I turned 35 I had a mock 21st birthday party to make up for the fact that I had missed out on having one at the time. I had chosen to spend that milestone day by myself out in the bush trying to rediscover a lost colony of an endangered species of bird. Instead of having a photo board at the party I put all those portraits up along the stairwell of the share house I was living in. I thought it would be a bit of a joke but most people at the party commented on how moving it was to see her work up there. One friend told me later he thought that the work that went into those portraits was the most exquisite, heart-rending act of pure love he had ever seen. Suddenly it seemed like a rather weak joke.

As I was going through Di's studio to sort out what was to go to the cousins, I came across a series of drawings she had done in 1943. A child's triptych of a Willie Wagtail, a sprig of wattle and an Australian flag, it is the earliest surviving example of my mother's art. To be honest, it is not particularly outstanding: the stars on the flag are misshapen, the wattle sprig looks severely drought affected, and the wagtail's head is the size of a moose. But then, she was only six at the time.

Further on in her collection I found a couple of pieces from just a few years later: a pastel of a bush hut and a sketch of her Uncle Bob. Both are profound advances on the earlier work. There is a sense of perspective, an eye for detail and an unerring accuracy in what is still admittedly a pretty basic style. Quite simply, you can see by this age that there was artistic talent there. Where this came from is something of a mystery as Di's family was not of a particularly artistic bent. From what I know of the women who raised my mother, they were a bunch of starchy, misanthropic Presbyterians who would find all that art palaver just a little too unsavoury.

Di's mother and three aunts owned a haberdashery shop in Smith Street, Collingwood and ended up all living there together, where they would spend the day hiding from the evils of the world, playing endless rounds of gin rummy, five hundred and – without any sense of irony – old maid. They were the sort of sisters that Elvis Costello or Robert Forster would write a song about. At a stretch you could perhaps draw a link between Di's painting and her mother's haberdashery. Perhaps being surrounded by all that cloth and coloured fabric rubbed off on her, creating some sort of creative aesthetic. Perhaps there was some artistic gene that was passed on. But I doubt it.

It must be noted that I am relying on Baz as my primary source here. My maternal grandmother died a few months before I was born and of the sisters who raised my mum, I only knew Aunty Mary. I actually adored her, and would spend idyllic summer holidays with her on her son's farm, but then I was only eight when she died, so I got no inside dope from her about the family and I was too young to see her in anything but a glowing light. Baz's view that Di's family were a kooky bunch of man-haters may very well be prejudiced but it is backed up by some things that distant cousins have said, and by the fact that, oddly enough for the times, particularly among devout churchgoers, all four of the MacDonald sisters were divorced.

Not that the sisters didn't have legitimate reasons for their misanthropy. Within the MacDonald family there seemed to be something of a genetic curse on the men, who by all accounts turned out to be losers and low-lifes. Certainly in the oral history of the family the men were very rarely mentioned, seeming ghostly presences who only ever appeared in brief cameos. The few that I ever heard snippets about seemed to confirm the worst. The only one ever referred to with much affection was their brother, Uncle Bob, but by all accounts (well, Baz's), he ended up a bit of a hermit, a mad old coot living on the banks of some inland river in a tin shanty, spending his days taking pot shots at cockatoos.

Around the time I was born we were apparently graced with the presence of Di's cousin Max, a merchant marine who in the brief weeks he stayed with us before Baz turfed him out managed to strain all ties of kinship due to his seedy, sleazy nature. For years afterwards, local taxis would boycott our house because of the treatment drivers suffered at the hands of Max. Even in Frankston there were limits to how many times you could vomit in a taxi, abuse the driver and do a runner when it came time to pay the fare, before you ended up being black-banned.

Apparently this was typical behaviour of the MacDonald men, who were all either con-men, drunks, work shies or all three, whereas the women were all paragons of upright, teetotal virtue. Or was it really that way? Maybe the men were all outright rogues and villains – maybe the starchy uprightness of the women of the family drove the men to stray off the moral path? Maybe no man could meet the clucking strictures imposed by the MacDonald matriarchs.

I don't think there was much of the deviant in Di's father, Fred Bray, for I met him and you could not find a more peaceable, well-regarded man. Yet he too fell foul of the sisters MacDonald. Perhaps he was not deemed good enough for the youngest sister, Teeny (short for Christine), as during the Depression he had, like so many men of his generation, hauled his swag along the Wallaby Track looking for itinerant work in the Outback as a shearer. Jack Thompson may have made the life of a shearer seem romantic in the revival of Australian cinema in the seventies but back then, for city matriarchs at least, it was just a form of common labouring to look down their noses at. But this attitude doesn't explain why, when Fred was showing genuine prospects and planned to move to Sydney to take up an opportunity to run his own roof-tiling business, Teeny baulked and refused to leave her sisters. So when she was twelve, Di's father became an absence in her life and she was not to see him again until I was born (and Teeny had died), when Baz orchestrated a reconciliation. He was not there for Di's wedding or to see her blossom into a shy but assured artist.

Like Baz, Di left school at fifteen. Drawing and painting were all she was interested in, and her studies in the other subjects soon fell behind, though at the Westleigh College for girls, run by a couple of elderly spinsters in Northcote, I suspect that graduating academic goddesses who would go on to study at university was secondary to producing proper young ladies who would present well and make compliant, supportive partners for their future husbands. Di's academic progress wasn't helped any by Teeny regularly taking her out of class so that they could both go to the old Westgarth picture palace in High Street, Northcote to see the latest Hollywood release. It seems unimaginable now, but Teeny deemed it more important that Di got to see the latest Alan Ladd picture with her than stay in a maths or French class. When Di used to tell me about how her mum helped her wag school to go to the movies, I thought my grandma must have been so cool, but looking back on it as an adult, I can't help thinking she must have been a desperately lonely woman to do that to her child.

Not that Di seemed to mind – she loved the movies. Especially Alan Ladd, the pint-size matinee idol who, it was said, used to have to stand on boxes when he kissed his leading ladies in the close-ups. All of the MacDonald ladies loved Alan Ladd – an ironic choice, really, for though his lack of height (and of expression) may have made him the 'safest' of the matinee idols to adore, he harboured a dark side, becoming an alcoholic and dying of an overdose of booze and sedatives. Even their fantasy men went bad.

Di's first job was as a window-dresser at the now defunct Manton's department store. This was a common route for young women of an artistic bent to follow as it gave them a respectable outlet for their aesthetic sensibilities – at least until marriage, when it was expected that they would sublimate their creative tendencies in order to run a household. If a woman pursued her art it was generally relegated to the realm of crafts and hobbies, no matter if she was every bit as talented as her male contemporaries. There were the occasional exceptions, but Di was certainly not unconventional enough to be such a maverick, due in no small part, I suspect, to the cloistered environment in which she grew up.

It is staggering to contemplate just how unworldly Di was, considering the work crowd she hung around with. Many of her work mates were on the fringes of Melbourne's avant-garde artist scene centred on John and Sunday Reed's 'Heide'. Indeed, a few years later Di was to find work painting pottery designs for the Guy Boyd studios. Guy, a member of the legendary Boyd family, eventually gave away the pottery business to concentrate on sculpture, but in the fifties and early sixties he ran a highly successful studio that created a fascinating amalgam of modernist design with kitsch Australiana motifs (although she would never have met an Aboriginal person, Di must have painted thousands of stylised figures of piccaninnies and warriors carrying spears and woomera) that has had something of a resurgence in popularity over the past few years.

Despite all these connections, Di remained a naïve suburban girl. Bohemia was not for her. For instance, Di had absolutely no clue that the fey men she worked with (and sometimes dated) were gay. Baz once told me that he was dragged to the 21st party of one of the 'beautiful boys' that Di worked with. Upon arrival Baz was aghast to behold a room full of 'arty' types listening to jazz and, horror of horrors, sipping wine. Baz made a hasty beeline to the laundry to put his bottle of big browns in the ice trough. Standing there was a glum looking guy who, much to Baz's relief, was drinking a beer. Baz introduced himself and said to him, 'Is it just me, mate, or is this party full of cats?' (Cats being Baz's term for homosexuals.)

His newfound friend replied sadly that this was the case and the only reason he was there was that the guy holding the party was his brother and he felt obliged to turn up. At least Baz had found a kindred spirit and the rest of the night passed without incident. On leaving, a pleased Di, who had been very nervous about introducing her uncouth boyfriend to such a refined crowd, commented on how Baz had seemed to enjoy himself. He said to her, 'You know they were all homos, don't you?' Di was stunned and refused to believe it. She thought Barry was being uncharitable and that her wonderful friends couldn't be gay – they were merely 'festive'.

But for one so conventional, Di still managed to live rather unconventionally for her times. She supported herself through her painting, did the overseas trip to England which included hitchhiking around the continent on an artist's pilgrimage with another female artist friend and managed to stay unmarried until she was 28, which in that era put her dangerously close to spinster territory. It wasn't that her immediate family had put her off men, for she had many boyfriends. But it was the most ill-suited of them all who eventually won her over. He was laddish, loutish and had no interest in art or any of the finer things in life, save for a decently cooked steak and an appropriately cold beer, and his name was Baz.

By the time Baz met Di, her family had sold up their dress shop in Collingwood and had moved in together with their children at the family beach house at Edithvale. They sarcastically referred to the flea-ridden, sandy shack as 'Tara' after the mansion in *Gone With the Wind*. I could imagine how those women must have identified with Scarlett O'Hara – the strong woman who was thwarted by conniving men, be it the guileless Ashley or the roguish Rhett Butler types.

How Baz even got his head in the door I have no idea. He was the complete antithesis to Di. Twenty years before Charles had chosen his princess, my mum was already known as Lady Di. She was a quiet only child; he had to compete against nine rambunctious elder siblings for attention. She was shy, reserved, elegant and artistic; Baz was cheeky and as gregarious as a seagull. She really was as straight as a die, her vices extending to an occasional wine with dinner and the odd social cigarette. Baz's life revolved around having fun, and that meant drinking, gambling and smoking, all in the company of his seemingly endless cavalcade of mates. The two of them met at a local youth group badminton tournament. Di was a keen and talented player who used her height to advantage at the net. Baz had never held a racquet before in his life but had been talked into going by the priest in charge of the local YCW (Young Christian Workers), who had bribed Baz and his mates into entering a team by saying that it would be a good way to meet girls.

Di told me that her first memory of Baz was of this skinny, red-haired kid with big ears and a loud mouth who took great delight in smashing the shuttlecock at the faces of his 'proddo' opponents. She thought he was totally uncouth, but for some reason, by the end of the night she had agreed to go out with him. She was probably too polite to say no, though I do wonder whether there was just the hint of a rebellious streak in Di and if she, like so many other 'good girls', was thrilled to be in the company of a 'bad boy'. Neither of them could remember where they went on that first date, but both agreed that at the end of it, seventeen-year-old Baz had said to her, 'Well, Disey, I suppose we better get married then.'

According to Di, they hadn't even kissed at that stage. She replied with a firm and adamant no, but Baz had found the woman of his dreams and wouldn't let the small matter of her not being interested deter him. The chase was on and for the next ten years Baz kept asking and, eventually, in her late twenties, Di relented, and they were married in the fibro Presbyterian church in Edithvale in January 1965. In marrying Di in a 'proddo' church, Baz was effectively excommunicated from the Catholic church, but there was no way known that Teeny would have stepped into St Joseph's in Chelsea, let alone allowed her only daughter to get married there.

Growing up, I never knew Baz to go to church outside of weddings and funerals. This seemed unfair because Di being a Sunday School teacher at the local Uniting Church, meant Wok and I were dragged along kicking and screaming every Sunday.

We would return each week to find Baz, feet up with his second beer of the day, watching *World of Sport*, with the smell of the roast of the day in the air. Baz would delight in telling us what a great morning he'd had out in the real world, but beneath his seemingly happy secularism beat the heart of an unreconstructed papist. And when, twenty years later, they renewed their vows, this time under the auspices of a Catholic priest, Baz took to religious life with relish and never missed a Sunday mass for the rest of his days. Interestingly, Di accompanied him for the first couple of months but eventually stopped going, and by the time she died she was essentially non-religious. Maybe the Catholic hymns didn't rock the same way that 'The Lord said to Noah, there's going to be a floody-wuddy' did.

It was one thing winning Di over, but it would be another to win approval from Teeny and the cabal of old maids residing in 'Tara'. Many a decent lad had tried and failed. This uncouth larrikin with bad habits didn't stand a chance, or so you might have thought. Baz described his first evening at 'Tara' as quite surreal. The only man on the premises was Len, the Down syndrome child of one of the aunties. Other than him it was all women, including Aunt Marge, who had some condition that made her sensitive to light so that as they played gin rummy she would sit at the table wearing a poker dealer's visor with a translucent green shade. They were all staunchly teetotal. And in walked a cheeky young Catholic bloke who, at seventeen, was already an experienced drinker.

But somehow over the years he managed to charm them,

because when he put his mind to it, Baz could be very charming. He even managed to win Teeny over. This was remarkable in itself, but the real miracle was that he did it with alcohol. Overhearing her complaints of insomnia, Baz suggested a medicinal ale as the answer to her problems. Despite her tut-tutting, the next night Baz brought over a bottle of beer and poured her a glass. While she tentatively sipped, he joined her, necking the rest of the bottle. Teeny had her best night's sleep in decades and this became their ritual for the rest of her life. Baz was in.

As I grew older and became more aware of the nature of relationships, it seemed ever more unfathomable that my parents had got together, let alone stuck out 30-plus years of marriage. In the days before Di died, knowing I would never get another chance to find out, I plucked up the courage to ask her.

'Mum, how come you married Dad?'

A sly smile crossed her face as she lay in the hospital bed. 'Because I loved him,' came the expected but unsatisfactory reply.

I wanted more than this, so I tried to hide my impatience and press on as tactfully as I could. 'Yeah, I know that, but why did you love him? You're so different. Why Dad? What was it about him exactly? I don't understand why you chose him.'

I worried that I had gone too far, that she would take it to mean I thought that she had somehow made a mistake. Despite several relationships I had still not worked out how one chose a life partner, how anyone knew that they wanted to be with the same person forever. While I had fallen fiercely in love before, I had never had that inner voice telling me that this was *the* person. I really wanted – *needed* – to know how she had made that choice with someone who, on the surface, seemed so clearly unsuited to her.

Luckily Di took it the way it was intended. She knew she only had days to live and I guess that gives one the ability to cut to the chase and do away with the superfluous social niceties that bind up so much of our precious time on the planet. Her smile returned.

'Because of the Dooley family. Right from the first time I met them, they were all so friendly.'

I hadn't expected this exactly, but I understood. The Dooley family was big and boisterous and always lively. Like Di's family, they would play cards at night, but it wouldn't be under a single gloomy bulb to protect Aunt Marge's eyes. The house would be blazing, there would be music blaring and roaring laughter and beer, and people dropping by and Alma throwing another few spuds in with the roast to feed unexpected visitors. People weren't guarded, the world was not seen as something to steel yourself against, it was something to be embraced, to suck the marrow out of and enjoy. At first it was all a bit overwhelming, but Di soon found that all the sisters and sisters-in-law took pity and welcomed her into the fold. I could understand that but it still didn't exactly answer my question.

'Surely you didn't marry Dad just because you liked his family?'

Her smile broke into a broad grin. I hadn't seen her smile like that for months. 'Because he made me laugh,' she answered.

I must have looked surprised because she continued, 'I always had a good time when I was with Barry. None of the others ever made me laugh the same way.'

While Baz had been certain from their very first date, Di had been extremely unconvinced. She had many boyfriends, but somehow Baz managed to insinuate himself back into her life, often just at the right moment – he had the uncanny knack of reappearing in her life just as she was starting to get serious with someone else, and he would turn on the charm, ramp up the fun and leave the other poor bloke floundering in his wake. They may have had little in common, but over the years Di came to realise she always felt good when she was with Baz.

Over the course of their marriage as I saw their divergent interests draw them further away from each other and that delight in each other's company seemed to wane, I wondered whether Di would have been better off if she had taken up with some of the men of more artistic sensibilities that she associated with. They were certainly more cultured than Baz and wouldn't dismiss art so readily as something that only wankers bothered with. Perhaps her artistic career would have flourished more had she married an artistic type herself. Maybe she was suited to a more refined life than sharing it with a beer-drinking bookie. But then artistic temperaments are notoriously fickle, and I doubt that if Di had hooked up with any of her other young courtiers they would have survived the onset of the Swinging Sixties that in Australia seemed to arrive sometime in 1973.

Di was certainly not the key-party, wife-swapping kind

and, perhaps surprisingly, neither was Baz. While she was a virgin on her wedding day, Baz would not deny he had played the field leading up to their marriage. But I have no doubt whatsoever that once that ring went on his finger he was strictly a one-woman man. I firmly believe this, not because of anything my parents told me but because it tallies with what I knew of his moral compass. In his own way, Baz was every bit as black and white in his morality as was Di; he took his marriage vows as a sacred commitment of fidelity – although before you were hitched, well, in Baz's view that was pretty much a free-for-all, regardless of what the parish priest might have said about saving yourself for marriage.

I knew for certain that Baz was scrupulously faithful during their marriage because as he knocked the top off another stubbie one night the week after Di had died, he regaled me with tales of when he had been unfaithful before they got married. As someone who all too easily felt guilty kissing somebody months after I had broken up with a previous girlfriend, I found Baz's ability to corral his moral code into different zones fascinating. He may have been dating Di, but he hadn't committed himself to her through marriage, so until he did he saw nothing wrong with straying. I guess Baz was able to justify it morally because he was of that generation of men who divided women into girls you married and girls you ... well, one story in particular stayed with me.

About a year before Di finally relented and walked down the aisle, Baz had picked up an older woman at some bar in the city and they began an affair. I am not sure whether he knew from the beginning, but she was married to an older, wealthier man whom she was no longer intimate with, though they were still very much together. According to Baz, both of them knew that this relationship was nothing more than a recreational exercise and once he was married it would be over. Imagine, then, his surprise when he and Di emerged from the fibro church to the confetti strewn cheers of friends and family (even Di's family – the photos of Teeny from that day show her as proud as punch) and Baz noticed sitting in a car parked across the road the woman he had been having the affair with. I imagine Baz's heart would have been in his mouth. But then, he said, she raised a glass towards him, smiled a wistful smile, drained the champagne from her glass and drove off. Baz never saw or heard from her again. He told me, all those years later, that he felt she was just checking up on him, to make sure he had chosen well. Her lack of contact after that, Baz surmised, meant she approved of his choice.

For a long time I wrestled with whether I should reveal this story. It is a tale that Baz said he had never told anyone until he related it to me that night, and in writing it I worry that I am betraying his confidence, and somehow Di's as well. But I include it for two reasons: one to show that Baz was no saint, and I am not attempting to paint him as such; but more importantly, I believe it shows in a sense just how devoted Baz was to Di. Many others would have probably ended up continuing the affair sometime down the track. That thought never entered Baz's head. And as a bookie who dealt in cash and spent a hell of a lot of time away from his family, there would have been plenty of opportunity to stray. But when it all boiled down to it, Baz really did think Di was the only woman for him.

For all those years when I could see them drifting apart, niggling at each other, preferring to lead almost completely separate lives, and thought to myself 'Why the hell do you two bother to stay together?', what I was unable to see was the abiding, incorruptible love that flowed between them. It would take the gut-wrenching reality of Di's illness for me to see how embedded those bonds of love were.

6 GIVE ME A HOME AMONG THE TEA-TREE

And so Baz and Di were all set to settle down to a conventional lower-middle class Australian existence. Aspirational they'd call it these days, but back then all they aspired to was having a couple of kids, paying off the home loan, and having enough left over to have friends around for a barbie on the weekends and a trip to Surfers Paradise every few years. Actually, that's a bit harsh – they only ever went to Surfers once in their lives. It had been their honeymoon destination but they only made it as far as Port Macquarie. This was partly because they were in no rush to get going in the mornings, and partly because Baz would make sure they rolled into a town with a decent pub as early as possible. Those were still the days when some pubs wouldn't allow women into public bars on the grounds that their constitutions were too delicate to handle the rough and tumble of the company of drinking men, so on more than one occasion when there was no ladies lounge, Baz would have to bring a shandy out to Di, who'd be waiting in the car. So romantic.

By the time I had got to uni and had supposedly become more politically aware, I wrestled with the seeming ordinariness of my parents' ideals and on one occasion arrogantly condemned Di's middle class mores with a sneering, 'God, Mum, you're so bourgeois!' Di was mortified that I had said something like that to her, though she was slightly less offended when she learnt that 'bourgeois' was not actually a swearword.

But looking back many years later it became apparent to me that Baz and Di never quite led the conventional lives they might have outwardly projected. You don't get many artists marrying bookies in the suburbs, for starters. While the first house they built, on a block of coastal tea-tree scrub in the bayside suburb of Seaford, was of a typical housing company template, the angle on which the house sat was slightly askew in relation to the rest of the block, which proved a bugger when they tried to fit two cars in the driveway – the angle just prohibited the second car from squeezing in. Not that we had two cars for long as Baz was involved in an accident that totally wrote off his HR Holden and he never got around to buying another car for years; we all had to make do with Di's Valiant Gallant. Baz and his passenger were pretty banged up from the accident. Baz had to stay in bed for a week and his mate was hospitalised. They were both blind drunk at the time. Unfortunately, so was the bloke that sideswiped them. Ah, 1972: the fun, the freedom, the horrific road toll.

My parents' plan to live the conventional suburban life with a dog and 2.3 kids hit something of a hurdle when after a couple of years of marriage there were no children in the equation. Eventually it was discovered that Baz was infertile, caused, the doctors said, by a severe case of mumps as a teenager. If they wanted to have children, they would have to adopt. And so in 1968 Baz and Di drove up to the Royal Women's Hospital to collect me, aged two weeks. Di was not much of a drinker, but as they had arrived early, Baz suggested they go for a drink at a nearby pub. Two champagnes later Di was, in her words, 'a little bit tipsy' as she held me in her arms for the first time. With Di giggling and swaying unsteadily as she accepted me from the nurse, I can imagine the adoption case worker watching and thinking, 'Oh no, we've just made a huge mistake!'

Now for some readers the fact of my being adopted is going to colour everything else they read in this book: 'Ah, that's why he thought that – he's adopted.' The notion of adoption seems to do that to people. Ever since I can remember, whenever I told someone that I was adopted, their automatic reaction was, 'Oh, I'm sorry,' as if it was some heavy burden that I carried around, like I had a degenerative disease or my puppy had just died. This was probably made worse when I was very young and would, according to Baz, mispronounce 'adopted' so that I'd tell people proudly that I was 'a-doctored'. But even when my mastery of the English language had improved and people realised I hadn't had some sort of hideous corrective surgery on my genitals, I still invariably got the same reaction. And if I protested that being adopted was never a huge issue for me, people automatically concluded that I must be in denial so, basically, I won't go on about it here.

Except to say to those who think that growing up in a family that I didn't resemble physically or temperamentally must surely have had some effect on my sense of self, I would argue that feeling a sense of distance from your closest relatives is just as common among people who share the same DNA as their parents as it is for adopted children. How many people who grew up with their biological parents have looked around at their family members and wondered, 'How on earth was I beamed into this group of alien creatures?'

I know for some, the fact of being adopted renders their lives full of unresolved angst; it just didn't for me. Whether this comes about because of some biological predisposition not to get fussed about such things, I will never really know, but I suspect the reason I am so sanguine about what many might imagine is a great trauma is that right from the start, Baz and Di were always open about the fact. I don't know how they did it. I certainly can't imagine how you would approach such a conversation with a child who is too young to correctly pronounce the word itself, but for as long as I can remember I have always known that I was adopted and it seemed the most natural thing in the world. Even though I am not their biological son, I have never known any parents other than Baz and Di, so I never had a problem with it.

It was problematic for my brother, whom Di and Barry adopted (from different parents to mine) twenty months later. From a fairly early age he would threaten to 'find my real mum'. He usually uttered this when he had just gotten into trouble but it nonetheless must have been hurtful to hear. Baz and Di never reacted badly, though, and when Wok was legally old enough to search for his natural parents, they were more than encouraging. Unfortunately for Wok, it turned out that all of his birth family shared the same short fuse that he had and within a year or so they had pretty much all fallen out and he now rarely talks to any of them. Finding his biological family hadn't really been the answer he was seeking and although we didn't speak of it often, one time when we did, Wok said one of the things that most turned him off his birth mother (apart from the fact that if she had kept him, she was going to call him Ronald) was her insistence that he call her 'Mum'. That was too much for Wok, who earnestly explained to me, 'She's not me mum, Mum's me mum, can't she see that?' I understood exactly what he meant.

Around the time Wok was finding out about his origins, Di asked me if I wanted to do the same. I think she was far more interested than me in finding out where I came from. The fact is, it was never much of a priority and my curiosity never got the better of me. At one point, in my early twenties when riven with existential angst, I did have a desire to track down my father, hoping that he might have the answers to unlock the mysteries of the universe that I definitely wasn't getting from Baz. I hoped that my biological father might have gone through some of the same philosophical conundrums I'd been wrestling with and come out the other side wiser, though I suspect if he was anything like me and I did meet him to ask, he would shrug his shoulders and say, 'I dunno; life's complicated.'

In the early nineties my Uncle Bernie, husband of Baz's

sister Joyce and one of Baz's closest mates, was diagnosed with bowel cancer. Unlike Baz, Bernie would not recover. It dawned on me that, as my parents' generation headed towards their sixties, the incidence of people dying was going to increase rapidly. I had always imagined that my birth mother was probably quite a few years younger than Di (who was 31 when I was born), given that she was more likely to have been young and single when she got pregnant with me, but that still would have put her well into her forties and about to enter that cohort in which cancer, stroke and heart attack begin to take their toll. I thought it would be a great tragedy that if I did want to find her it might be too late. Giving up a child, even voluntarily (and who knows what pressures my birth mother was under), would surely have to be the most heart-rending thing anyone could go through, and I really didn't want her to spend her life not knowing whether I was OK. I wanted to be able to let her know that I was, that I was healthy, happy and that I harboured no resentment towards her whatsoever. In fact quite the opposite, I would love to be able to thank her for giving me life.

But then Di found out she had myeloma, and for the next four years much of my emotional life was taken up with that fact. Then seemingly straight after that came Baz's lung cancer. At least there was one advantage of being adopted – I wouldn't have inherited their appallingly cancer-susceptible genes. (Though having lived under the same roof as them for the first eighteen years of my life, if their cancers were lifestyle related, I guess I was still rooted!) By the time I had surfaced from both these events, almost ten years had passed since my resolution to find my birth mother. By then it felt a weird thing to do, as though I would have been saying, 'Hi, I've lost one set of parents, you can be my new mum!'

One of the definite advantages of being adopted is that you don't have to face up to the disturbing fact that your parents have ever had sex. Biological children simply can't get around the incontrovertible truth that at some stage their parents had to have done it, at least once for every child. As both my brother and I were adopted that causal link was lost and it was possible to dismiss that gross prospect. That is until the day Baz – after he had had a few – decided to fill me in on all the gory details of how he found out he was infertile. As I squirmed in horrified discomfort he told me how, after a couple of years of unsuccessfully trying for children, Di had been checked out medically and was given the all-clear. It was now Baz's turn to be scrutinised and all that was required of him was to supply a sample for testing. This was in a more modest era, when presumably the concept of getting down to the business at hand in a cubicle in the medical centre was not on, so Baz was required to fill the specimen cup in the privacy of his and Di's nuptial bedroom.

'Trouble was,' Baz continued, oblivious to my blanched, traumatised face, 'I'd be enjoying myself with your mum too much to bother reaching for the cup. It took me months before I got a sample back to them.'

So I guess I can thank Baz's love of being in the moment for the fact that they didn't adopt earlier. It is amazing how life can turn on fate's toss of a … coin, I was going to say coin, and but for Baz's lack of self-control, I may have ended up with an entirely different family. Food for thought, though it's an image I really could have done without; truly, too much information.

Aside from this revelation, mine was an untroubled childhood. Our family had its ups and downs – the fork stabbing incident being a clear frontrunner for the downs – but generally things flowed pretty smoothly. Wok continued to have a knack for getting into trouble; a volatile combination of a short fuse and a trusting nature meant he would get himself into a position where he felt people let him down. That and sometimes he was just a little shit. As an older brother it was my God-given duty to beat him up periodically, but really this wasn't too often and generally our fights were pretty harmless. In fact the most damage I ever inflicted on Wok was when, inspired by watching the boxing during the Montreal Olympics, I convinced him to don shorts and singlet and gloves (though not boxing gloves) for a bit of a gold medal bout. I was Australia, he had to be Brazil for some reason. Not realising that boxing gloves provide a lot more padding than the thin woollen variety, I delivered a series of joyous uppercuts to my six-year-old sparring partner, leaving a spray of blood across the lounge room. The physical fights between us stopped around the time he turned fourteen. Not because we'd matured enough to sort out our differences with dialogue and détente, but because one day when I fought him he wouldn't go down and no matter how hard I hit I couldn't make him cry like he usually did. And as his return blows were really starting to hurt, I thought it was a good time to bow out of the ring an undefeated champion.

Baz continued to spend more time getting drunk with his mates than he probably should have, but we never felt bereft of a father's love. It wasn't until I hit adolescence that the differences between us began to matter and become more noticeable. Things came to a head rather unexpectedly when I was about thirteen. Wok and I had followed in Di's footsteps and were quite into badminton (Baz had pretty much given up badminton after that first night when he met Di) and Di took us to a regular Friday night juniors' comp. Unusually for a Friday, Baz had come home early from the pub, though he had drunk enough to be a little bit argumentative. As he sat in his chair with another beer, and I was opposite him putting my shoes on, he barked something at me. I can't remember what it was about now – me not having done something he'd asked me to, perhaps. I gave him a barely acknowledging grunt in reply. Baz had a go at me for either not replying or not having done whatever it was I was meant to have done. Something in me snapped and I screamed back at him, 'What would you know? You were pissed, you're always bloody pissed!'

I had never raised my voice like that in my entire life. The whole house stopped in shock, me included. Then I burst into tears. The dam had burst with this first act of defiance and although I didn't know why I was sobbing, I just couldn't stop myself. Baz sat there looking stunned, not knowing what to say. After a long silence he had another swig from his beer. He immediately looked a bit shame-faced, and not knowing how to hide his embarrassment, took another swig. I rushed out of the room and Di followed. She started berating me for talking like that to my father, but her anger toward me wasn't of the sort that is characteristic of, say, a battered wife, who will defend her tormentor to the (sometimes literal) death, as I was soon to find out.

I spluttered between sobs, 'But it's true, Mum, he is always bloody pissed.'

'Oh I know that, we all know that,' she replied testily, 'but you shouldn't use language like that. You could just as easily have said that Dad was always drunk or inebriated. And I don't appreciate you using the word bloody. There really is no need.'

You could take the woman out of the Presbyterian church but you couldn't take the Presbyterian church out of the woman.

It may appear as though I have painted Baz as a raging alcoholic. While it is true that unless he was sick he did have a drink every day of his adult life, and would have got drunk on a sizeable percentage of those days, I am not sure that he should be saddled with such a label. I might now sound like a battered child blindly excusing the poor behaviour of a parent, but while Baz's drinking certainly used to annoy me, that is about as extreme as it got – me finding him tedious and embarrassing when he was drunk. There was no violence or threat of violence or any sort of nastiness. All that happened when Baz drank was that he would bore us stupid. For those who don't come from a drinking culture it may be hard to fathom but in the world I grew up in, the world of the Sports Club and the local pub,

Baz was not an alcoholic, but rather a successful exponent of the social art of drinking. He never drank in secret, it rarely affected his work performance, and alcohol for him wasn't an emotional crutch to fend off a scary world – it was the culture itself that was alcoholic. Baz was just fairly proficient at the caper.

To this day I still enjoy the process of drinking, especially when getting drunk is not the primary purpose. This is a trait I must have inherited from Baz (you don't have to be biologically related to inherit certain behaviours or tastes). The difference between Baz and myself, I suspect, is that I have never particularly enjoyed the feeling of being drunk itself. I don't like the loss of control or exposing myself to potential embarrassment. This may be a genetic difference between me and Baz, although it could just as easily be environmental conditioning. I spent so much of my youth rolling my eyes at how embarrassing my old man was when he'd had a few that it became ingrained in my nature not to let that happen to me.

In this sense, I suppose I take after Di. She had gotten over her mother's and aunties' abhorrence of alcohol but she never attacked it with great relish either, perhaps because she too was worried about making a fool of herself. Baz was more than capable of doing that for the both of them. It was funny, really, the very things that had attracted her to Baz were what frustrated her the most. It was almost as if, after so many years together, they would automatically fall into their designated roles – Baz making mischief (he was always the sort of bloke who wouldn't make a public speech himself but would be the loudmouth lobbing in comments from the back of the room whenever someone else was trying to speak) and Di getting testy, telling him to tone it down.

This is not to say that Di was always the hapless victim of Baz's exuberance. As evidenced by her comment to me, she was fully aware of Baz's nature and wasn't about to be totally sublimated by it. That she would stand up to Baz about his excesses was the greatest cause of friction between them but at the same time I think deep down Baz actually liked the fact that she was able to pull him back into line on occasion. It always amuses me how men of my dad's generation (and I think I am beginning to see it creep into some of my male friends too) make such a fuss about their wife being the handbrake to their having a good time, yet are actually grateful for an excuse to detach from the vicious circle of blokey camaraderie. I've noticed that often the only honourable way for a bloke to get out of the next shout is to claim 'there'll be strife if I don't get back to the missus' when in fact they had already entered the red zone with their wife somewhere after their third pot. Everybody knows the poor put-upon man could keep on drinking if he really wants to but it saves face if he can lay the blame at the feet of external forces. Much better to do that than to admit that for once in their life they wouldn't mind trading in that extra beer for the joys of their wife's cooking.

And in our house it was definitely Di who cooked the dinners. And the lunches and breakfasts. Well, actually Baz did cook the majority of breakfasts, at least for himself. Virtually every new parent I know complains about not getting enough sleep because the babies are always awake at an unseemly early hour. In our family it was the reverse: it was us kids who were woken almost every morning by the sound of Baz clattering around the kitchen as he listened to a badly tuned AM radio station before he headed off to work. And once he had retired from a nine-to-five existence he didn't let up – in fact he was actually out of bed even earlier, anywhere from around five thirty. And not even a big session at the club the night before would put a dent in his early rising. If anything, he would be up earlier and making even more of a racket – even if he was only making toast, Baz managed to bang every pot and pan in the kitchen. But breakfast for Baz was rarely that simple. He was a big fan of the cooked breakfast and I would emerge sleepily to watch my daily round of morning cartoons before getting ready for school to find Baz finishing off a plate of bacon and eggs. Or steak and eggs. Or sausages in a tomato and onion sauce. Baz would even cook a roast for breakfast, particularly on a race day, and it was not uncommon for him to be tucking into a roast pork chop before the paper had been delivered.

If you got up early enough you could get to share in the feast. The trouble was, when you wanted to sleep in Baz would bustle into the room, turn on the light and bellow his breakfast invitation. As I got older and into my twenties, whenever I stayed at home Baz seemed to have a sixth sense about whether I had had a big night and seemed to double his incursions into my room. As sweet as it may have been, having someone come in four times before seven o'clock to ask you whether you were sure you didn't want beef rissoles and mashed potato is not what you want if you got home at three in the morning. Just when I thought I'd gotten the message through and had drifted off again, Baz would stick his head in the door and loudly ask, 'If you don't want mashed potato with the rissoles, how about chips? I could fry some up now, it wouldn't take me long!'

And if you did get up and share Baz's breakfast of flathead he had gone out and caught that morning, he would sit across from you and wait until you'd forked in your first mouthful before inevitably telling you, 'I bet Liz and Phil aren't sitting down to this at Buckingham Palace. Better than their kippers on toast, don't you reckon?'

Baz seemed obsessed with what the Queen and Prince Phillip ate for breakfast. The royal couple were his theoretical yardstick by which he measured the quality of his cooking. Sometimes he would cast a few aspersions on Prince Charles' breakfast, but usually it was the Queen's. I don't know if the Queen ever does eat kippers for breakfast – I certainly hadn't and I suspect Baz hadn't either, but in his imaginings they paled by comparison with his latest breakfast offering. And he would be at you to agree that, had they known what we were eating, Liz and Phil would have been green with envy. (If not green with eating badly cooked kippers.)

No meal that Baz cooked was ever simply a meal: it was an event. Just making soup on a Sunday night, even if it was from a can, Baz brought a sense of occasion – of performance – to his cooking. He didn't necessarily need praise for cooking, but he certainly wanted acknowledgement that he had been in the kitchen. And generally he got no argument, for the stuff that he did cook was usually pretty good. To this day I still haven't tasted better roast spuds or pork crackling.

Even Di seemed to agree that Baz was the better chef. She wasn't necessarily a poor cook herself – in fact I still miss some of her dishes. I may be biased, and perhaps everyone reckons their mum's spaghetti bolognaise is the best ever, but I have yet to find one that to my mind matches hers – it was just that she lacked the flair and self-promotional skills of Baz in the kitchen. While Di always cooked with love, she never really had the passion for food that Baz did. Then again, it is probably hard to cook with passion when you are doing it every meal of the week for a largely unappreciative audience. Occasionally Di would get praised for her efforts, but generally our approach to food was far more prosaic when she cooked for us.

Baz's magic in the kitchen only went so far, however, and that was because he was very good at cooking for himself, cooking the food he loved to eat, but when it came to making meals for others because he had to, he was somewhat less than inspired and inspiring. Take the case of sandwiches. Wok and I would despair on the extremely rare occasions that Baz would have to make our school lunches. When he put his mind to it, Baz could make a monumental sandwich, but that would only be when he was in the mood for a sandwich himself, and a lot of fanfare accompanied its construction, which included going out and buying special bread and fillings. The production of a simple sandwich would become bigger than Ben Hur. When it came to slapping a bit of chicken loaf between two slices of white bread for his kid's lunches, though, Baz's heart wasn't really in it, and somehow he'd manage to bugger them up almost every time. Maybe sandwiches were beneath him but not so for Di. By contrast, every sandwich Di ever made us hit the spot because she knew what we liked, she made it with us in mind, not how she thought she would be regarded for making it. Sitting right next to the bluebird of happiness in the Pantheon of Mothers is the chicken loaf sandwich of love.

7

HOLD ME CLOSER, JIMMY DANCER

Until September 1984, the only sandwiches made by Baz that I had ever eaten were his Melbourne Cup specials – chicken sandwiches that he would make up at six in the morning of Cup Day for his staff because the queues to the food outlets would be too crowded for them to grab a bite in between races. But that month the expected trajectory of our family life came a cropper when Di was diagnosed with ovarian cancer. Suddenly Baz was forced to make up school lunches for Wok and me while Di was in hospital. After a few ham-fisted attempts at sandwiches, with chunks of ham the size of fists that tumbled out of brusquely buttered bread before you could get them up to your mouth, I suggested to Baz that a far easier solution was to give us money for a pie at the tuckshop. He readily agreed.

School lunches were the last thing on Baz's troubled mind. He was always a bit of a Jonah when it came to people with cancer, always quick to declare them on the way out once he heard the news that they'd had a brush with 'Jimmy Dancer'. So when, almost without warning, the surgeon was removing a malignant tumour the size of a grapefruit from where Di's womb used to be, Baz was really struggling to hold it together. We all were, the certainties of our former, comfortable lives had been unalterably shattered. I didn't seem to be quite as upset as everyone else, but I think that was simply because I was utterly convinced that Di would pull through. The idea that she might not recover never really registered with me, and as distressing as it was to see my mum in so much fear and pain, I found Baz's display of maudlin grief rather irritating, as only a self-absorbed sixteen year old can.

When I think back now to what my life would have been like had my mother died when I was sixteen it is an aching chasm of horror, so maybe I was just in self-protection mode. Maybe it was a classic case of denial: I was pretending it wasn't upsetting when really it was eating away at me. For the amateur psychologists among you there were plenty of clues that this might be the case. I had hit my teenage angst poetry phase with a vengeance and one of the works I was most proud of at the time was an endless series of stanzas (which not so coincidentally could be sung to the tune of 'Pop Goes the Weasel' – I had entered my nascent rock star phase as well, but didn't have the ability to come up with my own tunes) wherein, like a Derek and Clive sketch, virtually everybody I knew from my dog to Ronald Reagan had cancer.

My mate likes to smoke on a bong
Spinning out when he can
What is it that he has done wrong?
My mate has got cancer
© Sean Dooley, *Misunderstood Bedroom Poet Music*, 1984.

As I wrote those lyrics on my bed one weekend, I remember thinking that if 'the social workers' read these words they would all nod their heads sagely and pronounce me seriously disturbed. (I don't know why it was, but there was always a fear among the kids of Seaford of social workers taking us away, though it had never happened once that we knew of.) But to my mind they would have been completely wrong because, sure, cancer was naturally on my mind, but this was more a musing on the state of moral and physical decay of our society and political systems. I was far more concerned about the environmental cancer of a uranium mine in the Outback (I had just discovered Midnight Oil at that stage too) than I was about my mum dying from her ovarian cancer but of course 'the social workers' would never be smart enough to figure that out. (Though this was the time I was also reading *Cancer Ward*, so you be the judge.)

There was in actuality very little cause for optimism. The tumour was so well advanced that it was thought there must surely have been secondaries. These are what usually kill you if you get cancer. Unless the cancerous growth is in a vital organ such as your brain or your lungs, the initial tumour is rarely what finishes you off. It is when cells from the original tumour enter the bloodstream or lymphatic system that the cancer can become seriously life-threatening. These systems are pathways to the rest of the body and can deliver the escaped cancer cells directly to some fertile ground in another organ, from which they can fester and grow. Cancer cells are essentially normal body cells that have gone out of control and continue multiplying beyond what they should. Generally a particular cancer cell will only continue to survive and multiply in a part of the body that provides similar conditions to the site of the original tumour. Thus the cells that survive and move around the body through the bloodstream or lymphatic system can latch on to similar territory the same way a plant or animal from one country can get a hold in a new but similar environment in another land and, with no natural checks in place, run rampant. Cancer is our own internal cane toad. For example breast cancer, which exists in a calcium-rich environment in the milk ducts, often finds its way into the bones where, of course, the most calcium is concentrated. The liver, with its rich blood supply, is one area that is attractive to many cancer cells and becomes a prime source of these secondary colonies known as metastases.

The size of Di's tumour had the specialists believing metastatic growths were inevitable. Miraculously they had never developed, though waiting to find out if her cancer had metastasised was an extremely tense time, one that was exacerbated by the tumour bursting as the surgeon was removing it. He thought he had mopped up all the spilt material but couldn't guarantee that he hadn't missed some and that it could take hold and develop into further cancer. We had to wait for more exploratory surgery twelve months later before he was able to confirm that she was indeed free of the disease and the initial surgery had been a success. I remember that Di did have some chemotherapy in that time but I am fairly certain that the effects weren't too debilitating and after a few weeks, she was back to making our lunches (along with doing all the other cooking) and, despite our heartfelt vows during the treatment, the rest of us were soon taking her for granted again.

In times of crisis such as a cancer diagnosis it is a common reaction to try and make deals with God, or to vow to live better or more fully, but I am reminded of what some stand-up comedian said (or was it Homer Simpson?) about how, if you lived every day as if it were your last, you would spend it crying your eyes out for everything you were about to lose, or just pissing off everyone around you by going on a major bender. Why should it be that we need a major trauma in our life to give us a kick up the bum? I have a feeling that the happiest people are those who have somehow learnt to appreciate what they have before it is gone, those who have the ability to live every day well regardless of whether it might be their last. These are the people who, if catastrophic news comes their way, are far more likely to cope because they will have fewer regrets about the way they have already lived. They won't need to make up for lost time – they will continue to make the most of what time they have.

Just in case our family hadn't got that message, the fates decreed that within one month of Di getting her all-clear we were back in hospital sitting around the bed of another parent who had just been diagnosed with life-threatening cancer. This time it was Baz. Looking at a photo of him taken just before his diagnosis it is amazing that we didn't pick up that something was seriously wrong. There he is in our backyard (cigarette in hand) looking as emaciated as a famine victim. But the weight loss had been so gradual that nobody had really noticed it happening. Baz had been a bit crook in the guts for a couple of years by this stage, so his recent discomfort hadn't set off too many alarm bells. He had initially been diagnosed with stomach ulcers two years earlier and after much nausea and reflux and discomfort, they managed to find the right combination of medication and things had settled down. So when the stomach pains returned we all assumed it was just a return of the ulcers.

It was only when Baz's doctor saw him that he immediately knew something was terribly wrong. He asked Baz if he had had any bleeding when he went to the toilet. Baz said no, he hadn't noticed anything like that. Dispensing with social niceties, the doctor asked Baz if his stools had been a black colour. They had. Contrary to what you might think, if you bleed from the bowel the stools aren't usually blood red but black because the blood has been sitting inside your colon, mixing with your faeces. Charming stuff, I know, but it is information that could actually save your life. The doc sent Baz straight in for tests and his suspicions were soon confirmed – stage three bowel cancer. They rate bowel cancer in terms of its extent, stage one being the earliest – and more treatable – stage. Stage three is where it is so far advanced that few people survive. At least they didn't back then. When you have family members who experience cancer you become something of an armchair expert and even years later pick up and retain snippets about the subject. I know that survival rates for bowel cancer are far better than they were in the mid eighties but I don't know if that is because with more extensive screening they are picking it up earlier or because they have become more effective at treating stage three.

With the tumour so far advanced, the specialists held out little hope for Baz. We didn't know this at the time as medical practitioners are adept at the art of holding out some hope no matter how grim things look. In fact it wasn't until Baz was seeing another specialist about his lung cancer that he found out how serious the bowel cancer had really been. The specialist (not Dr Nick, who would never have allowed himself such an unguarded moment) was looking at Baz's medical history and whistled in surprise: 'Stage three bowel cancer. Can't say I've met many stage threes fifteen years down the track.'

Miraculously, the surgeons were able to remove the entire tumour so cleanly that Baz neither had to have chemotherapy, nor did he have to wear a colostomy bag. Another inch of bowel and he would have been saddled with one. Baz made a complete recovery, and the only sign that anything had ever been wrong was that occasionally, if I used the toilet after Baz, I would find an intact cashew floating in the bowl. I quizzed Baz about it once and he said that he no longer had enough large intestine left to digest things like whole cashews and they would pass through unmolested. When I asked him why he hadn't actually chewed the cashew in the first place, he replied matter-of-factly, 'What can I say? I like cashews. Sometimes I just get carried away when I'm eating them and forget to chew.'

Of course, at the time Baz went into hospital none of us knew what the outcome would be, though again I was supremely confident to the point of being totally unconcerned that the operation would be anything more than a temporary inconvenience. I had no inkling or sixth sense about the outcome, I was just, at the age of seventeen, unable to conceptualise that my father, as annoying as I found him, might not pull through. As a result I was even more callous about Baz's operation than I had been about Di's.

The day before Baz's operation we had the annual Dooley family Christmas party. These had been started by George and Alma in the fifties as their children began to have kids of their own and it became logistically impossible for the entire family to be together on Christmas Day. By 1985 George was long gone, but Alma was still very much alive and kicking and would lord it over the party, dispensing specially wrapped gifts for every person. And with ten children, 38 grandchildren and an ever-burgeoning population of great-grandchildren in the Dooley family, not to mention all the in-laws and ring-ins such as Ace and Chris, who were considered honorary Dooleys, Alma's gift-giving went on for longer than a Fidel Castro speech to the party faithful.

What I now miss most about those parties was what, at the time, I think I loathed the most – the rough-house growl of the Dooley men. Essentially the men in the family left all the present giving and salad making and conversation to the women and would pretty quickly gather somewhere down near the shed in the backyard of whichever family was holding that year's do and get stuck into a riotous game of two-up. Uncles, cousins, mates of mates would all be getting loudly stonkered on copious bottles of beer as they laid down wads of notes in anticipation of the swy stick throwing up those two coins. I was too young to participate and would stand behind the circle of the two-up school, looking through the legs trying to work out what the roar was about. At the time it was mystifying and unfathomable and just a little frightening, but I was never to be initiated into this ritual of Dooley manhood, for by the time I was old enough, the elders of the Dooley tribe had started to drop off the perch. First George (prostate cancer) then a couple of years later it was my Uncle Ken (breast cancer – yep, men can get it too), then a hiatus of seventeen years, followed by a seeming rush with uncles Peter (cardiomyopathy), Norm (pancreatic cancer), Pat (who having beaten breast cancer died from prostate cancer, though he also had dementia so it is hard to know what it was that actually killed him) and the brothers-in-law Bernie and Alby (bowel and lung cancer), along with various cousins and family friends. (You can see why I was glad I was adopted – who would want to share the same genes with these people?!) By the time I was an adult (and had enough cash to afford to play two-up) the Dooley Christmas two-up games had ceased, the voluminous cheers of the men silent forever.

At the pre-op Christmas party, Baz was particularly raucous. I guess he was fearful it could be his last. I left the party early as I was going to a Midnight Oil concert that night at Kooyong Tennis Courts. As I said goodbye, a very drunk Baz shook my hand and pulled me close as he tearfully told me how much he loved me. And just in case anything went wrong the next day, he asked me to look after Mum and Wok as I'd be the man in the family. Not only was I embarrassed at my old man's drunken public display of affection, I was actually annoyed with him, thinking he was overdramatising his medical situation because he was pissed. Why else would he have used such hackneyed clichés, I thought to myself, not wanting to acknowledge the depth of the meaning of those words. I know it seems callous, and it was, but my attitude came about partly because I was utterly convinced that the operation would be a success and Baz would be fine.

I was so unconcerned that after the Oils concert I stayed up at the flat of my best friend's sister as it was close to the venue. As we were catching the train home the next day I could feel my throat becoming increasingly scratchy. By the time I got home, nobody was there. I figured correctly that Di had taken Wok to the hospital to visit Baz once he had come around from the operation. As there were no messages I assumed that all was well and as the sore throat had now developed into a raging cold, I took myself off to bed. The phone rang a couple of hours later and it was Di. I have never heard her more ropable in my life; it is the only tongue-lashing I ever remember getting from her and it was excoriating. She was incensed at how insensitive I had been.

I protested that as the operation had been a success, I couldn't see why she was so upset. It is the only time in my life I ever heard my mother speak with fury in her voice: 'Sean, your father could have died today and you don't even seem to care. I can't believe you, of all people, could be so heartless.'

We were incredibly lucky that both of them beat their cancers at this time. I was exceptionally fortunate because not only did it mean I had my parents around to see me into adulthood (not that I seemed to appreciate it back then), I also had enough time with them to become aware of what it would mean to lose them, and to make sure that the time I had with them was worthwhile. Those surgeons who saved my parents' lives also saved the quality of my life, and for that I owe them more than they could ever know.

8

THE STINKPOLE

The diagnosis of bowel cancer was a turning point in Baz's life but perhaps not in the way one might expect. While it was undoubtedly a sobering experience, this was only in the metaphoric sense. Once he was fully recovered, Baz's drinking habits barely slowed down. Neither did his pack a day smoking habit (though he would eventually give up seven years later) or his low fibre, high animal fat diet. No, the change in fortunes for Baz that arose from his brush with death was financial. He had left his job as a customs agent conveniently around the time I started high school. Simultaneously, the bookie business went through a rough trot, so money was tight. While I had won a scholarship to a private school, it was not a full scholarship and for the first year, with Baz out of work, they really struggled to pay the one-third fees each term. I was gladly offering to drop out and go to the local state high school where all my mates from primary school had gone, but Baz and Di wouldn't hear of it. Before things got too dire, Mick Hogan, an old mate of Baz's from his Chelsea days, got him a job with the old Gas and Fuel Department testing gas meters in a workshop in Port Melbourne.

The sheltered workshop was what Baz called it. This was a workplace with the triple crown of inefficient work practices: it was technically part of the public service; it was highly unionised; and it was populated mainly by men from Port Melbourne, who developed their working culture from the docks where for decades hard work was part of the job, just not a regular part of the job. On his first day Baz had tested his quota of meters by eleven o'clock and was admonished for working too hard. For the next four years he made sure he had finished his quota by eleven as it meant he could go for an early counter lunch at the local with the blokes and not have to make it back till knock-off time. He came to know nearly every pub in Port Melbourne, and would put that knowledge into full use on race days when he would stop for a pre- or post-race tipple.

After his operation Baz went to see the Gas and Fuel doctor. He looked through Baz's charts and said to him that if he really wanted to, there was no medical reason why he couldn't come back to work. But if Baz so desired, the doctor was willing to recommend that he was too sick to work so that he could take an early retirement package. Baz's brother-in-law Bernie had taken an early package from Telecom a year or two before and had bought a boat and was spending a lot of time fishing out on the bay. Baz didn't need to think about it too long.

And so thanks to his bowel cancer, Baz was able to retire at forty-nine. The package was enough to pay off the remaining mortgage on the house at Seaford and, as so often happens in life, Baz's luck turned elsewhere, particularly at the track, where he started to progress through the bookmaking ranks, taking on ever bigger clients and reaping ever bigger rewards. With money suddenly streaming in, Baz and Di sold the house at Seaford and bought a block of land at a canal development in the next suburb, Patterson Lakes, where they would build their dream home. Baz and Di started going on plenty of holidays, including cruises with Ace and Chris. After such a shocking and pessimistic time, both felt they'd had a major reprieve and Baz in particular set about making sure he enjoyed the bonus years he had been given.

It was around this period that I started working for Baz at the races, and for twelve years until his retirement in 1997 I was to see my father every Saturday, at least in a work context – probably way too often for a son to see his father. But then if I hadn't worked for Baz, there would have been a distinct possibility that we would have ended up hardly ever seeing each other. There was even a point where we both talked about me taking over from him, creating the third generation of the Dooley bookmaking dynasty.

That I could have become a bookie would probably come as a complete surprise to all those who have known me. They wouldn't think I was the type. Then again, I wouldn't have thought I was the type either. Bookmaking was never a natural fit for me as it clearly was for Baz. While I had occasionally accompanied him as a kid on his journeys around the state where he worked a stand at small-time country race meetings, I was usually more interested in catching the locusts and crickets that hid in the fissures of the dry, cracked earth of the racecourse car parks than I was in the actual horseracing.

When Baz eventually worked his way onto the city tracks I would sometimes tag along but my main passion was not the drama of the betting ring, but trying to get my head on the television racing coverage. My personal best was being filmed by the side of the track at Moonee Valley for every race on the card, including standing next to the starter's gate at the beginning of the final race. I learnt an early life lesson here – even though there was no way known a ten year old should have been hanging around bucking, agitated beasts that weighed up to half a tonne, as long as I acted like I belonged there, nobody asked any questions. It was my first direct experience of Baz's favourite observation that 'Bullshit baffles brains.'

For that particular race, the starting gate was at the finishing line and the horses had to run an entire lap of the course. As they made their way around the track I invented a little drama in which all my money was on the second placegetter. The camera recorded the horses whizzing past the finishing post for the last race of the day (what Baz called 'The Get-Out'), and there was this strange ten year old in a tracksuit top waving his arms around in a woefully over-the-top impression of a down-on-his-luck punter. Those who saw me in my later stab as an actor would say that nothing had changed with my technique.

I actually began working for Baz at the races when I was fourteen. My first job was as a runner during the Melbourne

Cup carnivals of 1982–83. Normally the term 'runner' applies to someone who lays off bets, that is, has bets with other bookies in order to lessen the potential financial damage a particular horse would cause if it won. In my case I was literally running up and down an escalator in order to get the odds for each race. Baz had secured himself a spot on the top floor of the new grandstand on the hill at Flemington, but come Spring Carnival time the racing club turfed him out of his usual location and out onto the escalator stairwell in order to make way for corporate clients.

To add insult they provided no PA system for Baz to hear the odds as they changed. It was my job to run down to the main betting ring a floor below where my cousin Greg was recording any fluctuation in the betting market. I would then sprint back up the escalators to tell Baz of the changes. Greg, who was studying accountancy, got the sedentary gig partly because of his numeric skills but more so because as an adolescent who hadn't undergone a major growth spurt, I was deemed small and skinny enough to squeeze through the milling throng of drunken revellers who packed out the grandstand, trying to take advantage of the views directly across from the winning post.

For my troubles I got thirty bucks a day, scalding hot coffee tipped on my scalp as I pushed through the crowd knocking punters' elbows, thighs like a Russian gymnast, and the opportunity to watch two of the greatest Melbourne Cups ever run unfurl before my eyes: The first year Gurner's Lane saluted to record a rare Caulfield–Melbourne Cup double and in doing so edged out the mighty Kingston Town, widely regarded as the best horse since Phar Lap; then in 1983 I got a bird's-eye view of Kiwi's amazing run from nowhere to snatch an incredible victory within inches of the post.

I must have done a halfway decent job (or Baz's nepotism ran deep) for a couple of years later I found myself working as one of his regular bookie's clerks. Early on my main job was to replace the betting sheets after every race. I mentioned earlier how once the horses had jumped for one race, Baz and the other clerks would dump all the gear with the payout clerk and head for the bar. If there weren't winning bets to settle, the payout clerk – who in those days was either my Uncle Bernie or my Uncle Norm – would hand everything to me and race off to the bar too, leaving me to pay out any outstanding bets as well as slot the sheets with the list of horses for the next race into the board and then await the call of the opening odds for that race to be broadcast over the racecourse speaker system.

Baz handled bets on Adelaide, Brisbane and Sydney races, which meant I was up and down on the stand twiddling knobs like an obsessive-compulsive mad scientist in a thunderstorm. The on-course speakers weren't always of the greatest quality, and if there was a large number of punters crowding in on the betting ring, or if the broadcast of another race was in progress, it became impossible to hear anything of the call of the card. A few years later they replaced the speakers with screens that would show the progression of all the odds, but when I first started I had to rely on the potency of my sixteen-year-old hearing.

Not being into horses much myself, I knew bugger-all about

form lines, so I was totally reliant on the announcements being correct and being able to interpret them accordingly. In order to stop keen-eyed punters taking advantage of any mistakes I might have made, I was always supposed to put up the 'board not set' sign as I was adjusting the odds for each horse. One particular day at Flemington I forgot to put the sign up. I misheard the price for the favourite and put up 33 to 1 instead of 3 to 1. Immediately a punter leapt from the crowd and demanded to bet fifty bucks on that horse. His unseemly haste triggered alarm bells and I looked across at the other bookies' boards and realised with gut-dropping horror that I had got the odds wrong. At 33 to 1 it was a payout of $1650, at 3 to 1 it was $150.

'Sorry, the board's not set,' I stammered.

'Bullshit! Where's your sign?' the punter demanded.

I looked up at the board and with a sinking heart realised I hadn't put it up. I would have to take his bet. Thankfully, at that moment Baz arrived back from the bar. He knew immediately that something wasn't right, not because he had assiduously followed the form and knew what the favourite in the seventh race in Brisbane would be, but because he could see how the weaselly looking punter had literally leapt over the other racegoers to try and get a piece of the action. The punter had that shifty look of someone doing something dodgy (though the expression was probably so permanently etched on his features that he could have been donating to the church collection plate and the priest would automatically have checked his wallet hadn't been pinched). He argued vehemently that he was entitled to get his thirty-threes.

The rules of racing say that once you have bet with a bookie, there is no going back on the bet from either party, but that is contingent on handing over your money and receiving a ticket. In this instance Baz was still well within his rights to reject the bet, but once he found out that the 'board not set' sign hadn't been up, Baz accepted the bet, all the while pointing out to the punter that he was an unconscionable scum for taking advantage of a young kid's mistake. But he took the bet nonetheless, the horse duly saluted and Baz wore the extra fifteen hundred dollar loss.

I learnt more about my father that day than I had in the previous sixteen years: (a) that though he had a short fuse (who wouldn't if their idiot son had just lost them the cost of a return trip to London?) he would soon get over it; (b) that his sense of honour was very strong, even when dealing with those whose sense was not; and (c) that money would never ruin his day, nor get in the way of the important things in life, for as soon as the next race was over, he was back at the bar, laughing with his mates as if nothing had happened.

Until that day, the clerk's job had just been something for me to do to earn a bit of pocket money. To be honest, I didn't really care for it either way. But watching the payout clerk hand over all those fifty-dollar notes to the smirking weasel brought home with a painful thud the reality of my father's occupation. I was mortified by my mistake, and perhaps for the first time ever I could see the implications of my actions. I calculated that if I offered to work at half pay for the next two years, I would be able to compensate Baz for his loss. I made the offer on the drive home with Baz and Ace. Baz simply wouldn't hear of it.

'You're not planning on doing it again are you, Rupe?' he asked.

'Not if I can help it, Dad,' I offered.

'All right then, don't worry about it. If I had a dollar for all the times I cost my old man money … Hey, Ace, remember that time Knackers O'Brien wanted to lay off on Big Philou when George was down at the trough?' and off Baz went with a trail of reminiscences that would last the entire drive home, from stopping for some 'travellers' (takeaway beers to be drunk on the way home) at one of his many local pubs in Port Melbourne, to the second pit stop at the Royal Oak in Cheltenham to restock supplies, with Baz barely drawing breath between anecdotes. Man, I used to hate listening to Baz on the drive home. Once I was old enough to drive, I became designated driver and hence couldn't even seek the solace of the back seat, wedged between my Uncle Norm and my Uncle Bernie. Occasionally I would have to break from my grim-faced contemplation of the traffic to turn and acknowledge whatever it was that Baz was banging on about. Forget waterboarding, if you want to devise a torture technique guaranteed to crack any eighteen year old, then stick them in a confined space with their father and his middle-aged mates when they have had a skinful, and the kid will confess to anything after just fifteen minutes.

It wasn't that what Baz had to say was necessarily boring or way off beam. To someone who had just met Baz, his stories would have been thoroughly engaging and delightful but, sadly, familiarity does breed contempt and there were times when Baz would launch into some particular diatribe for the eight hundredth time and no amount of 'Yeah, I know' could dissuade him from continuing. I would seriously contemplate crashing the car into a lamppost just to shut the bastard up.

As a writer I now really wish I had paid more attention to his stories, as they were often great tales that spoke of an Australian way of life that even then was rapidly disappearing. Stories such as the time when a famous pioneer aviator (whose identity seemed to change with each retelling) emergency landed his Tiger Moth in the paddock next to the school oval in Yarrawonga. Baz and his schoolmates swarmed over the plane excitedly and after the famous aviator had got the engine going again and flown off, they revealed to each other all the nuts and bolts they had souvenired from the fuselage. Or the story about an old World War I veteran, Morrie, who worked as a penciller for George. After Morrie's wife had died, he would invite Baz and Ace in for 'one quiet one' when they dropped him home after the races. With big Saturday nights planned the boys would reluctantly agree because they could see his loneliness, but as soon as they entered the kitchen Morrie would knock the top off half a dozen bottles and say to them that they may as well stay as he couldn't drink all that beer by himself. Or Baz's claim that he went out on the piss with the 1956 Olympic gold medal high jumper the night he won the event. An African-American, he was the first black man Baz had probably met, and in those days there were still discriminatory laws against serving alcohol to Aboriginals, but with that gold medal around his neck they got into every pub in town, as well as, the way Baz told it, the pants of half the girls in town.

They were not bad tales, it was just that I had heard them all before, and they were utterly predictable. For instance, whenever we drove through St Kilda junction and passed the Chinese restaurant that nestled incongruously with its laminated tables between a brothel and a tattoo parlour, Baz, if he wasn't already rhapsodising about his mates' boozy adventures at the Wagga races or how much Di's proposed cosmetic dentistry was going to cost him, would launch into a reminiscence of how, in the fifties, it had been the closest 'Chows' to where Baz lived in Parkdale. They'd drive the thirty minutes to the restaurant armed with their own saucepans (no plastic takeaway containers in those days) for their serve of special fried rice and sweet and sour pork, and then drive home again.

And that story would inevitably lead to a retelling of the time when George and Alma were away on holiday and had farmed eighteen-year-old Baz off to some relatives because they knew their youngest, only unmarried child couldn't be trusted to look after the house by himself. But Baz and Mick O'Connor, an impish, perennially single and often drunk (perhaps the two were somehow connected?) mate of Baz's had worked out how to gain entry to the house by squeezing through the milk delivery chute, a task made easier using Mick, who was as close to a leprechaun as you could find outside of a storybook.

They were well into old George's beer supply when Baz's sister Judy turned up unexpectedly with one of her girlfriends. The party really got going then, and after some while it was decided that Chinese was in order. Mick and Judy volunteered to undertake the drive, leaving Baz and Judy's friend to mind the fort. After another couple of drinks it suddenly dawned on each that the other was a good sort and by the time Judy and Mick returned armed with their rapidly cooling saucepans, Baz and the friend were passed out naked in each other's arms on the lounge room floor.

A great story, aside from the vision of your father having a premarital romantic interlude (or any love life for that matter), but when you've heard it every second Saturday night for five years, that lamppost becomes a very attractive proposition.

But the prize for enduring the most tortuous Baz story doesn't fall to me, but to my brother who, once I had left the family home, briefly had the job as Baz's chauffeur. One night Baz instructed Wok to give St Kilda junction a miss and head up past the 'stinkpole'. Poor, unworldly Wok made the mistake of asking what exactly Baz meant by the term 'stinkpole'. A fair question, and one that you may well be asking yourself.

The short answer is that a sewage vent used to stand at the intersection of Alma Road and Barkly Street. This long, narrow pipe was intended to allow potentially volatile sewer gases to escape harmlessly into the atmosphere rather than blow up the streetwalkers and gutter crawlers in a freak accident. The pole is no longer there so presumably the water authorities devised some other way to deal with the excess methane – at least one would hope. Whether or not you feel this might be an interesting topic to hear about, you'd also probably assume it would take no more than a minute to explain. It took a tanked-up Baz the best part of forty-five. Forty-five minutes on a sewage vent – we have a winner! Poor Wok. I was almost sorry I wasn't there for that one. Almost.

What I found with all Baz's stories, amusing or not, was that they weren't really a form of conversation. It was just him banging on about his world, situated more often than not in the past, and allowing no incursion into the sanctity of his diatribe. He certainly never seemed to be interested in anyone else's world and, particularly after he had a few beers in him, there were no gaps long enough for anybody else to actually contribute anything. When he was on a roll, even his mates couldn't get a word in edgeways. Sure, a lot of people get like this when they are drunk – alcohol allows their self-centredness to play the main stage of the rock festival of their lives, whereas it may normally just have a gig in the 3.30 am slot in the jazz-fusion/world music marquee down by the overflowing toilets, but Baz was like this for pretty much most of the time. If you weren't into the things he was on about – the races, beer, football, beer, sport in general, a good steak and beer – then you could waste an awful lot of energy trying to get him to take an interest in anything beyond his own world.

Now this is hardly the worst thing in the world that can happen to a child – they certainly wouldn't let me into the 'misery memoir' club with something as lame as 'my father was not on my wavelength'. But though I was angry with Baz for a period there in my late teens over his lack of understanding, by my early twenties I had worked out that that was the way he was. I knew that he loved me and wanted the best for me, but if I was searching for a connection beyond that, I was looking in the wrong place. I came to believe that Baz didn't really have the imaginative capacity to 'get' who I was and as that was something I couldn't force if I wanted to maintain a connection with him, I had to sit at his table. I would always be able to share his love of steak; I just had to learn not to serve him up lentil and chickpea curry if he ever did come to my table. And to never, ever mention the stinkpole.

9   A LITTLE DITTY ABOUT BAZ AND DIANE

It wasn't just that Baz and I were different personality types, we were also of different generations. I was born smack in the middle of Gen X, though I never really felt plugged in to the pop culture of my times. This feeling of isolation from my own generation is a trait I am assured is the very thing that identifies me as a typical Gen Xer. My generation came of age in an era post feminism, post civil rights and post postmodernism when the excesses of the previous generations, both social and environmental, had been curbed by the rise of AIDS and global warming. Well, the excesses continued, but we all just felt guiltier about them. Basically it was an era in which the old certainties of the past had gone, particularly if you were male. Baz belonged to the generation that fell between the 'Greatest Generation' (those who had come of age during the Depression and fought in World War II) and the Baby Boomers. This was a generation that got the best of both worlds without really having to fight for either of them. Benefiting from the post-war prosperity that preserved the old order for a decade or two, Baz's generation were young enough to enjoy the fruits of liberation that the social revolution of the sixties brought without having the spectre of the Vietnam draft hanging over them.

Perhaps the big difference between us was that I was of the first generation of men that grew up with an awareness that the social rules had changed and as such were negotiating new ways of being a man within this new order. When confronted with these changes to the old orthodoxy, Baz's generation either couldn't comprehend them or fell back on the claim that it was all 'political correctness' gone mad. And while, in some ways, the pendulum may have swung too far in its correction (I am sure I would have got a lot more sex if I hadn't spent so much of my twenties fretting over whether a woman would feel oppressed if I tried to make a move on her, when all she probably wanted was a good shag), I can't help feeling that the main objectors to political correctness are middle-aged men offended by the fact that they can't get away with being the rude pigs they had previously been allowed to be.

Not that I am saying Baz was much of a bigot, far from it, just that he was a product of a certain generational mindset. When Baz and Di got married we still had a prime minister who had also been PM in the 1930s. The great social and economic changes of the previous couple of decades had yet to wash over Australia's isolated shores and in so many ways it really was a man's world. Baz went straight from living at home with his parents and having his mum cook and clean for him to being married and having his wife do the same. His lifestyle barely changed. Listening to Baz's stories I couldn't help but feel slightly envious at the amount of freedom he and his married mates had. I seriously doubt that any man of my generation could get away with what Baz did during the first twenty years of his marriage.

Maybe they do and I am just ignorant of what goes on all around the country, but to me it seemed in some ways as if Baz's Sports Club was one of the last vestiges of that blokey culture where the men could grog-on free of any feminine influence. In this hallowed space, boys could be boys, within reason, and fathers could boast about getting their sons laid, while others could refer to their wife, whom they clearly loved and were devoted to, as 'The Sow' and suffer no censure. It was probably no worse than any group of women getting together with their girlfriends over a few wines and running down their hubbies. But the difference was that for many of these men, the attitude of the club had been the prevailing atmosphere of the society they had grown up in.

Perhaps an illustration is in order. This one comes courtesy of Baz on one of those interminable drives home from the races, though this was a story that Baz only told once, and it is one I would have welcomed hearing again. At the time Baz was only about 21 and single, but his brother Ken was well and truly married with at least two kids. Ken lived in Geelong but would come up to the city on a Saturday to work at the races for old George. As they were having a beer at the end of the day, Ken casually asked Baz what he was up to that night. Baz said that a girl he fancied (not Di) was having a nineteenth birthday party – a pyjama party. Ken's interest was piqued so he invited himself along. Baz protested that Ken probably wouldn't like it as the party-goers would mainly be eighteen-year-old girls. Eighteen-year-old girls *in pyjamas*, Ken corrected him, and could not be dissuaded from going, any thought of getting home to Geelong to tuck the kids into bed totally forgotten.

Ken insisted they arrive early so they headed straight from the races to the party, and were indeed the first there. The girls were happy to see Baz but weren't so sure about Ken, who, at 32, seemed like an old man to the teenagers. Ken didn't seem too fussed but after a few minutes of strained pleasantries he sidled up to Baz and said he was going out the front for a smoke. The pyjama party got into full swing, courtesy of the boxes of beer Baz and Ken had brought along, but one thing was amiss: aside from Baz, none of the boys invited to the party had shown up. The girls were a bit worried, but they were having fun with Baz, who was lapping up the attention, so they soon forgot about it. After about an hour Ken rejoined the party and when challenged that he wasn't wearing any PJs, shut them up by proclaiming that he slept in the nude. The girls allowed him to stay in the suit he'd worn at the races.

Baz couldn't believe his luck and at one point as he and Ken were out in the backyard watering the lemon tree, he commented on how no other blokes had turned up, giving him the pick of the chicks. Ken smiled and explained to Baz that when he was out the front having his 'smoke', he confronted every young bloke who turned up in flannel PJs, asking in a fierce tone, 'Who the fuck are you?' When they responded, 'Well who the fuck are you?' he answered, 'I'm the birthday girl's father. Now fuck off before I really get shitty.' It worked every time and Baz and Ken had all the girls to themselves.

Not that Baz divulged whether Uncle Ken actually did have any of the girls at the party. Ken's wife, my Aunty Norma, was still alive at the time that Baz told me the story and he could be surprisingly discreet. It may have been that Ken was just looking out for his younger brother, but whether Ken did or didn't was beside the point. It was the fact that he had no compunction about leaving his wife at home with a couple of infants, completely in the dark as to where her husband was on a Saturday night. The fact that Ken and Norma ended up having six children is testament to the fact that he couldn't have got into too much trouble for staying out, and he and Norma remained together and, as far as I know, devoted to one another, as unfathomable as it might seem to us by today's standards.

Not that Baz always got away scot-free with his shenanigans. I remember Di saying that when Baz and Ace failed to return home for dinner after the races (or even during the week when they would have met up at lunchtime when both of them were working in the city) she and Chris would get on the phone to each other and tearfully resolve to take the kids and leave. It might have been a close-run thing – I remember waking one night to hear Baz and Di arguing (probably about his drinking but I couldn't be sure) and Di mentioning the D word – but it never actually happened. I was young enough at the time to be horrified at the prospect that my folks could break up and after the row had settled down Di could hear me sobbing above Baz's snores and had to reassure me that she hadn't meant it and had just said it in frustration. Her soothing words didn't really convince me but as I had never known her to lie, I had to take her at her word. Still, it was a long time before I got back to sleep.

At that age I was devastated at the thought of them splitting up. By the early nineties, I thought it would probably be inevitable as they were living such separate lives under the one roof anyway. And by then, it didn't particularly bother me – I thought they would be happier that way. For the couple of years leading up to Di's second cancer diagnosis, it seemed at times that they barely tolerated each other's presence. There were still many occasions when they were united and seemingly happy, but I could see a tension building in those years. Maybe I was only noticing this because as I emerged from my teenage self-obsession I was becoming aware of the way people interacted with each other. Maybe I was identifying with Di's frustration because I was feeling a similar disillusionment with Baz's seeming narrow-mindedness. I remember reading aloud to Di a semi-autobiographical theatre monologue that I had written and in it the protagonist says of his father, 'Everyone says my old man is a living legend. That may be the case, but the problem with living legends is when you have to live with them.'

Di tried to defend Baz to an extent but in the end was more sympathetic towards me, saying I would just have to learn to accept Baz for who he was as he would never change. When

I told Baz about the play, he responded, 'Is this one I have to go and see?'

I thought about it for a second, imagining how maybe a few home truths would be delivered if he came and saw it, and then said, 'No, I don't think you'd be interested, Dad.'

'Thank Christ for that. Do you want a beer?' Then he added, responding to a not so subtle glare from Di, 'But I'm sure it would be good though, Rupe. Just not my bag, right?'

This was at the root of what I saw as the problem between them: anything that was not Baz's 'bag' he was not interested in. And as she got older, that wasn't enough for Di, particularly as her painting career increasingly took off. Baz had never been discouraging of her art, in fact he was quite proud of her abilities, and when building their dream house together at Patterson Lakes Baz was very keen for her to have as much studio space as she wanted. It was just that Baz wasn't into art that much himself. Di could be into it as much as she liked, just so long as Baz didn't have to be involved in the details.

As Di had been president of the Peninsula Arts Society in the seventies it meant that Baz would on occasion have to be dragged along to art events. Did he accept these with grace and forbearing? Not bloody likely. Getting Baz to an exhibition opening was like getting a child to the dentist. As the president, Di had met the local MP, Phillip Lynch, at a couple of gallery openings. Lynch went on to become deputy prime minister in the Fraser government. One election day, Di decided to join Baz when he went to vote early so he could get to the races. In truth the whole idea of going early was not so much to get to the races early, but to get to the pub opposite the racetrack by ten o'clock and with Di taking so long to get ready, Baz was already half an hour behind schedule by the time they arrived at the polling booth. Baz was in and out, probably voting for the guy at the top of the ballot paper so he could get out of there as quickly as possible. Baz confessed to me once that in his time he had voted for pretty much every party, particularly since the DLP had lost relevance. (Even though they booted him out of the church, Baz had an amazing loyalty towards the Catholics.)

He looked around and could see Di talking to the Liberal candidate. A furious Baz stomped over and told her they had to go. Di responded, very excited (until Bob Hawke came along, Di would never think of voting anything other than conservative) and said, 'Barry, I would like you to meet Phillip Lynch.' As Sir Phil, the second most powerful man in the country, extended his hand, Baz looked Di straight in the eye and said, 'Bugger Phillip Lynch, I've got to get to the races!'

I am sure that it is not necessary to share the same passions in order for a couple to stay together, and that so long as each other's interests are respected diverging tastes are no barrier to a successful relationship. Perhaps it was their ability to live separate yet shared lives that meant my parents did manage to stay together all those years. But such an approach doesn't guarantee closeness and it was this distance that I noticed more and more.

Ironically, it was building their dream home that probably sowed the seeds of discord. Baz became a subcontractor and oversaw the construction of their new house, which was modest by ostentatious Patterson Lakes standards. (This is the suburb where they filmed *Kath and Kim*, and in our neighbourhood there was a replica of both Elvis's 'Graceland' and 'Tara' from *Gone With the Wind*, and the latter wasn't named ironically.) Di had a big hand in the design – a snooker room and wet bar for Baz, a studio for her – and in the year and a half it took them to build, they were quite united. Di would even drive out on a hot summer's day with an esky full of cold stubbies for Donny, Baz and the rest of the boys working on site.

But once the house was built Di, now ensconced in her studio, really threw herself into her painting. With the kids grown up she had more time to concentrate on her career and it really began to take off. Di probably didn't have the outrageous artistic temperament to ever make it big in the art world. Quiet, polite, conservative suburban types don't tend to exhibit in the fashionable galleries. Nor did she have any sort of high-minded artistic manifesto she was promoting – she just loved to paint. And she had an incredible talent. Her landscapes were of the realist school, which is perhaps not so cutting edge, but they were impressive examples of the genre. But it was her talent at portraiture that really advanced her career. Just before she got sick she received her first major commission, and I was in no doubt that she would soon crack into the rarefied league of successful artists as her work was flourishing.

Yet all the time she was in the studio, she was spending less time in Baz's life. Not that he actually minded, as he got to continue in the lifestyle of his choice: the bookmaking, going fishing with his brother-in-law Bernie, drinking down at the club, and going on trips around the country with his mates. Baz went to the Birdsville and Darwin Cups with the Spaniard (who was not Spanish), the Wagga races with the Port Boys (who mostly no longer came from Port), and the Warrnambool Cup with Fatty Byrne (who, contrary to the logic of most of Baz's nicknames, was actually fat – well, he had been in the early days, but by the time they were all in their fifties Baz and most of his mates were actually just as fat as Fatty).

During this period, Baz went on his first major overseas trip. Ten weeks in Canada, the States, England and Ireland. Without Di. Instead he went with Tony Wilson, an ex-bookie mate from Albury who had become an undertaker after he won the business as part of the settlement of a gambling debt. That Di and Baz didn't go together never seemed to strike anyone as strange at the time. Baz would rather be visiting racetracks and bars around the world and Di would relish having more time to spend in the studio, without having to worry about cooking meals for Baz or cleaning up after him. They were both happy doing what they wanted to do. Baz was loving his life, Di was loving hers. It was just that, aside from their socialising with Ace and Chris and the regular trips they would all take to New South Wales to play the pokies, they weren't loving their life together.

Then came the day that Di broke her arm hanging out the washing and, yet again, the trajectories of their lives were to be drastically altered by a diagnosis of cancer. Among the many facets of this nightmare, Di was to discover that her shattered arm was still too weak to withstand the rigours of holding up a paintbrush. The career that had taken a lifetime to start paying off looked to be over. But she could not let go of her life's passion so easily and taught herself the techniques of watercolour painting which, being done on a horizontal surface, allowed her to work without straining her damaged arm. Within weeks she was producing astonishingly accomplished works and would continue to do so until the very last couple of months.

Given his track record over the previous few years, Baz was the last person anyone expected to pull something extraordinary out of the fire when Di got sick but Baz, too, found his life suddenly cleaved from its expected path, and had to rise to new challenges. The way he responded to them was quite remarkable.

10 BAZ HATCHES A PLAN

There was no bleaker time than when Di was first diagnosed with multiple myeloma. She was so extraordinarily frail that there was none of that bravado that families put on when somebody is given the news that they have cancer. You hear it all the time: 'Oh, she's a fighter'; 'He's a tough old nut' – that kind of upbeat, stiff upper lip talk that I think we all feel we need to tell one another because the reality can be truly terrifying and unthinkable. We particularly reserve these sorts of affirmations for famous people, especially sports stars. Old team-mates, family and supporters will rabbit on about fighting spirit and grit and determination. 'If he was able to grind out an unbeaten half-century on a venomous last day green-top in the heat at Calcutta then he'll be able to fight this' is the sort of thing you hear people say, as if being able to apply yourself to a game that you enjoy and have trained for is in any way analogous to being able to stem the advance of rabid cells in your body.

With Di, there was none of that upbeat talk. It was hard for us to believe she would last until the end of the year. And before she could even start the fight against the cancer, she first had to recover from the operation on her broken arm. The specialist said the disease was well advanced, so it was an excruciating wait that Christmas as her weakened body built up enough strength to withstand the onslaught of what the doctors, pulling no punches, warned would be a particularly harrowing round of treatment. First she had to undergo intensive radiotherapy to try to reduce the tumours in her bones, and once she had recovered from the ravages of that, she would start a brutal course of chemotherapy.

Di was incredibly stoic throughout. In fact the only time she broke down was when she was told that she would most likely lose her hair. This had not happened during her fight against ovarian cancer. I could understand she would be upset but I was shocked at the strength of her reaction to the news. My mother had always been a well-groomed woman, but I had never thought of her as particularly vain about her looks. I guess she saw losing her hair as the final indignity, the stripping away of her true essence. I suspect also that her grief over her potential hair loss was a conduit for the grief she had otherwise been able to contain. But there was never any question as far as I was aware that she ever contemplated refusing treatment. Even though she already looked shattered and defeated, it was clear that she was determined not to succumb to this thing just yet. She knew it was going to be exceptionally gruelling, but she also knew that if she refused treatment she would certainly not see another Christmas.

Not that the Christmas of 1993 was much chop. Not only was Di hospitalised in the city at Peter Mac, but Baz was due for, as he so delicately put it, 'a reboring' of his prostate. I spent much of the weeks leading up to Christmas travelling between Peter Mac (thankfully they had moved to the new premises by then, so the Gulag ambience of the old place was but a shuddering memory) and the private hospital in Frankston where Baz's procedure took place. Baz's operation was not a great success. He loved his surgeon, mainly because he was a curmudgeonly old bugger who used to upset the nursing staff. Baz found it hilarious, and kept banging on about how Old Jim was a top bloke. Unfortunately Old Jim should have retired years ago, for no matter what sort of bloke he was, he had by this stage become something of a butcher as a surgeon. After the op, Baz was in agony as what should have been a quick recovery turned to days and days of bleeding. After visiting Mum, who was bearing up with remarkable fortitude, I would then drive down to sit with Baz, who would be writhing in searing pain as I watched what looked like great big globs of flesh travel down his catheter into a blood and urine filled bag. Best Christmas ever.

About a year later Baz's prostate was playing up again (he had never fully recovered from the first surgery) and he had to go in for another operation. I think Old Jim had retired as Baz got a new surgeon of Chinese background. Like Dr Nick in later years, this guy was not Baz's type of bloke — no doubt because he wasn't a grumpy old white guy — and Baz was very sceptical of getting a better outcome than the last time. When he was able to walk out of hospital the day afterwards with a spring in his step and no pain or post-op bleeding, Baz was singing the Chinese doctor's praises.

By the time Di was ready to start her chemo, Baz had made a full recovery. He and I would share the driving as we had to take her up to the city for her sessions. Di got through the radiotherapy relatively well (aside from the nausea and lethargy and constant diarrhoea because one of the tumours they were targeting was in the pelvis so there was incidental damage to the bowels) and the specialists told us that the tumours had all but disappeared after being bombarded with those radioactive waves.

This didn't mean she was cured by any means as the myeloma itself inhabited the blood cells and there was no way of ridding her of it completely. Left unchecked it would make a comeback and form new tumours in her bones, particularly where there was any pre-existing weakness. In a sense the radiotherapy, as harsh as it had been, was just clearing the way of hazards for the shock troops of the chemotherapy to come in and do the real work. It had taken almost six months for Di to be ready for this mopping-up operation. She had sprung back well from the radiotherapy but had to be as fit as possible as this was some serious chemo she was about to receive.

The treatment hit her like a ton of bricks. Chemotherapy is basically pumping toxic chemicals into the system of a cancer patient in the hope that they will target the rapidly expanding cancer cells. Although they are always refining treatments there is still a great deal of incidental damage. Cancer cells are actually the body's own cells that have gone feral and are growing out of control, consuming other cells in the body. As I understand it, most chemotherapy is targeted at these rapidly multiplying cells, so it is not surprising that they affect other areas of the body that constantly produce new growth cells, such as the immune system or the hair cells. Both can be compromised and hence hair falls out and a patient can be at risk from the most innocuous of infections because they have very few healthy white blood cells left to fight any invading organisms.

The chemicals they pumped into Di were so potent that the nurses administering it did so wearing masks and gloves and full surgical gowns lest they splash some on themselves. If they were worried about a drop splashing on their own skin, one can only imagine the damage chemotherapy inflicts when pumped directly into the body. Di thought the radiotherapy had been harsh – it is essentially burning parts of your body from the inside – but it was a walk in the park compared to the chemo. Many cancer survivors I have heard speak have said the great irony is that the only time they have ever wanted to die is when the chemo, the very thing that is meant to save you, is having the greatest impact.

Within days the effects began to show in Di. She was wracked with nausea, vomiting, headaches, aches in her limbs, crippling lethargy and, yes, her hair did begin falling out – at first just a few strands, but pretty soon in great clumps. Di had steeled herself for this and handled it pretty well. The people at Peter Mac were incredible; not just the nurses and medical staff, but all the support people. She was in there often, staying for up to a week at a time during the worst of both the chemo and radiotherapy and came to know many of the staff. These people have to deal with some horrific stuff and are probably trained to be positive and supportive, but it was amazing to see them in action. Whenever nursing and other support staff go on strike for more pay, my immediate reaction is that they should double whatever it is they are asking for. And if such a pay rise would endanger the functioning of the health system then I reckon the politicians and doctors should tithe some of their own pay to cover the difference. That's how good and important they are.

Di was even visited by a wig consultant who gave her strategies to deal with the loss of hair. Di had been unconvinced but bought a couple of wigs. She soon found that they were too hot for comfort and that no matter what the consultant said, they never looked stylish, more like small rodents clutching on to the top of her head. Fortunately Di went with a range of scarves and became so adept at coordinating them with her wardrobe that you barely noticed her hair loss – one wouldn't have been surprised to learn she was just wearing them as a stylish fashion statement.

Her loss of appetite was a big worry. Di's oncologist had said that while she had built up some strength since her diagnosis in December, she was still starting from a very low base. Unfortunately even when the chemo wasn't making her feel as sick as a dog and the nausea had subsided after a few days, it still managed to suppress her appetite. It also dulled her tastebuds so even when she could manage food it was very unpalatable. Di would make an effort to eat but she could barely put away more than a few scant mouthfuls. Rather than building up her strength,

Di was slowly starving herself. After a couple of treatments, the oncologist said her blood count was beginning to level out – a very good sign – and if all went to plan it would soon plummet back to normal levels. But he was very concerned with her fragile health, which if it kept declining would necessitate a rethink about continuing treatment. Things weren't looking promising.

At the time of her diagnosis I was temporarily at home, as I was throughout my student career when one rented household wound up and I needed to save money to move into another. Now that Di was sick I had forsaken plans to move back up to the city so that I could help Baz look after Di. It wasn't that he was doing a bad job, nor was I actually doing much that was useful, but it meant that I was able to take the load off Baz when it came to things like driving her to Melbourne for treatment.

Baz had seemed rather at a loss as to what to do for Di. He watched with great concern and offered what support he could but I often felt that, at first, there was a kind of emotional barrier between them – I suspect mainly because Baz didn't want to communicate his fears for Di and so shut up emotional shop. It seemed to me that Di was better able to talk to me about what was going on emotionally. I don't know if I was really all that suitable to be someone's emotional rock given that, as a mid-twenties student, my head was as often as not wrapped up in studies – or avoiding them – and certain passions in my life such as relationships, politics, theatre and the whole birdwatching thing. After thirty years of marriage there were, naturally enough, emotional things only my parents could share, but there were also thirty years of non-communicative patterns, guilt and resentments that had become entrenched, and throughout those first months of Di's treatment I stood by feeling helpless as I watched Baz standing by helpless, not knowing what to do for Di.

One day I came home after a particularly brain-numbing intellectual property lecture to find Baz bustling around the kitchen. This was not an unusual event as he had been doing the bulk of the cooking since Di had been crook, but he hadn't been tackling the task with much relish, seeing it as something of a burden and a reminder that so much had changed in the household since Di's diagnosis. There was certainly very little joy about Baz's cooking in those early days. This particular night, though, he was banging about in the kitchen with renewed vigour. (You always knew when Baz was cooking as he was the noisiest chef going – why pull out a saucepan quietly when you could rattle through the entire pots drawer clanging every single one of them together?) He even wore an apron and there was real purpose to his bustling.

'What's up, Dad?' He'd piqued my curiosity.

'We've been to see the specialist again today and your mum is losing strength too quickly. He reckons if she doesn't pick up soon he might have to stop the treatment.'

'Yeah, so what are you doing?'

'I've worked it out. Your mum needs to eat. But she isn't.'

'That's the chemo, Dad.'

Baz was not to be deterred: 'I know. But I was thinking, what if I was to create the perfect dish? A meal that was so irresistible that she couldn't refuse? That would get her eating, get her strength back.'

He was positively humming. I didn't want to burst his bubble though I was pretty dubious. 'But you know she hasn't got any appetite.'

'Yeah, but once she tastes this she won't be able to stop herself.' Baz was rubbing his hands together like a man about to tuck into a beer after a week lost in the desert. He was almost dancing a little jig.

'What are you cooking?'

'Spicy Japanese fish parcels with udon noodles!' he proclaimed with great pride. 'She won't be able to resist,' he said, looking down at some recipe he had cut out of the paper. 'It'll be bloody beautiful, Rupe.'

And true to his word, the meal was fantastic. It was quite a fiddly dish to prepare and I was surprised that Baz, not known for his patience, cheerfully kept at it. He laid the dish out on a tray and took it in to Di who was propped up on pillows in her bedroom. He had even picked a nasturtium from the garden that he placed in a small vase, like they did in hospital, and with great pomp laid the tray out in front of an unenthused Di.

'Here you go, love, get that into you,' offered Baz, barely concealing his excitement.

Di, looking very pallid, turned her nose up at it and complained, 'I don't feel like fish.'

Undeterred, Baz pressed on, 'Yeah, but you haven't tried fish this way before. I can guarantee it.'

Di picked up the fork and poked at it dubiously. She broke a bit off and put it to her lips. She chewed and swallowed with Baz looking on. Di took a mouthful of the noodle salad and after eating it began poking at the fish again.

She stopped, put her head back on the supporting pillow and simply said, 'I can't eat any more.'

'Oh come on, you can do better than that,' encouraged Baz.

'Barry, I don't want any more!' She turned away and wouldn't look back while Baz cleared the plate, keeping her eyes averted as he left the room.

Baz handed me the plate and said I could finish it if I wanted. It was bloody delicious. While I ate, Baz took out a cookbook and started scanning the pages.

'What are you doing, Dad?'

'I'll get her yet,' he mumbled as much to himself as to me as he pored over the recipes, 'I'll get her yet.'

THE TRACKSUIT GANG

The onset of Di's illness coincided with Baz's ascension to the ranks of rails bookmaker, so while he was looking after her during the week, on race days Baz was suddenly dealing with stakes far higher than he had been used to in his previous twenty years as a bookie. Living at home and working with Baz, not to mention driving him and the boys to and from the track, meant that I was seeing far more of my father than was probably healthy for a 25 year old. And while Baz was still as infuriating as ever, his stories still as interminable, seeing him operate under such immense pressure from the dual scourges of rampant cancer and rapacious punters, I started to notice a different side to my old man. And I have to say, I was beginning to be rather impressed.

Worries at home had done nothing to dampen Baz's love for the fight with the punters. If anything, the races became an outlet for his frustrations and he was even more emboldened to take them on. Baz's catchcry of, 'It's only money, boys!' (usually offered as a palliative to himself after a losing race) seemed to resonate deeply with him. When you are dealing on a daily basis with somebody who is struggling for life, who is so wracked with nausea that they cannot even enjoy a simple meal, it does put money into perspective. Not that Baz was the Dalai Lama when it came to losing money. If any of us contributed to the loss on a particular race by failing to let him know there was a plunge on for a particular horse, or by taking a large bet from a winning punter, Baz would let us have it with both barrels.

I had been there with Baz through the years: the wages were enough to get me through uni, though this was not wholly the reason I stuck at the job. Partly it meant that I didn't have to do any other part time work, leaving my evenings free for play rehearsals and the various other activities that a young university student gets up to at night (studying Shakespeare, Foucault and High Court judgements, obviously), although it was a downer having to be up and fresh on a Saturday morning. I soon learnt that it wasn't advisable to try and process bets on an average of 24 races in five hours with a raging hangover. Partly it was just that I couldn't find a way to tell my dad that I didn't want to work with him. As much as it (and he) annoyed me, I could never find a sufficiently good reason not to work there.

And I had to admit that Baz was a generous and flexible boss. He didn't mind if you had a drink on the job (in fact it was almost mandatory), and he wasn't averse to throwing in a bonus if he'd had a particularly good day (and sometimes we would get a 'sling' on a losing day, just because he thought we had done a good job). He understood that sometimes I had to miss a meeting or two around exam time, or if I had a matinee to perform during the day. What he couldn't fathom was when I asked for time off to go twitching – that is, chasing after rare birds that had turned up around the country. Baz never got why I was a birdwatcher. I think that he came to terms with the fact that I was an intellectual, even that I was what he would term 'a theatre poof', but the whole birdwatching thing eluded him. I took a year off between school and uni and when I wasn't travelling I was saving up for travel by working with Baz and, at one point, doing a stint in a paint factory. When a Northern Shoveler, a type of duck from the Northern Hemisphere, turned up in Adelaide, I figured I had enough money in the bank from the paint factory job to afford to take a day off from the races and catch the train to try and see it.

It was almost the last day I worked for Baz. He wasn't happy that I dashed off at a moment's notice, taking the job for granted. Especially for a bird. (And one that I dipped out on seeing anyway.) Baz made it very clear from then on that this was no charity gig, this was a serious business involving large amounts of money, and if I wanted to continue, I had to treat it as such. To back it up, he started giving me more responsibility and over the years I progressed from being just the kid who changed the betting sheets between races to doing every job that was going, from payout clerk to penciller, from writing the tickets to swinging the bag as a bagman.

The job of the bagman, or baggie, is to stand there with the bookie's bag around his neck taking the punters' money and calling the bets. A good baggie can make all the difference to how effective a bookie can be. They can coax punters to place a wager by sheer force of personality. They are also another pair of eyes for the bookie – someone who can watch the betting ring and know who is betting with whom and on what, who is looking shifty, who is looking too eager to bet on a certain horse and what prices the bookie on the next stand is setting. The betting ring during a plunge before the horses jump can be a crazy place, with desperate punters thrusting wads of cash at you, screaming to be let on, so a good baggie needs to be able to stay in control and remain calm while keeping track of all that money floating around in the bag.

I was never a great baggie. I could do the job, but got the fumbles when the rush was on. I much preferred doing the pencilling, which involved writing all the bets down. This too could get insanely busy at times, as for each bet you had to write down five figures – the amount of the bet, the amount it would pay if it won, the cumulative totals for money held and money to be paid and the ticket number, as well as a sixth column if it was a place bet – all the while keeping a running tally of how much money you were holding on each race and which horse was costing too much should it win, so that you could warn the bookie that he should turn that horse's odds down. On some of the big race days such as Derby Day at Flemington or Cox Plate Day at Moonee Valley I would literally have to brace myself against the mob of punters crowding in to get on. In that feeding frenzy they would try and climb over me to get their wad of cash into the baggie's hands, and at times I was almost writing bets upside down as the sea of desperation pushed the betting book over my head.

It was actually a great rush and I loved the challenge of keeping on top of all those figures, much preferring it to being on the bag, which took a certain kind of skill, physicality and chutzpah that I didn't really have. For years Ace was Baz's bagman, and when they were more small-time his warm personality was enough to do the trick – he had the ability to call every punter 'knackers' and never offend one of them. Baz's only complaint was that Ace, never fastidious at the best of times, would end up making a total mess of the bag, and by that I don't just mean merely mixing up the twenty-dollar notes with the tens (if our figures ever matched the actual money in the bag at the end of the day, Baz would call for an inquiry). Sometimes a plunge would happen unexpectedly and Ace would literally drop whatever he was eating or drinking – pie or beer – to take the bet, so that by the end of the day, the bag would be sloshing around in half a litre of beer and Ace would be handing out soggy bank notes to the payout clerk.

Eventually Ace (whose first name was actually John) left to pursue his own gambling pursuits at the track. Stepping up to the plate was another John, universally known as Toby. Toby was an archetypal fiery redhead whose stint fighting in Vietnam had done little to soothe his volatile temperament. Like all of Baz's staff, Toby had been a drinking buddy first. He was recruited initially as a penciller. When he took up the satchel, I took over the main pencilling duties. But Toby didn't last too long on the bag as, though he could be exceptionally charming (his success with the ladies was legendary), he didn't have the requisite patience and, particularly with a few sherbets in him later in the day, he would often crack it with an indecisive punter – ripping the money out of their hand and pointing at a horse's name on the board, his swelling capillaries adding to the neon rouge of his cheeks, he would scream at them, 'You want this one? You want this one, you idiot?!' Baz put Toby back on the books with me pretty quickly. Not long afterwards, Toby left his wife of twenty years and shacked up with 'a youngie'. They moved to the country, had two children in quick succession and Toby stopped working for Baz, much to the relief of many a prevaricating punter.

His replacement was yet another John who was also rarely called by his given name. If you have a son and don't know what to call him, why not opt for John, because odds on he will end up being called something entirely different anyway. This John's nickname was Whispering Jack, because he had the loudest voice on the racecourse. He could out-bellow the best of them. This is a good trait for a baggie to have, as they need to be like butchers at the market, yelling out the prices above the din of the crowd. The first few times I tried broadcasting the odds I was a dismal failure as, selfconsciously, I would try and yell out in my natural voice. It was too thin to penetrate the crowd. It was only when you expel air from deep down in your gut and force it out through your nose that you get that piercing, nasal tone that can cut through concrete. It is a completely unnatural way of speaking but it works and, surprisingly, when I used this voice at the track I actually felt less conspicuous. Whispering's problem was that he had no volume control – or more precisely, no mute button. He would talk just as loudly in a private conversation, so his inquiry into another clerk's health – 'Hey, Smithy! How'd the haemorrhoid operation go?' – would be louder than the course broadcast system.

The pencillers tended to be a more introspective lot than the baggies, Toby notwithstanding. For a while, my uncles Bernie and Norm were pencillers for Baz, though as they got older they willingly shifted on to the role of payout clerk as this usually involved much less stress and gave them a lot more time to spend at the bar, which was how Baz liked it. The more mates he had to drink with between races, the better, in his view. A couple of younger blokes were given a tryout on pencilling duties, including one called Bertie who lasted a year or so. But it wasn't until Baz tried out a mate of Fatty and Ace's, rather unimaginatively nicknamed Hally given that his surname was Hall, that Baz's rails team was locked in. Hally was the perfect combination for Baz: he was a bit quieter than Toby or Whispering Jack but still loved a beer and a laugh so he fitted right in.

Hally arrived just as we switched to the computerised betting machines. It was a good thing he had a sense of humour as Baz was a bit of a technophobe and if that ticket didn't appear the instant you had punched in the bet he would seriously lose it. On the occasions when the screen was refreshing or the computer had a brain freeze, Baz was known to throw his hands up in the air and jump off the stand, yelling, 'You can throw that bloody machine to the shithouse!' Hally and I got on pretty well and at times like these, when Baz was raging and fuming, we'd have to avoid each other's gaze or else we'd both crack up laughing.

Hally's greatest asset as a clerk was his unflappability, though this was tested at times as you would always get some mug punter who was either a total imbecile or was trying to scam us by claiming a losing ticket he had was actually a winning ticket and we had tried to rip him off. This sort of thing happened fairly often and I was gobsmacked at the audacity of some of the scams people tried to pull. Baz often used to give in to some of the minor frauds, reasoning it was easier to pay the mug his twenty bucks than have him disrupt the serious money that was trying to bet with us. But that punter was guaranteed they would never get on with Baz again. The trouble with calling someone on a dodgy claim was you never knew who you were dealing with, and one time when Hally got shirty with some scammer, it almost came to blows, something that wouldn't have been advisable as he was one of the 'Tracksuit Gang'.

The Tracksuit Gang, associates of the now infamous Tony Mokbel, were a bunch of unshaven gorillas wearing shiny tracksuits, slicked-down hair and ostentatious bling, as it is now called, who would lurk furtively on the edge of the betting ring. Normally they'd be written off as your typical racetrack desperados, but they would swoop in the final seconds before a race in Brisbane or Adelaide and pull out huge wads of fifty- or hundred-dollar notes from their tracky daks to bet on the short priced favourite. They were never massive amounts, certainly well below the ten grand that would have obliged the bookmaker to report the transaction to the authorities, but over a day it would add up.

What took a few months to sink in was that these guys were not just ugly losers who were getting lucky, they were ugly losers who were part of something bigger. (And if any of the Tracksuit Gang are reading this, I certainly don't mean to say you were the ugly one, it's just that some of your mates' personal grooming left a lot to be desired, but not you, sir. I applaud your bold and stylish choice of matching chunky gold chain necklace with the luminescent nylon sheen of open tracksuit top offsetting that thick tangle of jet black chest hair – a sartorial triumph, sir!). Not that there was much we could do about it except take their bets. As it turned out, they were laundering drug money in small increments, but it never seemed a brilliant way to do it as they still had to win the money back from the bookie. And while they may have had the inside dope – or even, on occasion, been able to fix races – sometimes the horses didn't understand the plan and still lost. I wonder just how much the Tracksuit Gang ever actually won off Baz.

Tony Mokbel himself never won very often, and unlike with some other bookies, he always seemed to pay up with us. At this stage I still had no idea of his infamy – he was just this big-spending guy who had credit bets with us from the members stand. To me he looked like the typical flash Jack who splashed his money around to impress the acolytes and much younger women that seemed to hang around him. I was surprised to hear he was a major underworld figure, but even more surprised to find out that he was only a couple of years older than me – I would have said he was at least ten years older. I guess money can buy you power and influence and put others in fear of your very presence, but it can't, it would seem, buy you a wig that makes you look youthful.

My only personal run-in with a member of the Tracksuit Gang echoed a family situation that Baz had found himself in decades before. All of his brothers had worked for George at the track at some stage, and aside from Baz, the one who took to it the most was my Uncle Norm. One day in the madness of the main ring at Caulfield, as Baz was sitting pencilling, he saw a ten-pound note flutter from a punter's wallet onto the ground in front of him. Ten quid was a substantial sum in those days. He was too flat out writing bets to pick the money up and called Norm's attention to it. Norm was on the bag so it was a simple matter for him to reach down and pocket the tenner. But there was a bit of a miscommunication and at the end of the day when Baz asked Norm for the tenner, he refused to hand it over. Baz said he would share it with Norm, but Norm was firmly of the finders-keepers school of jurisprudence. This sparked a falling-out between them that lasted upwards of twenty years, and while they were still civil to each other, they were no longer the mates they had been.

They eventually made up and Baz brought Norm back on board as a way of helping him out after he lost his job. They were great mates from then on, and until he got sick with terminal liver cancer, Norm's driest of humour and connoisseur's palate for beer were much appreciated by Baz. In fact, Norm was like Baz's official beer taster. On entering a pub, Baz would wait for Norm to take a sip of the first pot and pronounce the quality of the product. If he gave his nod that the lines had been cleaned and the beer hadn't spoiled, Baz and the boys would all get stuck in. The slightest frown meant that they'd be switching to bottled beer or heading off to another pub. He rewarded Norm with the cushiest job of all, taking the bets of Baz's biggest credit punter, Harry the Horse. Harry had won big with Baz in the early days, but Baz eventually wore him down and though he wouldn't bet big, the Horse would bet often, so by the end of a day he could easily be ten grand down.

After making a few instalments on his debts, it became clear after a year or two that Baz would never see the money in full but as they had become great mates, he allowed Harry to continue betting with him. By the time Baz died, the nominal figure owed by the Horse was well over $200 000 but by this stage Baz treated it as if it was Monopoly money and never bothered to call the debt in. After all, why spoil a good friendship over something like money? Norm's job entailed sitting over at the bar and waiting for Harry to come and give him his bets, which Norm would duly write down in a racing guide for Baz to transcribe at a later date, though the bets never ended up in the actual books, because as everybody implicitly knew, they weren't real bets.

Anyway, the reason I mention the story of Norm and the ten quid was that the identical thing happened one day at Flemington, but this time it involved me and my brother. For a while Wok worked for Baz and while he was far more tuned in to the punting and racing side of things than I was, he was even less suited to the business of bookmaking. The mathematical side eluded him, and he certainly didn't have the effusive personality, that element of a showman, that every bookie needs. Baz thought Wok was a handsome bloke who might attract some of the young fillies to the stand so he would whack a bag on him on slow days and have him out on the members' side of the rails in the hope that he would attract the pretty young things to bet with us. It would have worked, but Wok spent most of his time gazing shyly at his shoes.

This particular day at Flemington, Wok was actually working out the front of the stand as the second baggie, taking bets from the general public that Whispering Jack couldn't cover. Whispering could cover a lot of punters, and as it wasn't a hugely busy day, Wok spent more time looking at the boards of nearby bookies working out what he was going to bet on than he did taking any bets for Baz. In a replay of thirty years previously, as I was writing down the bets I saw a fifty-dollar note land near my feet. I looked up. The fifty could have belonged to any of a dozen punters who were crowding around trying to place bets. I wasn't about to ask whether anyone had dropped a fifty as a dozen hands would have shot up claiming ownership. It was mine for the taking. Except that I was too flat chat to get up and collect it myself so I motioned to Wok as surreptitiously as I could, nodding in the direction of the note lying invitingly on the asphalt. Wok stared back at me uncomprehendingly.

I nodded again. Wok looked back at me, impassive. I tried again and still nothing but a quizzical stare. I began nodding my head in the direction of the fifty like one of those bobble-headed dogs you see on the back dash of cars and still Wok didn't cotton on. But one of the Tracksuit Gang did and swooped upon the fifty like a seagull on a chip. I leaped up from where I was seated and challenged him: 'Oi, that's not yours, mate!'

'Yes it is,' said the slick-backed bouffant in the glistening tracksuit.

'Bullshit,' I called him on it. You could tell he knew he was caught out but he spat back at me defiantly.

'Prove it.'

At this point Baz had taken an interest in proceedings: 'Is that your fifty, Rupe?'

'It's not his, Dad.'

'Can you prove it?'

'… No.'

'Then you take it, mate,' Baz said to the Nylon Wonder, who smiled a real 'fuck you' smile in my direction as he went to pocket the fifty. Baz added, 'But if you take that money, you can forget about betting here again.' He took the money and swaggered off into the crowd.

Whispering Jack approached me for a quiet word: 'I'd be careful, Seany, you know he's one of Mokbel's mates.'

'So?'

'You know who Mokbel is, don't ya?' John continued. 'He's not someone you want to cross.'

Whispering Jack then went on to tell how he had been out in Lygon Street with his wife one night when they bumped into Tony Mokbel entering a restaurant. He recognised Whispering from the track and invited them to dine with him, and though he tried to decline it was an offer too good to refuse. He said Tony was a delightful host who shouted him and his wife their meal. They didn't enjoy the dinner though because Tony insisted that they sit with their backs to the window onto the street, and the entire time they ate, Mokbel repeatedly looked nervously over their shoulders. Whispering Jack reckoned if a car had backfired in the street he and his wife would have been on the floor in an instant. All of this Whispering told me in strictest confidence. Pity that the rest of the betting ring also heard the story. I just thank God that Whispering never decided to become a priest – that's one voice you wouldn't want sitting on the other side of the confessional.

So Wok and I never even got to squabble over who should get to keep the fifty dollars, all because we didn't have that unspoken, empathic communication kind of thing going that brothers are supposed to have. Some might say it's because we are both adopted, so we don't have those blood ties or kinship. I would say that it was more because we had long ago stopped spending much time together and were no longer really on each other's wavelength. Either way, the same process happens in lots of families – siblings just don't end up being that close. This is not to say we don't care for each other, but it was fairly clear early on that we were on different paths in life.

While we used to play together as kids, I had a rich imaginative life and would often prefer to play by myself. I don't know how much of this was to do with the fact that if Wok didn't get his way he was likely to throw a tantrum – whenever we played cricket, he would insist on batting first, and then refuse to go out, more often than not throwing the bat down in a huff and abandoning the match – or whether I was just so caught up in my imagination that I had no room for him. From an early age I took to playing football by myself in the backyard, commentating on the action as I went along. Pretty soon Wok had a footy of his own and would do the same. It must have looked hilarious (and just a little sad) to see two kids booting balls around the yard, managing to have two entirely unrelated matches going on at once.

And whereas I had got the scholarship to the private school, Wok had gone straight on to the local high school. After a year, though, Baz and Di were worried that he was falling in with the wrong crowd. I don't know how they managed it financially but they sent him to my school the next year. For two years Wok had been giving me grief for having to wear a uniform with a tie to attend what he termed 'that poofter school'. I didn't hesitate to point out to him that he was now one of the poofs too.

Wok and the new school didn't exactly hit it off and he only lasted two terms. It was actually rather mean to try and get this round peg to fit into such a very square hole. Starting behind academically, Wok was always going to have trouble catching up, even if he had been keen in the first place. And when he made serious efforts to tackle his studies he always found a way for his endeavours to be sabotaged. After going dreadfully in French class, Wok fronted up one day and announced to the class that from that day on he was going to pull his finger out and work really hard. The teacher was so impressed he asked Wok to bring his workbook up so he could help him correct the assignment from the previous class. Unfortunately for Wok he hadn't been so conscientious in the previous class and where his work should have been he had written 'Stanhope sucks cock'. Stanhope failed to see the joke and Wok was dragged to the vice-principal's office to be issued with yet another detention. Wok got to see the vice-principal an awful lot that year.

The vice-principal took a real shine to Wok, though, and tried to help him out. He brought in a psychologist who, apart from recommending that Wok would be better suited to a more technically focused, less academic school, also suggested that many of his problems stemmed from having me as a brother. I had spent most of my life going about what interested me, which happened to be academic study, but the psychologist deduced that my achievements, and the favour that arose from them, were exacerbating Wok's feelings of inadequacy. I remember feeling rather put out by this as I never thought I was rubbing anything in Wok's face, just getting on with what I liked to do. This was the way things worked in our family. I was good at schoolwork, Wok was good at footy. We each would have liked to be better at the other, but what were we going to do? I didn't expect Wok to play footy any less well because I couldn't pull down a speccy, so why should I have to lessen my performance at school? The thing was, Wok felt pretty much the same way and once he went to a school that wasn't trying to make him good at something he had no interest in, many of his problems disappeared.

But before Wok left our school, he did pull off one achievement that really impressed me. Outside a Catholic school, ours seemed to have the highest number of dodgy teachers in the country. While I was there one teacher was found out and committed suicide before the police could lay charges, but there was a whole slate of teachers (at least three or four) whose improprieties with students were only exposed in the years after I had left. There was one teacher whom I particularly despised, and though he was not one of those who physically or sexually abused anyone, he was certainly not averse to psychological torture of his students.

He was a small man in so many ways, hiding behind the respectability afforded those in the teaching profession. He was clearly a disturbed character, one who couldn't abide being proved wrong, which is perhaps where his love of discipline came from. He once told us in class that when his toddler daughter had shown curiosity about the stove-top, in order to stop her getting seriously burnt he had taken her hand and burned it on one of the hotplates. 'Not enough to scar her,' he announced to the appalled class, 'but she never went near the stove again, let me tell you.' Yeah, and she was probably never able to have a trusting relationship again for the rest of her life. That's the kind of man he was.

He also loved to bullshit, particularly when it came to discipline. He claimed to have fought in Vietnam, but given the shaggy dog nature of most of his stories, I found this hard to believe – though if he had spent four years in a bamboo cage as a captive of the Viet Cong, it might have explained some of his behaviour. He once interrupted an algebra class to give a dissertation on why hippies were evil, claiming he was at a party where they had injected the oranges with LSD and one of his friends had eaten one *and had instantly become addicted to LSD*. At this stage of my life I was fascinated with the drug culture and had done a lot of reading up on the subject. I called him on his blatant lie (who serves oranges at parties anyway?), piping up that it was physically impossible to become addicted to LSD. He fixed me with an icy stare and screamed back: 'Doesn't it? Doesn't it? That beautiful girl is now a prostitute on the streets and had to sell her babies for drugs!'

I caved in and let him rant some more, just waiting for the bell. I was more of your silent (that is, gutless) rebel. I had to leave it to my brother to really sock it to the fruit loop. After all Wok's jibes about me having to wear a tie, it turned out that he just couldn't master tying one for himself. Di would have to do it for him before he left for school, and if, during the day, it somehow came undone, I would have to surreptitiously knot his tie for him behind the bus shelter before we went home. Not only did Di make sure Wok's tie was done up, she also made sure his blazer was pressed, pants ironed and shoes shiny, so that he at least looked the part of a private school boy.

One day as Wok, under threat of yet another detention for being late, was rushing between classes, he was pulled up by the teacher on duty – our disciplinarian friend. Impatiently, Wok demanded to know what was wrong. The teacher began rhapsodising about Wok's state of dress, saying admiringly, 'Now this is what I like to see – a student who takes pride in his appearance.'

As Wok fidgeted fearfully the teacher began fiddling with Wok's tie.

'Your top button is done up, your tie is on, and is it – ? Yes, I do believe it is a Windsor knot! Immaculately knotted, if I may say so.'

All the other kids had disappeared into class. Wok was genuinely agitated now, but his tormentor was on a roll as he looked Wok up and down.

'And those shoes! I can see my reflection in them. You must have been up all night polishing them. Your trousers are pressed, shirt tucked in, your blazer spotless. You, young man, make me proud to teach at this school. A finer example of what this school stands for I couldn't imagine. What do you have to say for yourself?'

And Wok, with an eye on the closed classroom doors, turned to his admirer and said, 'Would you just fuck off, I'm late for class!'

He was immediately frogmarched to the deputy principal's

office where the teacher demanded something be done. The deputy assured him something would be and took Wok into his office, closed the door behind him and pissed himself laughing for the next half-hour. The school ought to erect an honour board for my brother.

Very occasionally, Wok would come out with something like that that would have me in absolute fits. Once at the races as I was paying out a winning bet to Andrew Peacock, who at that time was leader of the federal opposition, the alternative prime minister of the country, Wok sidled up behind me and whispered in my ear, 'Ask him if he really has got a pea cock!'

Puerile I know, but given the inappropriateness of the circumstances in which it was uttered, it had a devastating impact and it was all I could do not to splutter with laughter into the honourable member's suntanned face.

Sadly, these shared moments between us weren't all that frequent, and by the time Di was sick, Wok was only a bit player with Baz at the races. By this stage he had moved out of home and was living with his girlfriend just around the corner in Carrum and was busy establishing his own life. We saw each other fairly regularly but our interests were so divergent that aside from remembering shared childhood events such as the day he told the blowhard teacher where to go, we seemed to have less and less to talk about.

We were still sufficiently close that Wok asked me to be best man at his wedding a couple of years later. Di had said, at the time she was diagnosed, that she was staying alive so that she could see two things: Wok get married and me get my uni degree. Or a haircut. At that point all three things seemed as unlikely as a cure for Di's cancer being found, but at least Wok came through with the wedding. So, as a surprise, I went and got a haircut the day before the wedding – my first in about four years – much to Di's delight. It turned out to be a great night, paid for by Baz, which he didn't mind as Wok's new in-laws weren't doing too flash – though Baz wouldn't have minded if they'd at least made a token offer to pay for something.

Wok got married by the beach at Baz and Di's place at Patterson Lakes. The wedding photos, like most such photos, look a little stiff but it is impossible to miss Di's radiant beam. Although she looks very thin, you wouldn't particularly think that she was ill. By this stage she was in remission and feeling well – her own hair had even grown back. There was still much to come, but for this brief interlude everything was going about as well as it possibly could. It had taken a hell of an effort to get this far, and not just on Di's part. For her recovery, Baz was to play an unexpected role.

12 BAZ'S KITCHEN NIGHTMARES

When some people get sick, particularly with degenerative diseases such as cancer or dementia, it is said that often as well as creating physical ill health, the disease also eats away at the veneer of civility that people have armed themselves with to get through life. All pretences fall away and the elemental being that lies at the core comes to the surface, and often it is not pretty. My mother was always a very polite, even-tempered soul who radiated calm. The only people she ever seemed not to get along with were highly strung neurotic types who mistook her shyness for a sense of superiority, but most people recognised her as a gentle soul. Even as she battled the ravages and indignities of her cancer, she did so with a calm grace that touched even the most hardened medical professional. She managed to retain a dignified yet determined stance to her fight and throughout was still as nice as pie to everyone.

Everyone except Baz. Man, did he cop it. For that first year, I was also living at home, and Di was rarely terse with me, radiating nothing but love even in her darkest, most painful moments. But Baz could do nothing right. I don't know whether it was some form of payback for all his misdemeanours throughout their marriage – all the cold dinners never eaten, all those late nights staggering in rotten drunk, all the times he had embarrassed her in public with his loudmouthed exuberance – but she would snipe at virtually everything Baz did. He became the vent for her pain and darkness. Every time I did something for Di, no matter how trivial, she was incredibly grateful. Baz could have taken a bullet for her and she would merely have snapped, 'Don't bleed on the carpet!'

What amazed me, though, was how Baz copped it on the chin. Patience had never been his forte yet here he was, taking Di's needling with as good a grace as I'd ever seen. Before Di got sick I would have doubted his capacity to look after her, but he really stepped up to the plate. He took on all the cleaning – in fact the running of the entire household. I would be amazed to come home from uni to find Baz ironing. He would be in Di's room every few minutes acquiescing to her requests to rearrange the pillows she would be sitting up on. He was forever opening and closing the curtains in Di's room according to her capricious whim: the light would be too bright, then it would be too dark and depressing. She wanted to see the water of the lake so could he open the curtains wider. And sit her up. The she-oak outside was making too much noise scratching up against the window so Baz was out there pruning branches, with Di barking orders from her bed telling him he was doing it all wrong.

I was amazed at how Baz put up with it. Not that he didn't grumble. He would leave her room muttering under his breath like Muttley from the *Wacky Races* cartoon series, but he rarely lost his cool, particularly in front of Di. I think the way he maintained his composure was through his sense of humour. The clothesline was next to Di's bedroom and when he was hanging out the washing, Baz would yell out to her, 'I've got hold of your knickers, Di – I reckon it's the closest I'll be getting to them for a while.' She'd always hated it when Baz spoke so loudly. When I was growing up in Seaford I remember that Baz would shout at random, 'Diane, put that knife down!' just to get a rise out of her; she would hiss back, 'Barry, what will the neighbours think!' And now she was bedridden there was nothing she could do about it but chide him to be quiet. He'd keep going until eventually he had her laughing.

And so it went with his plan to cook Di the irresistible meal. Never one with much meat on her bones even when she was healthy, Di was wasting away before Baz's eyes. She was in and out of hospital for the brutal chemo rounds and then back at home where she barely had the energy to get out of bed to go to the toilet. Her oncologist reiterated to Baz that with her immune system taken out by the chemicals coursing through her, any nutrition he could get into her was vital to help her body fight off infections that would be harmless to us but devastating to Di. Some days Di could barely keep down a piece of toast and even when she wasn't nauseous she showed no interest in food. Every culinary treat Baz concocted was rejected, but still he persisted.

The previous year my studies had been severely interrupted because I had been on the road with the *Melbourne Uni Revue*, a sketch comedy show that in the past had given the likes of Barry Humphries, David Williamson, Steve Vizard and the D Generation their start. While our show was not destined to become quite the same launching pad for our careers, there had been enough interest in our group from the TV networks for us to put on a showcase season at Melbourne's Last Laugh theatre. The timing of this season couldn't have been worse for me – while all the others in the group had graduated, I was still in the middle of my degree and the performances were scheduled during the same weeks as my exams. I didn't sit a single exam and when no offers were forthcoming from the networks, I had to beg to be let back into uni. The only way the academic progress committee would allow me to return to study was if I undertook not to involve myself in any shenanigans in the theatre for the next twelve months. Over the course of that year as I tried to apply myself to serious study with no extracurricular activity, I almost went out of my skull with boredom. I ended up genuinely failing a subject at the end of that year and I realised that I was someone who needed to be stimulated or else I would stagnate. Being stuck down in Patterson Lakes, away from the inner city action, did little to provide said stimulation, but I had determined that I would be there to help Di in any way I could.

What it meant was that when I was home from uni there was often not a lot to do as Di was confined to bed and slept a lot. And most of what needed to be done was handled by Baz. So

I spent the year not really studying that much but watching a lot of late night telly and feasting on the remains of Baz's masterpieces. This was the one bright spot of moving back in with my parents. There were always leftovers when I came home from classes as Di would invariably take one spoonful of Baz's latest concoction and turn her nose up at it, saying she wasn't hungry. Most nights I was eating two meals. It was around this time that my body shape started to change from skinny and lanky as I began to fill out. I always put this down to genetic programming, but it has only just dawned on me that perhaps it was all that rich food coming from Baz's kitchen.

Baz, your typical steak and chops kind of bloke, started branching out into all manner of cooking styles. East Asian was his specialty, though in an effort to tempt Di's tastebuds he would even condescend to cook pasta, which he loathed. As I polished off yet another plate of untouched prawn and pea fettucine with white wine sauce, Baz would say in wonderment, 'Fair dinkum, you must be a wog; the way you knock off that spaghetti, you must have had Dago parents.'

Within a few months Baz had turned a general disinterest in the kitchen into an obsession, particularly with Japanese food. And for the first time in his life his cooking wasn't about Baz showing off. His motivation to cook was coming from an entirely new place, though he couldn't help turning it into just a little bit of a performance. I'd come home of an evening and before I could put down my bags, Baz would have grabbed me and led me into the kitchen where he'd proudly display his latest work in progress.

'I've discovered the secret of tempura, Rupe!' he declared one day, showing me the bowl full of ice cubes in which a smaller bowl of batter mixture sat. 'The key is to keep it chilled as you make it. You can even put it in the freezer.' And it was true, he had cracked the secret as his tempura vegetables were as good as anything I had ever tasted in any Japanese restaurant. It wasn't just that he carefully followed the recipes and techniques, he had a flair for it, a true artist's calling. He could turn anything into a tempura triumph – pumpkin, broccoli, prawns. His experiments in the world of tempura were boundless and I half expected him to tempura the dog's biscuits for her.

Not that it made any difference to Di, who was resolute in her rejection of anything Baz came up with. The tempura bream (the fish caught fresh that morning by Baz in the lake) came back from Di's room with a couple of bites out of it and a complaint that the smell of the fish cooking had made her feel sick.

Another day, another attempt: 'What I'm doing here, Rupe, is a type of Japanese hotpot. I've bought these special Jap pots for it, see?' and he would enthusiastically shove one of the pots filled with eggs and rice wine and sprouts and shitake mushrooms and God knows what else out for me to inspect. Di would later return the pot barely touched, moaning about how she was sick of all this fancy stuff and why couldn't she just have something simple like corned beef or a roast.

So the next night it was roast pork. Nobody cooked roast pork like Baz, but this night he was like a madman, obsessing over making this joint of pork the best that was ever cooked.

And it would have been pretty hard to beat. Baz cooked the most amazing crackle I have ever tasted and the flesh was succulent and juicy. Di ate about half a mouthful and pushed the plate away, griping that the whole thing was tainted by the taste of the crackle.

Baz returned from her room, scraped the meat onto my willing plate and put the plate into the dishwasher, all the while mumbling to himself like Muttley. As he closed the door of the dishwasher his mumble rose in volume and he sang out to Di, 'You haven't beaten me yet. I'll get you yet, Didy. One of these days, I swear, you won't be able to resist, you hear me?!' And with that he lapsed back into his mumbling.

Once the dishwasher was packed he would pull out a cookbook or a recipe he had snipped from the paper and bring it over to me.

'What do you reckon about this for tea tomorrow night? It's a new recipe for braised lamb shanks with polenta. Have you heard of polenta? It looks all right.'

And he would sit down with the recipe thinking of little improvements he could make, every now and again looking over to Di's bedroom and muttering, 'I'll get you yet Didy, I'll get you yet.'

After a couple of months of constant rejection, you would have thought Baz would have given up on his quest for the ultimate, irresistible meal. But he was having none of it and every untouched dish only spurred him on to new heights of culinary inventiveness. He was a man possessed and would stop at nothing to lure Di's appetite back. The more treatment she had the less she felt like eating. The less she ate, the harder it was for her body to recover and the less effective the treatment would be. All his traditional sure-fire winners had failed to impress, as did each elaborate new recipe he tried. Aside from the occasional piece of Vegemite toast, Di was still not really eating anything. Baz could see her strength to fight wasting away.

I walked in one night as Baz proudly produced his latest concoction – tea-bag chicken. He never quite explained the mystery of how he cooked the chicken breast with the tea-bags but I had to admit that it didn't look half bad. He placed it on a serving plate and entered Di's room with his usual pomp only to be greeted with the inevitable, 'Oh shut up, Barry.' But he took it with good grace as usual, put the plate down and came back to the kitchen where he and I shared the remainder.

At times I could understand why Di got so shirty with him. Baz could be a bloody pain the way he went on about what he was cooking. Perhaps that's the difference between a male and female cook – the man always wants to be congratulated for every little effort. When he was like this I would often be deliberately vague about whether I liked the meal or not. He was really banging on about this tea-bag chicken and it annoyed me to have to say that it was quite tasty. It probably wasn't the most amazing dish of his career, but it had a clean, simple freshness about it. We both polished off our serves with relish.

After half an hour Baz got up to collect Di's plate. I could hear him ask her whether she had enjoyed his tea-bag chicken. She said it was all right and left it at that. I would have taken no more notice but for the look of amazement on Baz's face when he reappeared in the kitchen. Di's plate was totally clean. She had eaten every morsel. Baz grinned like an idiot. As he put the plate away in the dishwasher I could see tears dropping into the cutlery basket. He collected himself and wandered back into Mum's bedroom and asked nonchalantly, 'So, Di, how about some ice cream?'

Over the next few weeks her appetite came back thanks to Dad's culinary efforts. Chances are it would have happened anyway once the effects of the chemo had worn off. She would have started to taste her food again, and as her body recovered it would have craved sustenance to help her get back on her feet. But it would have been pointless trying to tell Baz that. He was convinced that his tea-bag chicken had caused the breakthrough. And who's to say it didn't? The doctors at Peter Mac were very impressed with the way she bounced back from her treatment. From being perilously close to death, Di went on to have a particularly vigorous remission. She got back into painting, learning to master watercolours. She and Baz went on several trips together, reinstituting the pokies trips to New South Wales with Ace and Chris. For the best part of three years Baz got the Di of old back.

But even better was that Di got a new Baz. They were never happier together than in those last couple of years. Where I had seen a couple inexorably drifting apart, now they shared a closeness I don't think they had ever had before. You often hear people who have had cancer say that, in a way, having the cancer was the best thing that had happened to them. On one level that is bullshit, because if you had the choice, no one would choose to go through all that pain and sickness and terror. But I firmly believe that the diagnosis of cancer can be the catalyst that makes people take stock of their lives, sort out what is really important and actually begin living.

Multiple myeloma ultimately robbed Di of what should have been many productive years. Lung cancer took Baz before his time (though let's face it, with his lifestyle nobody was expecting him to end up ninety-nine not out). But if neither of them had got sick, they wouldn't have found each other again, they wouldn't have discovered in one another and in themselves what they cherished. Without their illnesses I would not have got to see them at their finest. I would never have got to understand them the way I did and, in the case of Baz, I would never have got to truly mourn him when he was gone.

Some may see this as a cruel irony. I see it as a gift.

13

ON THE ROAD (WITH BAZ)

The ironic thing about my birdwatching was that even though Baz thought it was completely weird, it actually gave us one of the few opportunities we had to spend time together. Baz loved travelling around Australia and as I was always out and about looking for birds, it seemed only natural that we could combine our mutual interests. Not that it happened too often. I think the whole idea of trying to birdwatch with my Dad had soured on our family holidays when I was growing up. Rather than hearing the eternal 'Are we there yet?' coming from the back seat, Baz had to put up with me pleading to stop at every swamp we passed or bird that I saw feeding out in a paddock or sitting on a wire. While Baz loved driving and didn't really care what the destination was, he was still impatient to get to wherever it was that he didn't particularly care about. And if there was the prospect of a new pub to have a drink in at the end of the drive he became even less accommodating in stopping to look 'at just another bloody swamp'.

But what Baz could never understand is that it was never just another swamp, or just another bird, for me; every bird, every habitat, held the exciting possibility that it was something new, something I hadn't seen before. The critical moment for me came on a hot, blustery summer's day in the backblocks of northeast Victoria, somewhere between Benalla and New Zealand. What had begun as a jaunt off the main highway had now become a 'we don't know where the hell we are' kind of tense family moment and nobody was happy. At the tipping point of Baz seriously losing his cool, I spied a pale falcon with black wing tips cruising over a paddock. It looked for all the world like the exceptionally rare grey falcon. I yelled at Baz to stop the car and go back. Baz refused, and to this day I have still not seen a grey falcon, one of the very few Australian birds not on my list. Not that I'm bitter. Much.

As an adult, it wasn't until the year after Di's myeloma diagnosis that I went on a road trip with Baz. It was to King Island in Bass Strait. Di was in remission and as a kind of reward for hanging in there with them, Baz shouted me an airfare so that I could be chauffeur for him and his mate, the Spaniard. The Spaniard, who looked about as Spanish as Baz (I know there are Black Irish, descended from the survivors of the Spanish Armada who washed up on Irish shores, but was there a movement the other way too, resulting in White Spanish?), was an ex-boxer who had gone on to run a sand quarry out the back of Frankston. We rented a house on the east coast of the island and though they made one half-hearted attempt at fishing, the real reason they were there was to feast on the local produce and drink crateloads of beer. My job was to drive them across to the island's only pub, which was on the west coast, and to get them home safely afterwards. The rest of the day I could head off birding by myself.

It worked out remarkably well. I got to see some of the island's specialties and Baz and the Spaniard got to drink with the locals. They were on a kind of secret mission to make contact with some local crayfishermen so they could get a direct supply of fresh King Island crays. Not for any business reasons, just because they loved crayfish. They hit it off so well with one cray man that we were all invited out on his boat the next day to join him as he went offshore to check his pots. I was keen as it was a chance to get out to sea and up close to some ocean-going sea birds like albatross that were often attracted to the fishing boats, hoping to cop a free feed courtesy of the by-catch.

The conditions were perfect for albatross: windy and very choppy. I saw several but I also spent the last half of the morning staring grimly at the horizon trying not to lose my breakfast. Baz and the Spaniard, neither of whom were regular sailors, seemed totally unperturbed in the rough conditions and by ten o'clock were quite happily cracking open tinnies of VB. I guess when you have spent half your adult life deliberately making yourself unsteady on your feet, the rollicking of the sea offers no impediment. Sadly for Baz and the Spaniard, not to mention the fisherman, his boat sank on a reef the next year and their anticipated flow of fresh crays dried up.

The next year they decided to try Flinders Island on the other side of Bass Strait to hook into the local cray trade. Again I tagged along as designated driver. As we were staying in the pub this time, I could have a drink myself and I remember Baz being quite astonished when I sat up drinking with them and saw both of them to bed before I had finished. Baz was particularly impressed that I had outlasted the Spaniard, who was no slouch when it came to putting the grog away, and he queried me the next morning: 'I didn't think you liked a drink, Rupe?'

'I don't mind it, Dad. I just don't like getting blind every night,' I explained. Baz looked at me rather puzzled.

Towards the last few years of Di's life I also did a few road trips with her as well, though these tended to be just short day trips from home during which she would paint and I would go birding. Di felt safer out in the bush with me lurking in the vicinity birdwatching, though what she expected me to do to if we ever did encounter some nefarious types I was never sure. Frighten them off with my powers of honeyeater identification?

We did one epic road trip together, though it was hardly the stuff of Kerouac, staying at country motels with your mum. Then again, from what I know of Jack's last few years, that's not so off the mark. We drove from Melbourne to Townsville to visit Di's cousin Kay, who was dying of breast cancer. Mum and Kay were more like sisters, having grown up together in that house of crazy divorcees on the beach at Edithvale. For the first seven years of my life Kay and her family had lived in the rented house next door to us. Her youngest son Michael, despite being five years older than me, was my best friend until they all moved up to Townsville for work opportunities and to be closer to their older son.

This was before Di had become sick herself and she could stand up to the gruelling ten-hour days in the car. It was really lovely to spend so much time together, something we hadn't done as adults. As I drove through the countryside she would record in my notebook any new birds I saw. I treasure those entries, not only because they are a reminder of that time, but because my handwriting is so atrocious; they are the only parts of the notebook that are still legible. I don't think I'd ever felt as close to my mum, though I'm not quite sure what she made of my adult life when one night as we sat up in our respective beds in the motel in the small town of Miles I noticed that the show my new housemate was in was about to air on the telly. I was away when my other housemate interviewed her and I got an excited call saying he had found the perfect person to fill the vacant room. She was a model, recently returned from overseas and had just landed her first acting role. My housemate was smitten with her but, sad to say, I found I had absolutely nothing in common with her and spent most of our time in the house together with my mouth agape, incredulous at her ditzy banter. Still, maybe she was a good actress, I thought, and, hoping to show Mum what sophisticated circles I moved in, I put the show on.

It was a soap called *Chances*. It had started as a genuine attempt to be a contemporary adult drama but rated poorly and the producers were told there would not be another season.

So they decided to have some fun with the remaining episodes and started to throw in lots of sex and violence and ridiculous plotlines about vampires and the like. My housemate played a nun (who wasn't really a nun) and in the first five minutes had her gear off and was humping the lead. I fumbled for the remote as my straitlaced mum looked on aghast. I don't think she ever asked about a housemate of mine again.

One day in May 1998, with the six-month anniversary of Di's death approaching, Baz rang me and asked whether I felt like doing a road trip. I was between jobs and had just split up with a girlfriend so jumped at the chance to get out of the city. We had no real itinerary and ended up heading in a vaguely westerly direction. It was a relatively quiet trip initially. I was still grieving from the bust-up and not unnaturally Baz was still grieving for Di. We both were, and in a way the long silences weren't that awkward as we each understood the other needed to be left to their thoughts. In those six months we hadn't really talked all that deeply about losing Di, though we had definitely spent a lot more time keeping in touch than we otherwise would have.

After we had passed through Ballarat and stopped for a cuppa at the small town of Beaufort (it was still far too early for the pub), where Baz told me about a mate who used to run the newsagency there until he was hit by an Adelaide-bound truck, Baz suddenly decided we would go to a place neither of us had been before, a little dot in the Western District called Willaura. Di used to have on her key ring a flat piece of metal that was shaped like an old-time jalopy with the name of her grandfather's garage engraved on it: 'MacDonald's Garage, Willaura, telephone 36' or some such. Baz had used it in the past as an emergency bottle opener and still had the tag attached to his key ring. Sadly, it is lost now.

We arrived at Willaura just after opening time and were the only ones in the pub that frosty Sunday morning. The publican was vaguely interested in the key ring but said the garage was closed. When we told him that it came from the 1920s he said he hadn't been in town that long (he probably wasn't born until about 1955 and we couldn't work out whether he meant it as a joke) and we should wait for some of the old-timers to come in. The old-timers never showed so we downed our pots and kept on meandering through the Western District. We stopped by a lake and watched a small flock of Brolgas fly in. The Brolga is Australia's only endemic species of crane, a magnificent bird and rare in those parts. They gather together at certain sites to feast on tubers in the ground and stage elaborate and stately courtship dances in what has been likened to a giant corroboree. We sat in the car watching their hulking grey frames prod in the wet ground for food and Baz didn't smirk once. He wasn't dismissive, or cracking gags about fancying birds himself. He sat there taking in everything I said and just enjoying the birds for their beauty. He even said as much. 'They're beautiful birds, Rupe,' were, I believe, his precise words.

It was one of those wonderfully wintry days, the sort where it is great to sit by an open fire, the sort of day that seems conducive to introspection. It seemed only natural that we ended up at Port Campbell, that dramatic cliff-lined stretch of coast where the seas roll in from the Antarctic trying to tear great chunks of the mainland away with every crashing wave. Baz and I stood rugged up at sunset watching the roiling surf crash in on the little harbour. We stood there lost in our own thoughts until the last skerrick of light had slipped below the horizon of the grey ocean. We headed to the pub for a counter meal, had a couple more pots, grabbed a six-pack and took it back to our room, and talked. And talked like we had probably never talked before. And every conversation wound its way back to Di.

We reminisced about all those meals Baz had cooked for her. The meals rejected. The meals that went into the dog's bowl. We laughed over how she would complain that the food was too spicy. Or too fatty. Or too ... whatever, when it was clearly delicious. We spoke of the enormous crayfish I had been confronted with as a kid down at Port Fairy, when crays were still affordable to the average diner, and how Baz had watched in awe as I demolished this beast of a crustacean that was bigger than my head. Baz told of how he regretted ever turning me onto crayfish as it meant there was always less for him, and how he had done the same thing with Di and oysters.

We remembered the last couple of months of her life. By that stage it was coming up to four years since her diagnosis and we had all become somewhat used to the patterns. A round of chemotherapy and then a remission of almost a year. Then signs would appear to indicate the unbowed disease was gathering strength so there'd be another course of treatment and then another, less complete remission that lasted maybe six months. And then there were the spot treatments: the short stays in hospital, the localised bouts of intense radiotherapy to knock off a few rogue outbreaks in her bones and put them back in their place. It was never back to normal but it was back to an altered type of normal. We thought it would go on like this for years.

She had started to go downhill again and another spell in Peter Mac was called for. This time it lasted longer than had been the case for a while and she spent her 61st birthday away from home. At her sixtieth all she had wanted, she said, was for Wok and me to play her a song. We had both taken up the guitar at various times but had never played a tune together. Wok had spent most of his time sitting around with his stoner mates trying to nut out a riff from a Kiss or Led Zep album, while I was usually locked away in my room bashing out chords to accompany my bad teen poetry – I barely knew how to play anybody else's songs. We cobbled together a version of John Lennon's 'Imagine' as requested and threw in a rendition of 'Wish You Were Here' as this was the only song we both knew by heart. It wasn't the greatest of performances. Wok, clearly the more talented player, had to cope with both my erratic time signatures and his own performance anxiety.

There was not to be a repeat performance. A couple of months later Wok had separated from his wife and had ended up tagging along with a mate from his Seaford days who worked on the sugar plantations up north. By the time of Di's 61st birthday he was ensconced in an old Queenslander house with a bunch of blokes in Tully, Far North Queensland. Baz and I celebrated her birthday by bringing some cake into the ward. The nurses got most of it. I guess there have to be some perks to their job.

Di ended up in a private hospital closer to home for respite care. Though I knew she was going downhill, I kept thinking she would simply get some more treatment and continue on. By this stage, there was an outbreak in the bones of her eye socket. One of her specialists told us that without another operation and more radiotherapy, the bone growth would cut off her optical nerve and she would lose her sight. We all assumed Di would have the treatment and we would get on with things as we had before.

But Di was tired of fighting. She couldn't face the gruelling regime again. When she announced she wanted to stop all but her palliative treatment we were stunned. I was actually angry with her. For the past four years I had been having dreams that she had died and would wake up howling in the night. Now it seemed to me she was willing to embrace my nightmare scenario. It took a long time for me to accept her decision, but eventually I realised it was her decision, not mine or Baz's or Wok's or anyone else's to make. I had been there through the darkest times and knew how tenaciously she had fought this bastard of a disease, so there was no question she wouldn't have kept fighting if she thought it was a battle she could win, but she was at the end of her tether and couldn't muster the energy to keep battling.

It took enormous courage to deal with what she had to endure. It took me a long time to realise that it took just as much courage to accept that she simply couldn't continue like that.

Di's decision would inevitably bring on her death earlier than if she continued treatment but it would be a death more on her own terms, one where she maintained a certain dignity amid the whole overwhelming process. I am not talking about euthanasia here, for she wasn't trying to end her life, she simply did not want to prolong it excessively. There is a subtle but crucial difference. But most importantly, and this is what took me too long to cotton on to, was that she wanted to face her death without bitterness, with a sense of peace, and that word again – grace – which to me Di seemed to personify.

If only I had arrived at the same awareness as Di earlier, I wouldn't now regret the wastefulness of those last few weeks. Though Di was fading before our eyes, all three of us Dooley boys continued on in denial. Baz would visit her every day, Wok (who had come down when we realised that things were getting quite serious) and I far less – a whole week would go by and I might only have spoken to her once on the phone, so busy was I with whatever the hell I was doing, so intent on not facing up to the glaring reality of the situation. Even though Baz was seeing her constantly, he wasn't talking with her about what was to come, always avoiding the topic. In her greatest need, Di had probably never felt more alone.

It took my Aunty Jan to set me straight. On one occasion I had been planning to visit Di but reneged because I had a bit of a cold and didn't want to pass anything on to her that would attack her weakened system. I got a call from Jan that night. There is no bull with Jan and she cut straight to the chase.

'You didn't see Di today.' It was a statement rather than a question.

'No, I'm a bit sick and I didn't want her to catch it.' How pathetic I sounded.

'Sean, your mother's dying and she's upset that you won't see her.'

Geez, don't sugar-coat it, will you, Jan? 'She's not dying just yet,' I replied stubbornly.

'Sean, she's dying. She might only have two weeks at most.'

'No. The doctor said –'

Jan cut me short: 'Two weeks, Sean, if that. She knows it. And yet none of you geniuses will talk to her about it. She wants you there. And you're not there for her.' And for the first time I could ever remember, tough old Aunty Jan started to cry. I could feel that familiar tightening in my throat as I assured her I'd be by Mum's side the next morning. I put the phone down. That's when I really began to cry. It didn't stop all night. This was no dream that I had woken from: this was reality.

The next morning I fronted up at the hospital. Di was overjoyed that I was there, and so began the hardest and at the same time most beautiful two weeks of my life. Every visit was gut-churning when I left but we sat and spoke openly about what was happening, what was to come and what we were feeling. I learnt so much about Di in that time – half the content of this bloody book came from what passed between us in those ten or so days. I more or less told Wok and Baz what Jan had said to me and they both spent plenty of time with her, enough time to say goodbye and feel like nothing was left unsaid. We were so lucky to have that. She could have died from ovarian cancer when I was sixteen. She could have died of a heart attack or a car accident or a freak penguin attack at any point since then. Not only had we had a bonus thirteen years of her sublime presence in our lives, but we got the opportunity to let her know what she meant to us and how much we loved her. I hated that fucking cancer with my very being, but what it did give us was the chance to say goodbye, the chance to celebrate a beautiful life that we might otherwise never have had.

At this time I was working for another rails bookie, Alf King. It was a midweek meeting at Flemington and things were very quiet. Apart from one or two minor associates of the Tracksuit Gang, the ring was virtually empty when Alf got a call on the 'bat-phone' as Baz used to call the line reserved for the off-course punters. Oddly, Alf didn't yell out a bet for me to record but handed the phone to me. It was Baz.

'You better get here quickly, mate, she doesn't look good. She's in a coma. They say she may not make it through the day.'

I'd known it was coming, I'd known that very soon I would get this call – Mum herself had steeled me for it – but I had not dared contemplate the true impact of what that call would mean. All at once there was both a release and an increasing of the tension that had been building up for the past weeks. I felt like someone had thumped the bejesus out of my solar plexus, yet my first reaction that I could barely keep in check was to burst out laughing.

I put the phone down and looked at Alf, expecting that I would have to work the rest of the day. Like many a bookie, Baz included, he could be a tough old bastard, but just from the look on my face he knew and before I had virtually said a thing he insisted that I go and be with her.

I howled the entire drive down there. When I arrived I was a little more composed. Baz and Wok were already there. There was not much to do but sit with her and wait. It was hard to say whether the coma was completely natural as her rattling breath would be punctuated by the intermittent click of the machine attached to her arm that would inject another dose of morphine. A couple of times she would vaguely stir but she would never come to full consciousness. This went on for the entire day and into the night. The way myeloma gets you is not by spreading to the rest of the body but by placing such a strain on your system that vital organs begin to shut down. This was happening before our eyes, though from the outside only her faltering breath gave away the tumult within.

At one point the hospital chaplain entered the room to carry out a blessing. Baz and Wok were very reverential as he went about his rituals. They couldn't work out why I was grinning like an idiot when he finished and solemnly told us, 'God was very important to Diane. She knew the love of God was with her and she took great comfort from that. As can you.'

What Wok and Baz hadn't been privy to was what Di had said to me a few days earlier when I arrived to visit just as the chaplain was leaving. Once he was safely gone, Di whispered to me, 'I let him talk because I don't want to be rude, but I don't believe it. He's just talking a load of crap really.' This from a former Sunday School teacher. This from a woman who wouldn't even say the word 'bummer' because it seemed uncouth – she would say 'bomber' instead. I couldn't help laughing because the God guy was so caught up in his patronising reassurances and platitudes that he had no idea he wasn't getting through and it was actually he who was being patronised.

By evening the nurses told us there had been no major deterioration of her vital signs and that they thought she would last the night. If we wanted to go home and rest, they would contact us if anything changed. I went back to Baz's with Wok and we spent a solemn couple of hours. On my way back up to the city I dropped in on Di again. It was about half past eleven. As I stroked her hair and kissed her face she stirred and grabbed hold of my hand. Through the fog of the morphine she looked up and said, 'Oh, it's you, love …'

'Yes, Mum, it's me,' I whispered strongly, moving in closer to her so she could see.

She closed her eyes and smiled, ever so slightly squeezed my hand and said, 'Good. I was just …'

And then she lapsed back into unconsciousness. I couldn't rouse her further. I believe it was the last time she stirred, the last words she ever said. I have had no greater honour than being the recipient of those last words, knowing that I was the last person she was ever conscious of, but God damn it, what the hell was she going to say?! When I was at uni I had written an inconclusive 'last words' scene like that for a production I was in, little realising that it would presage what was to come in my own life. Maybe it was Di's payback for having to sit through something so pretentiously enigmatic.

I had never known that the death rattle was a real thing, but for the whole of the next day we sat and listened as Di was unable to clear her passageways of the phlegm that was gathering. It is a horrible sound – a cross between snoring and strangulation – made all the more terrible by the knowledge that it represents death approaching at speed. Occasionally there would be vast gaps between rattles and we would lean forward, half in dread, half in hope, that her ordeal was over. And then after as much as thirty seconds, the rattle would fire up again.

After another day's vigil, the specialist checked on her in the afternoon and thought that though the end was near, it probably wasn't going to be immediate. I had some things to do back up in the city and Baz insisted I take a break. I no longer remember what those things were, and if I did them it was through a fug of grief, but whatever they were I ended up running late. I was meant to relieve Baz from his deathwatch duties at seven but I didn't arrive back at the hospital until twenty to eight. The nurse said Baz had left about twenty minutes earlier. I walked into the room and the first thing I noticed was that Baz had left the one-day cricket going on the television. Di had never had the slightest interest in cricket. I turned to her, smiling.

She was not moving. No surprise there, she hadn't moved for the best part of two days. But I knew instinctively this was different. There was no death rattle for starters and all the tension had gone from her body. I approached and all was totally still. Though she was warm, it was clear she was dead. I had read somewhere that as the brain shuts down in death, of all the senses they thought that hearing was the last to go. She had been alive twenty minutes earlier when Baz had left. There was every chance she had only just died. I cradled her head in my arms and put my lips to her ear and whispered over and over again, 'I love you, I love you, Mum.' If there was one iota of awareness in her, of life still there, I wanted her to go with that ringing in her ears.

I don't know how long I held her like this but eventually my incantation petered out and I just held her as the first sobs came. After a while I looked up at the cricket on the telly and saw Greg Blewett, my favourite Australian player at the time, get caught after fending off an almost unplayable delivery from South African bowler Allan Donald. 'Fuck you, Blewett, you dickhead!' I screamed at the screen. I really hoped Mum's consciousness had left the building, as I'd hate to think they were the last words she heard.

Well-wishers overflowed the hall at the funeral home for Di's funeral. Baz had come up to see her as soon as I had rung with the news. Wok hadn't at the time but on the day of the funeral he wanted to have one last look. Just before the service the three of us had a quick viewing. In some ways I think Wok wished he hadn't. The make-up people had done a good enough job, but they didn't know her and the rouge on her cheeks was way overdone compared to what she would normally have worn. But worse than that, she now had a waxy, dare I say it, lifeless complexion. Wok cried, but I couldn't at that stage because what lay in front of me had very little to do with the Di that I knew.

Her essence would live on in a million different ways, but that waxwork dummy was not one of them. Prime among my treasured memories of Di is the letter she wrote the week before she died. After I had visited her one time in hospital she had pressed three letters into my hand and asked me to give Baz and Wok theirs when she was gone. They weren't sealed but I never took a peek. I didn't even look at mine until after she had died.

What she said in that letter was in a way anticlimactic. There were no amazing revelations about life from the perspective of someone about to depart it. She had gained no searing insight that I could live the rest of my life by. It simply started: 'To my Sean, I can hardly put into words what I feel for you darling, you are the hardest one to leave my note …' And it goes on in very few words to say that she loved me and was so proud of me. Nothing particularly profound. But every time I get that letter out, she is with me. It is such a moving experience that I have to limit how many times a year I can open it. Even now, ten years on, the memory of her can leave me wracked with the pain of missing her. Often I don't think of my mum for weeks, but when I do it can floor me still.

Six months after her death that feeling was still overwhelming. Even though I had seen a lot of Baz, we avoided talking about Di too much as it was unbearable. But that night by the surf at Port Campbell as we debriefed after those first tough six months I suddenly knew in my heart, for possibly the first time, that I would also feel just as strongly about Baz if he ever dropped off the perch. But that was going to be years away, wasn't it?

14

Less than two years after Di had eventually succumbed, Baz started his treatment for lung cancer. It was the day before Grand Final day. Luckily one of the local private hospitals had their own chemo unit so Baz was spared the tedious process of driving up to the city to get his regular dose of poison pumped into his veins. Some types of chemotherapy barely leave a trace; others wreak absolute havoc on the body. The chemo for Di's ovarian cancer hadn't been too bad. The stuff for her myeloma was a bitch. I remember driving her up to Peter Mac hospital during her treatment and having to pull over to the side of the road in Brighton so she could open the car door and vomit into the gutter.

There is something inherently topsy-turvy in watching your parents being sick – they are the ones who are meant to hold your hair out of the way as you chuck. When the roles are reversed it just seems against all laws of nature. After Mum had finished and it was OK for me to drive on, I told her that next time, if she gave me a little more notice, I could pull over in front of the most opulent mansion in the street and she could fertilise their lawn. I didn't get the smile I'd hoped for, but at least she had the strength to admonish me for being an idiot.

Baz had been lucky enough to need no chemo after his bowel cancer, the surgeon had done the job so well. He was not so lucky now. I left him at the chemo day clinic as soon as was polite to do so. I offered to stay the whole course but he waved me off, for which I was grateful. Even though the nurses had done their best to cheer the place up – there were photos on the wall of the July Christmas ward party, and they had created a feature wall of patients' pets that reminded me of the employee of the month plaques at fast food outlets – the ward still felt rather creepy for the first few visits. All those hairless, pale-skinned, sunken-eyed people sitting around attached to their drips was just a tad distressing, made more so by the unavoidable, morbid speculation about which of the patients this torture would actually work for.

What made me want to get out of the ward even quicker was when Baz started to flirt with the nurses, especially the younger ones. Baz had reached the age that some men do when they can get away with flirting without being seen as lecherous, particularly if they are charming. Self-confident men who are comfortable in their own skin are always charming, no matter how rough they actually look. And while you wouldn't call Baz self-confident in the sense of being arrogant, he certainly had a rare unselfconsciousness about him, which often had the effect of making me squirm when I was with him in his 'charming' mode. Not just because he was my dad, but also because I could see in him the eighteen year old who had somehow found himself trapped in a sixty-year-old body. The nurses wouldn't have tolerated him if he was twenty or thirty years younger but because he had crossed that mysterious age threshold he was deemed harmless.

Long before Di was sick I had gone down to Queenscliff with Baz one hot summer to visit Uncle Norm, whose family had a caravan there. I had extricated myself as soon as I could from Baz and Norm as they headed down for a session on the grog at the bowls club and gone birdwatching along the shores of Swan Bay. When I got back hours later, Baz and Norm had been hard at it and Norm was snoring his head off. Baz was as pissed as a parrot. (Not just a quaint saying – one type of parrot, the lorikeet, actually can get drunk when the nectar of the flowers they feed on ferments in the sun. See, I really am a birdwatcher.) He wanted to go to the pub for a feed. As soon as we arrived he latched on to two dolly birds who were almost as tanked as him and started being 'charming'. I left him to it and went and watched the cricket on the bar's TV. Sensing he might have been losing their interest he called me over and displayed me in front of them like a prize pig: 'This is my boy, Sean – he's a good looking kid, isn't he? And he's going to be a lawyer.'

For one horrible moment it felt like he was recruiting me as a two-for-one package to try and pick up these forty-something women. (I was in my early twenties, Baz in his mid fifties.) As far as I knew, to that point Baz had always been faultlessly faithful to

Di so this was a bit of a shock. It took me a while to realise that he wasn't actually trying to pick them up as such, it was just that he wanted to keep their attention – although to this day I still haven't worked out whether he was trying to lend me a hand to get me laid.

Fair dinkum, how off the mark could the man be? Not only did Baz not get that being pimped by my father was not how I wanted to meet women – no matter how attractive they were – he even managed to get my career wrong. Although I had finally finished my law degree, I had never practised. Instead, I had been earning my living as a TV comedy writer (I knew all those hours in front of *The Flintstones* would pay off!), though Baz clearly never thought that was worth boasting about.

A few hours after his first treatment was over and I was driving him home, he didn't let me down. 'So, Rupe, what do you reckon of that Michelle? She was all right, wasn't she?'

'Oh Jesus, Dad,' I groaned in protest.

Baz slunk back in his seat and said sulkily, 'Don't know what's wrong with you.'

I rolled my eyes and, as I did with so many other things in relation to Baz, just let it slide. I had long learnt that unless it was really important, there were many things that Baz would never really get and it was far easier for me to just move on than waste energy trying to explain the situation from my viewpoint. Though it meant we were perhaps denied a certain closeness that comes from mutual understanding and empathy, it made for a far more harmonious coexistence.

The full debilitating effects of the chemo wouldn't take hold for another couple of days, so (much to Dr Nick's horror, I am sure) Baz was all set for a big day at his Grand Final celebrations. Despite having had a toxic cocktail pumped into his body, Baz was up half the night baking Cornish pasties for the boys. The next day he was out shopping for some streamers and balloons in the team colours, North Melbourne and Carlton. We arrived at the club early to set everything up, fire up the pie warmer and put up the bookie board in preparation for taking bets on the game.

As we were tacking up balloons, Dee the barmaid arrived to open up the bar. For the tenth time, Baz introduced me to her. 'Dee, do you know my son Sean?' Baz didn't add that I was a good-looking lad because he knew Dee was married – in fact her husband sometimes drank at the club and though it had very few rules apart from 'no two shots on the black', sleeping with the wife of a fellow club member was right out.

'Yes, Barry, we went to school together,' came Dee's stock response.

Baz never took in such details about other people's lives, but I was about to say something that would make him sit up and take notice. Without thinking about it I chipped in with, 'Yeah, Dee was my first kiss.'

'Was that your first kiss?' Dee asked, surprised. But the real look of surprise was on Baz's face. Throughout the years I had successfully imposed on Baz a virtual news blackout on any details of my personal life. I had let my guard down now and an explanation was in order.

It hadn't necessarily been all that romantic a kiss, really. Dee and I were in the same class in grade six at Seaford North Primary School. She was a twin who had only come out to Australia from Ireland a couple of years earlier. Girls must have developed more quickly in Ireland for the by time Dee was in grade six she was mainly hanging out with boys who were already at high school, not pipsqueaks like me.

She was very popular, so I assumed I was never in with a chance. But then the grade six teacher, in order to shake up the Australian Barbecue Phenomenon in the classroom, whereby boys always sat with boys and girls with girls, decreed that each girl in the class had to choose a boy to share a desk with for one week. To my amazement, Dee chose me. My immediate thought was that she must have wanted to copy from my schoolwork. To my delight, however, this girl who had seemed so distant when she was hanging out with the tough kids at the roller-rink with their skinny black Fabergé jeans, shark-tooth necklaces and packets of Winfield Blues wedged tightly in the upper sleeve of their Golden Breed windcheaters, was suddenly taking an interest in me and laughing at all my jokes.

In English class we had an exercise where we had to look up new words in the dictionary. Dee and I took great delight in finding big words to which we could construe ambiguous meanings, such as the word 'ambiguous'. 'Ambiguous: difficult to classify; of doubtful origin'. For some reason that had us in hysterics, as did 'egregious', though for the life of me I can't remember what exactly was funny about 'outstandingly bad;

shocking'. But, hey, we were eleven, to us this was the height of sophistication.

Around this time my best friend, Reevesy, and a couple of his mates had decided to form a gang, which they invited me to join. They called themselves 'The Gods', but the way they pronounced it, as if they were leads in a gladiator movie, always sounded to me like they were saying 'The Guards', and for the entire time the gang lasted I thought that was what we were called. In order to join you had to become blood brothers. The other three kids had cut themselves with razor blades to do so. I really wasn't keen on the idea but was able to find a loophole when I grazed myself playing with them in the local swamp and a quick consultation of the rules committee agreed it was OK for me to bleed on the other members.

The reign of these gods was brief and I reckon after two weeks nobody could be bothered with the charade of being in a gang anymore, so we went back to our ordinary mortal existence. But some girls in our class had taken notice and decided to form a club of their own. They went about it properly, setting up their club headquarters under one of the girls' houses, and their club survived the entire year. To be initiated the girls were required to kiss a boy of their choice. It had to be a proper 'pash', not a chaste peck on the cheek. One by one the girls chose their victims and dutifully through a week of lunchtimes, boys would be targeted in the playground and held down if necessary by a large group of giggling girls. Some boys reacted to this gross violation of human rights by spending all of lunchtime running around the school in terror. Most submitted after token resistance. While you couldn't be seen to be wanting to get pashed by a girl, most guys were secretly flattered by the attention.

At the end of the week all the girls in the gang had successfully passed initiation except for Dee. There were quite a few boys hoping to be targeted so I was pretty chuffed when at recess on the Friday she coyly brushed past me and whispered, 'You're my initiation.' Di's chicken loaf sandwiches were wolfed down extra quick that lunchtime and I was out on the oval awaiting my fate as soon as I could manage. Eventually a group of grade six girls assembled around me like sharks gathering at the smell of blood. I made a decent effort at pretending to escape but ensured that I didn't run fast enough for them not to catch me. Amid a cacophony of mini-Amazonian squeals I pretended to struggle as they held me down and Dee appeared above me.

It suddenly occurred to me that I had never asked anyone how you actually pash a girl, so adopting a pose from the movies, I lay there with my mouth wide open. As she got closer, Dee whispered urgently to me, 'Close your mouth, stupid!' I duly did, and the entire experience wasn't half bad. We actually started officially 'going with' each other after that and, oh, what a blissful two weeks they were. I think we split up when I saw Dee kiss one of the older kids at the rollerskating rink a couple of weeks later.

I looked at Baz who was clearly eager to hear all the juicy details. Dee was blushing slightly as she concentrated on the keg she was tapping and started to pour out the beer. Even though

Baz and I had become a lot closer since Di's death, it took me all of two seconds to consider whether I should share this slice of my life with him.

'None of your bloody business!'

Before Baz could protest, he was distracted by the first of the boys arriving for the day's festivities. It was a bloke called Stinky, who lived just across the road from the club and who had made the bar an extension of his lounge room. Funny how Stinky always managed to arrive just as the first keg was tapped; there must have been some kind of bat signal in his lounge room to let him know it was about to happen. Stinky entered with his customary roared greeting.

'Baz! What's going on?!'

Baz returned Stinky's salutations with a cheeky smile. 'Hey, Stink, did you know that Dee was Rupert's first kiss?'

Stinky's roar revved up a notch. 'You're kidding? Half his bloody luck! I'd have a crack too, if Leslie would let me.'

Leslie – Stinky's 'missus' – had walked in behind him. She also worked at the club, and was serving that day with Dee. She just raised her hands in mock exasperation and proclaimed, 'If Dee would have you, she'd be welcome! Trouble is, Dee's not stupid. Or blind.'

Leslie was your archetypal 'barmaid with a heart of gold' who, after a succession of arsehole men in her life, had finally struck a good one in Stinky. Not that it would immediately be apparent as Stinky had done his best to make himself look as messy as possible.

Sporting a moustache of Merv Hughes proportions and more ink than a giant squid, which he showed off by insisting on wearing a bluey singlet and stubby shorts in all but the coldest of weather, Stinky looked like the sort of drug-running Outback trucker who knows where the bodies are buried. And in fact he was. Well, I don't know if he ever was a drug runner but he had actually been an Outback truckie. He now worked driving concrete trucks. He would often come into the club covered in concrete dust and would happily spend the night drinking that way, only going home for a shower if Leslie was on duty and wouldn't serve him until he'd 'made himself decent'. As for the bodies hidden in the Outback, despite his incredibly gruff exterior, you got the sense that this really was a man who wouldn't hurt a fly.

Not so Big Terry, the next of the club's denizens to arrive. Terry also had a biker moustache even more impressive than Stinky's but, unlike Stinky, Big Terry had the menace to back it up. He was actually a pretty generous-spirited bloke but you just knew you wouldn't ever want to cross him. Unfortunately, the first time I ever met Terry I had crossed him. I was driving in the city in a hire car when this bloke opened his car door on Nicholson Street. It clean took the passenger side mirror off the hire car. I pulled up and stormed back to the bloke to give him a piece of my mind. Out loomed a mountain of a man with a mad bastard stare, who, though he was in the wrong, looked exceedingly pissed off – Big Terry. As we exchanged addresses and I was praying he wasn't going to king-hit me, I noticed he lived in Seaford. I mentioned I had grown up there and my old man still lived nearby, hoping that would stop him belting me. He just grunted. When I told Baz about it, he said he knew Terry and recommended that I didn't tell the car hire company I had his address. Not because Baz thought he would thump the living daylights out of me but because, as I was to hear a hell of a lot, 'He's a good bloke. A mate. He doesn't need this sort of thing.'

So I didn't dob Tez in, and when I finally met him at the club a few weeks later, he didn't smile when we were introduced, but came up to me a bit later and said, 'I better buy you a fucken drink then.' After that we were sweet. Or I liked to think so anyway.

Slinking in behind Big Terry was Jimmy. Jimmy had been a lovely kid, Baz told me later, quite bright, and his old man was the gentlest soul in town. But Jimmy had been conscripted to Vietnam and when he came back he was never the same. He spent most of the seventies and eighties lost and on the gear and after a disastrous marriage to another junkie, Jimmy was now a bit of a mess. Surviving on an invalid pension and a regular methadone handout from the chemist, Jimmy was a harmless soul but every so often (every full moon, Baz reckoned) he would go off the rails. No serious damage would be done – at worst he would yell some incoherent garble at one of the mystified drinkers and storm out and howl for an hour or two. These little episodes meant that he was occasionally banned from the club, but the bans were never really serious and he would sneak back in like he did this day, promising to be on his best behaviour.

Turning up soon after Jimmy was Dave the Pom. Sometimes Baz's nicknames could be incredibly inventive, sometimes not. Dave's name was indeed Dave, and he did hail from England. He and Baz were great mates, though you would never have known it as most of their time together was spent arguing. There must be some particular male gene missing from my make-up, because I still don't get how you can have such affection for someone that you are constantly calling a dickhead for disagreeing with you, but Dave was right at the top of Baz's Christmas card list.

Another bloke that Baz had been remiss in giving a decent nickname was Brucey. As his name was Bruce, I thought this particularly disappointing on Baz's part. I had initially avoided Brucey because the first time I met him we had a ten-minute, in-depth conversation but he was so blind that I couldn't understand a word he said. I just kept nodding and going 'yeah' or 'really' at what seemed the appropriate pauses. But then one day Bruce overheard me saying to Baz that a birdwatching boat trip I had been planning to go on out of Port Fairy had been cancelled due to bad weather. I braced myself for the usual gags that inevitably flowed from Baz's mates when they first heard that I was a birdwatcher. But I didn't get this from Bruce. He piped up that his family had been going down to Port Fairy for years, and that he absolutely loved the place. And though he did seem a little bemused that I would go down there just to look for albatross, he put it aside and began asking about whose boat we went out on. It turned out that Bruce was interested in anything to do with Port Fairy — folk music, fishing, history and a whole lot of other stuff besides. He even lent me a book about the history of Port Fairy which I have never actually returned so, Brucey, if you're reading this, g'day; I've still got your book and sorry about portraying you as a drunk, but you were pretty pissed that night, you've got to admit.

Next in line was Ando, one of Baz's neighbours who bizarrely enough was one of Baz's neighbours when they were kids. Well, it probably wasn't really that bizarre, but get a few sherbets into Ando and he could go on about it all night. At times like that you could see in Ando, who was about ten years younger than Baz, the little tacker who followed the older kids in the neighbourhood, yapping like the little dog in the Warner Brothers cartoons, always trying to impress.

Ando would bring along his mate, whom Baz called 'Fifty Bucks' because when drunk he was a chronic big-noter. Once Fifty Bucks found out I had worked in television he would sidle up to me and let rip with a comment along the lines of, 'Know who I went out to dinner with the other night? None other than Coxy. That's right, Coxy from the Roxy.' (For those not in the know, Coxy was a minor celebrity Aussie pub rock musician from the seventies and is now an occasional TV presenter.) Next Fifty Bucks would be telling me that if I ever wanted to, he could give me Ray Burgess' personal home phone number. Ray Burgess! 'I met him once at a New Year's Eve party and I can tell you, Sean, Ray is a top bloke.'

Then of course there was Donny, whom you've already encountered, and a host of other blokes like him who loved a drink, a smoke and a bullshit session with their mates, away from their wives and families. There were a whole bunch of them who drifted in and out of the club that I never really got to know, but this core group was, for the foreseeable future, going to feature prominently in my life whether I liked it or not.

At least that day I had the running of the book on the Grand Final to occupy me, forestalling any of the initial awkwardness of my first full day in their midst. Baz had retired as a rails bookmaker the year before Di died, but he had kept all the bookie paraphernalia: betting books, bookies' board and bag, and thousands of betting tickets. We had set up the lot in a corner, taking bets on the Grand Final. Well, after half an hour, I was. At first Baz was into it, but he had to go see to the heating of the pasties he had made the night before, leaving me to hold the fort. And then he got drinking with the boys and kind of left the whole show to me.

As the match was between hot favourites North Melbourne and Carlton, who had fallen in by a single point in the preliminary to make the play-off, the Dooley boys were offering more than a simple win/loss service. The boys could bet on who kicked the first goal, quarter-by-quarter winners and, of course, the Norm Smith Medal, awarded to the best player afield. By half-time it was clear that North were going to romp it in as they were cutting up Carlton in every department. I consulted with a by now particularly merry Baz (I didn't know whether the chemo had reduced his capacity or he was just drinking harder as a form of release from the tension of being given a death sentence) and told him that while we had lost a bit on the first goal and North winning wouldn't do us any favours, we were in serious danger of getting pantsed on the Norm Smith if Shannon Grant kept playing well. The North rover had picked up a swag of possessions in the first half and had busted the game right open. By half-time he was almost a shoo-in to win the Norm Smith and I asked Baz whether we should shorten his odds and try to lay off with some big fat odds on some of the other contenders. Unconcerned, Baz said to keep betting as we were till three-quarter time.

Given that I was all too familiar with Baz in that festive condition, I should have taken control of the situation; as soon as Shannon Grant had danced around his hapless opponent to kick that goal in the second quarter, I should have put up the shutters, closed the books, put the cue in the rack, the gun back in the holster, the hamster back in the trousers. But as the whole day was set up to 'give the blokes a bit of fun' and I didn't want Dad to think I was being a stingy fun-stopper, I kept taking bets for Shannon Grant long after the engraver had finished carving his name on that medal.

Baz and I lost about five hundred bucks on the whole day's enterprise. We'd agreed to go halves on whatever we made. Or lost. Losing two hundred and fifty bucks was no great loss for Baz, but I had come back from Europe broke, and with no TV work on the horizon was seriously thinking I'd need to go back on the dole. So for me this was a huge whack. As I steadied a staggering Baz home that night he offered to pay my half of the debt. I refused and after some argument he accepted. The last thing he said before falling asleep in his favourite chair was, 'Oh well, Rupe, we'll get 'em next time. Shannon Bloody Grant, hey. Who would have thought? Must have taken our eye off the ball.'

And he was snoring before the end of the sentence. When it came to bookmaking, Baz never took his eye off the ball, but I guess he had a good enough reason to that night. As I watched over my father flaked out at the dining room table, a half empty stubbie sitting in front of him, I mentally resolved that come what may in the months or years ahead, I would try and make things as comfortable and normal for him as I possibly could. It was the least I could do for this man who had made such a huge change in his attitude to care for Di throughout her illness. I vowed not to let my eye off the ball again and to make sure whatever time Baz had left ran as smoothly and sanely as possible.

In the silence of that evening it all seemed so simple, so straightforward. This wasn't what I had expected to be doing with my life in my early thirties, but I could do this. It couldn't be that hard, could it?

15   A LIFETIME QANTAS BAN

The Qantas flight from Brisbane on a Sunday night is one of the last to land in Melbourne, so the terminal at Tullamarine was disconcertingly quiet as I waited at the exit lounge for the arrival of my brother. A couple of dozen friends and relatives of the other passengers sat about in states varying from boredom to agitation, casting glances at the arrivals gate where their loved ones should have disembarked ten minutes earlier. The only ones who seemed in any way excited were a couple of little girls in pyjamas and dressing gowns who chased each other around rows of chairs, occasionally reprimanded by their parents for being too boisterous. But nobody seemed to mind. The distraction was welcome as surely there is nothing more heart-warming than seeing little kids out at night in their dressing gowns. Maybe it is a peculiarly Melbourne thing that arises from the tradition of loading the kids into the back of the car after their night-time bath to go look at the Myer Christmas windows in Bourke Street. Even now, the merest glimpse of a tiny tartan dressing gown, junior Grosby slipper or highly inflammable nightwear has the capacity to make me just a little dewy-eyed with fond memories.

I must have absorbed these good feelings from some residual cultural memory, though, as we never actually did the Myer pilgrimage as a family – Baz thought it was too long a bloody drive through the suburbs at night. Patience was never Baz's strong suit, particularly when it came to children's entertainment. He could barely tolerate being in a queue at the bar, so to be stuck in traffic on Skye Road waiting to get into the Frankston drive-in to see *Herbie Rides Again* was his idea of hell, but he had promised us our first drive-in experience so there we were, Wok and me, in our PJs and dressing gowns, getting more and more excited as the shimmering white screen loomed up from the suburban landscape. For a five year old, this was like being part of some amazing science fiction experience – this could push sinking a Play-Doh submarine in the dog's water dish into second place for greatest moment of my life. But within the shadow of that screen (which surely had something to do with the space program), Baz snapped and did a u-turn for home, cursing under his breath about how we probably wouldn't have gotten in anyway.

The reaction of the two kids in the back seat perhaps encapsulated our two approaches to life. Wok screamed. And screamed, and screamed some more. He briefly stopped screaming when we got home, but that was only so he could fully focus his energies on kicking the door of the car. Once he had been prevented from doing this, his screaming began afresh. I probably protested at first too but, unable to match the untrammelled fury going off alongside me, I just looked out the window and tried to shut out the noise (of both Wok's howling and Baz and Di's yelling at him to shut up) and thought to myself about how it had all seemed too good to be true.

Somebody once told me that anger comes not just from not getting your own way, but from having your expectations thwarted (usually) by the actions of others. I guess this could explain the fundamentally different natures of my brother and me. Wok automatically expected *Herbie Rides Again* by right and there was hell to pay if he didn't get it; me, I never really thought Herbie would truly happen anyway and was genuinely surprised when it did. Maybe this makes me a little too meek and accepting and I don't have enough mongrel in me to affect great changes, but when life is full of Herbie movies, you can waste a hell of a lot of energy fighting to get in to see each and every one of them.

As I sat and watched the two little sisters gambol around the terminal, I became increasingly anxious waiting for the now very late passengers to disembark. There was always one Herbie situation or another in Wok's life that he was railing against, and the thought of having to deal with that as well as with what Baz was facing meant that this was not a family reunion I was looking forward to with much relish.

Neither, it seems, was Baz. I had rung Wok to tell him of Dad's diagnosis. Baz sat in the background, not keen on breaking the news himself. He just didn't know how to say it. He had, however, expressly emphasised that Wok was not to worry and that there was no need for him to come all the way down from North Queensland at this early stage. On hearing Baz's news Wok's immediate response was, 'I'll be on the first plane down.'

I tried to assure him that there really was no need as Dad was currently well and starting treatment and would be focusing on that, and he didn't want Wok to disrupt his life and work by coming down. This is apparently a common worry among cancer patients: they often feel their disease is impinging on the lives of those around them, and when they should be focusing on looking after themselves they instead end up feeling depressed about being an inconvenience to others.

My brother would have none of it: 'Sean, you think I'm gunna sit up here when Dad's going through all this shit?'

I stammered a reply, but Warwick was on a roll, adding almost triumphantly, 'Tell Dad I'm comin' home!'

The trouble was, as Wok was telling me this, Baz was shaking his head, mouthing that he didn't want him to come.

When I hung up the phone Baz looked at me half in hope before asking in a resigned tone, 'He said he's coming, didn't he? I guess I can't stop him. If he wants to come …' and he trailed off for a moment before trying to rouse some enthusiasm. 'Don't get me wrong, it's good that he wants to come …' But then he just trailed off again into a contemplative silence.

I don't mean to give the impression that Baz didn't love his younger son; quite the opposite. In fact in many ways Wok was Baz's favourite. I know this to be true because I heard him say it.

Not directly to me, and not in the cruel way that some parents might in order to punish one child by favouring another or selectively withdrawing love. I overheard him say it to a mate one night when he was drunk and wasn't aware that I was listening.

I was eighteen and Baz, Wok, my Uncle Pat and I had gone on a road trip to visit Nick, a mate of Baz's who owned a sheep station in the backblocks of New South Wales. It was an interesting trip in many ways. Uncle Pat was Baz's oldest brother. There was a twenty-year age gap between them, and though Pat had once held the reputation as the wildest man in Chelsea who, with a bit of ink in him, would much rather a fight than a feed, that had been a very long time ago. Uncle Pat, by then almost seventy, would be straight to bed after a counter meal at the pub each night, leaving Baz desperately short of a drinking partner. (Wok was still too young, and though I had turned eighteen, it would be at least another few years before Baz and I would feel comfortable having a beer together.)

Having failed as a suitable drinking companion, Uncle Pat was turning out not to be the ideal driving partner either, as he was wont to say the same things over and over again. Pat's family, who lived in the street behind ours in Seaford, had owned a dog called Missy who was not particularly bright by all accounts. Pat likened her to a sheep in that she would follow anything, be it another dog or a human – any human. Every time Pat saw a flock of sheep he felt compelled to point and yell excitedly, 'Look at the little Missies!' As we were driving across the sheep-rich Hay Plains in a good season, the sheep to human ratio was probably only second to New Zealand, and so Uncle Pat was uttering his little Missy comments with intolerable regularity.

It was no surprise then that, when we arrived at the mate's sheep station, Baz launched himself into the drinking session that first night with more than usual gusto. Uncle Pat was out for the count not long after dinner and Baz's blathering had sent both Wok and me to our swags on the lounge room floor. Baz and his cocky mate (cocky in the sense of being a farmer, not in the sense of Nick having an arrogant manner) continued drinking in the kitchen. Being mid summer, all the doors were flung open to let any breeze through the house. Wok was soon asleep, but I was having trouble due, no doubt, to the noise of Baz and Nick banging on into the small hours.

At one point Nick was commenting on Wok and me, to which Baz drunkenly replied, 'Yeah, they're great kids. Sean, well, he's never given us a moment's trouble, and he's bloody smart – he's going to be a lawyer – but I have to admit that even though Wok is a little shit sometimes, I've got a soft spot for him. I sort of know where he's coming from.' Then he uttered those words that probably every child suspects but never wants to actually hear: 'Yep, if I was pressed I'd have to say that Wokka was my favourite.'

There it was, stated in bold. Out in the universe. My dad liked my brother better than me. I suspect in most memoirs such a moment would be of major import and as a reader you'd be in for a heart-wrenching, angst-ridden dragging over the emotional coals. Old Testament themes of sibling rivalry and prodigal sons might be invoked, along with Freud, Sophocles or Jane Fonda. If the author was famous enough they would soon be sitting on Oprah's couch, fighting back the tears as she laid a reassuring and empathetic hand upon their knee. And I must admit as I lay there in the dark, I felt a bit put out for about a second, but then I thought to myself, 'Yeah, that sounds about right,' shrugged and rolled over to go to sleep.

I relate this story not to garner sympathy points for myself or to say it had any profound resonating impact on me, for at the age of eighteen I had already been working for Baz for almost three years: three years in which I realised that he would never really understand me and that we really were quite different. So Baz's revelation that night came as no real surprise. I mention it primarily because otherwise it might seem like Baz didn't care for Warwick, which couldn't be further from the truth.

I had only seen Wok once since the sad weeks after Di's funeral and that was when I had been on holiday in North Queensland. Wok had headed back there and was working on a banana plantation and living with a bunch of blokes in a share house, where they were all in their own way hiding from the world. I thought it would have been rude of me not to pay my brother a visit while I was up there. Wok had been very keen, enthusing over the phone, 'Come around for a barbie on Saturday. It'll be unreal – the Dooley boys back together again!' I thought this was odd as we had never really hung out together since our early teens, but he was my brother, I reminded myself, so I should make the most of it.

I had been staying north of Cairns at a little birdwatching paradise called Julatten. Wok lived in Tully, a town that proudly proclaimed to the world that it was the wettest place in Australia. Tully was about four hours' drive south, but what with all my birdwatching stops in what are some of the richest habitats in Australia, it was well after dark when I arrived. It was the night of the 1998 Queensland state election, the one in which Pauline Hanson's right wing One Nation Party was making huge inroads into the political scene, particularly in that part of the world. Her strident, simplistic views had appealed to the rednecked, racist elements in the local communities and nearly every roadside tree I drove past that miserable, rain-soaked night seemed to be adorned with an electoral poster of Pauline draped in the Australian flag.

By the time I arrived at Wok's place, the radio coverage was declaring One Nation had won a swag of seats and I was tired, dejected and about four hours late. And what greeted me did little to lift my spirits, despite the massive welcoming smile and bear hug from Wok. After we broke our embrace, I looked at Wok's beaming face and my heart sank, because behind the broad smile was the soapy-eyed stare of someone who'd been sucking back beers for eight hours straight.

'Come on, man, I been telling the boys all about my big brother!', and with that he led me down to where the action was.

Wok's house was a classic old Queenslander that stood on stilts, and the party was set up downstairs, beneath the main body of the house where all were huddled, staring out into the barbecue fire pit as it sputtered and fizzed in the rain. (It may have been the dry season, but this was Tully after all.) Plates of uncooked chops and snags lay gathering puddles alongside the carcasses of several cardboard beer boxes.

It was a motley collection indeed. Wok's mates all wore flannelette shirts and long, hillbilly beards. They looked exactly like the sort of pig-shootin', ute-drivin', hard-drinkin' blokes that would chair Pauline Hanson around triumphantly at her electoral rally appearances. Not that these guys were One Nation voters – you'd have to register in order to vote and that might mean the child support people or the by-laws officers catching up with you. And they all thought Pauline Hanson was an idiot anyway, though as one bloke with two front teeth missing said, she did have some good ideas when it came to 'the boongs and the chinks'.

Even Wok looked embarrassed when his mate said this. He wasn't the only one looking uncomfortable. Sitting nervously in one corner of the party was a group of young backpackers who had been press-ganged into joining the festivities. Wok's house was opposite the start of the walking track to the national park. It was popular with visiting tourists, and that afternoon a bunch of English girls and a couple of Irish guys who were trying to crack onto them had emerged from the track and were headed down to the local backpackers'. At that precise moment, one of Wok's hillbilly mates emerged from the house across the road with an axe he had borrowed from them in order to chop wood for the barbie. Already tanked, he must have made an imposing if not downright frightening figure as he 'invited' them all to the barbie. With images of Ivan Milat flashing across their minds they decided it was not in their best interests to decline and so sat huddled together looking as nervous as goats at a devil worshippers' picnic as they fended off the clumsy pick-up attempts of Wok's mates.

It was like a scene from a slasher film. Hyper-tanned to the colour that only the Brits seem able to achieve – an orange glow that sits somewhere in the colour spectrum between a healthy tan and the shocked red of a lobster that has been plunged unexpectedly into boiling water – the English girls had stumbled into a cauldron of hairy, smelly backwoodsmen who were only a pluck of a banjo away from turning into an atavistic hunting party. Sitting defensively between them were the two pasty-skinned Irish boys, who had probably been lining these girls up for a shag for days and their capture by these Aussie rednecks was seriously denting their chances. They were not happy and you could see them shifting uneasily, caught between the chivalrous urge to protect the girls' honour and the knowledge that if they were to do so, they were outnumbered.

Needless to say, the night was not a success. The rain continued to tumble down and at one point one of the Yowies that Wok lived with, frustrated at his lack of success with the girls, pulled a burning log out of the fire and took a swipe at the Irish blokes, thereby bringing the party to a premature conclusion. Not long after, Wok was trying to take a swipe at me after I had the temerity to point out that it had been him, and not the backpackers, who had broken the tape deck on his stereo. Earlier in the evening Wok had kicked it while emphasising some point or other. When he noticed it was broken, he seemed to have forgotten all about his previous actions and wanted to chase after the backpackers who were clearly responsible for this atrocity of Herbie-like proportions. Wok took me pointing out that he had done it himself as an open invitation to war and turned on me screaming something along the lines of, 'So you're against me too!' but with several expletives beefing up the accusation.

After having bottled up my exasperation at Wok's behaviour for the entire evening, I finally lost it and started screaming back just as vehemently. It takes a fair bit for me to crack and once I had I knew that unless I left immediately we would be punching on. That was something I didn't want. Not because Wok could most probably, as he promised, 'beat the living shit' out of me (although in his drunken state I reckoned I might just be able to hold my own) but because if I did take him on I thought I could lose the last tenuous link between us. Very few people were ever able to get through to Wok or affect some semblance of calm when he was in a state of enraged fury. Baz was usually too impatient, and with Di gone I was about the only one. To fight him then would be to lose that connection and as much as I wanted to clock him, something within me thought it would be better to walk away.

So I walked away and spent the night in a motel by the highway with cane toads in the toilet and sugar trucks rattling the windows as they took their loads to the refinery. The next morning I wasn't sure whether I should go back, but thought I'd better not leave things as they were. Wok had calmed down and was contrite. He suggested we head out to the river for a swim. We didn't talk much on the drive to the waterhole. When we got there we stood by the banks of the rainforest stream and continued our silence.

After a while, Wok turned to me and said, 'I rang Dad this morning.'

'Oh yeah,' I replied, not quite sure where this was going.

'Yeah,' he continued. 'I told him what happened. I said to him, "I know I'm a dickhead sometimes, but I don't deserve to be talked to like that, not even from Sean."'

He had been looking away but half turned my way to gauge my reaction. I was more conciliatory than the previous night but was not going to just let it go without comment – that seemed to often be the case in our family: don't make Wok face up to too many home truths lest he fly off the handle again and we lose him.

I began: 'I'm sorry with the way I said it, but you were acting like a dickhead.'

Before I could go on, Wok burst into tears, howling, 'Sean, I miss Mum so much.' And he wrapped his arms around me and began sobbing like I had never seen him cry before, even the day of Di's funeral, when at the end, after all the mourners had gone home and the last stubbie had been drunk, Baz, Wok and I had embraced and cried the last tears that hadn't yet been wrung out of us that day.

I hadn't been expecting this and just stood there holding

Wok until his heaving stopped and eventually he wiped his eyes with those hands covered in deep scratches from the banana harvesting. We decided the crystal waters that ran out of the rainforest mountain looked too cold to swim in, and drove home as though everything was back to normal.

And so a year later I sat there in the arrivals lounge hoping that everything was OK. *Please let it be OK.* The plane had been docked for over twenty minutes before the doors finally swung open and disgorged the passengers. The first woman out was met by the man who had been sitting next to me. He rose concerned at her ashen face and asked what was wrong.

She replied, barely concealing her distress, 'It was the worst flight ever. It was just awful, I've never seen anything like it.'

My heart sank as he led her away as one would a trauma victim. All the other passengers wore similar expressions and I could hear snatches of their conversation:

'... an absolute disgrace ...'

'... just appalling ...'

'... I was so frightened ...'

As each passenger passed by a sick feeling in the pit of my stomach rose until it was oozing out of my ears. Surely not? But when all the passengers had disembarked and there was no sign of Wok, I knew I wouldn't like the news. Perhaps he had missed his connection in Brisbane. If only ...

After another fifteen minutes, Wok was led off the plane, escorted by a purser and two security guards. He spied me and slurred sheepishly, 'Looks like I got into a bit of trouble, Sean.'

The purser approached me and asked if I was here to meet 'the passenger'. I said I was and as Wok was sat in a corner of the lounge, flanked by the security guards, the purser relayed what had happened. He said that Wok had been disruptive, abusive and dangerous to the point where staff had felt threatened and passengers were intimidated. He went on to say that they were considering laying charges and that at the very least Wok would have a lifetime ban placed on him by Qantas, meaning he could never fly with them again.

I explained that he had just found out his father had cancer and that we had recently lost our mum, which seemed to soften the purser's attitude slightly. Then Wok stood up and suddenly started yelling, 'Don't let him tell you any shit, Sean. That guy's a fucking idiot poofter.'

I turned on Wok and snapped, 'You shut the fuck up now, and don't say another fucking word!'

Amazingly, Wok sat down. I turned to the purser and, apologising for my language, tried as best as I could to calm things.

'Just get him out of here quietly and we won't charge him with anything, all right?'

Given this lifeline I pulled Wok up and bustled him out of the terminal. As we walked he could see I was fuming and tried to explain how things had gotten to this state. The flight from Cairns left in the afternoon. Wok's mates had driven him up from Tully and said they would shout him a couple of bourbons before the flight. Only trouble was, they had arrived at the airport about four hours early. Wok said that in sight of the check-in counter they knocked back around a dozen bourbons, so he wasn't upset when the staff on the flight from Cairns to Brisbane wouldn't serve him a drink. He thought it was fair enough because they had seen him drinking and knew that he had drunk a few too many.

But then while waiting for the transfer at Brisbane, Wok downed a few more drinks. His reasoning was that as the airport staff at Brisbane could only have seen him drink those couple, what right would the new flight crew have to deny him a drink on the second plane? 'Fair dinkum, Sean, how could that poofter know I was pissed?' Wok demanded to know of the purser I had spoken to. 'It was just discrimination pure and simple. You tell me Sean, how could they possibly know?'

I looked at my brother – hair as wild as his eyes, eyes that had that same red-rimmed soapy aspect they'd had the night I visited him at his place in Tully. He was swaying like he was on a yacht and he stank of booze. How could they have known indeed?

I had almost got him out to the car park when he stopped violently.

'Ah, shit – me dog!'

Wok had forgotten that he had brought his dog, Cody, with him. We then spent the next hour trawling through a by now deserted airport trying to find his dog. By the time we'd tracked down poor Cody in the bowels of the airport, and I'd finally bundled both her and Wok into the car, it was well after midnight. Wok immediately crashed out and slept for the whole drive to Patterson Lakes.

Welcome home, little brother.

16   DOG SPOTTING FOR BEGINNERS

You are either a dog person or a cat person, so the saying goes. Much to Baz's chagrin, Di was a cat person. On the surface he barely seemed to tolerate any of Di's cats, but there were times when the public façade would slip and Baz would be discovered actually talking to the cats as opposed to yelling or throwing things at them. And somewhere in the family album is a surreptitious snap of Baz with our cat Ginny cradled on his lap. Moments of weakness aside, Baz was definitely a dog person. He preferred a real man's type of dog. Not as extreme as a Rottweiler or Rhodesian ridgeback, but from the time Baz was a kid and invented an imaginary dog called 'Tiger' that he would call out to whenever he was walking in the dark to frighten off any would-be attackers, Baz had always liked a dog with a bit of grunt to it. (Baz also had imaginary bantams called Fanny and Gus as a kid, but that's another story.)

It was kind of ironic then that we never really had big, blokey dogs in our family. According to the game where you take the name of your first pet and first street you lived in as your porn star name, I would appear under the moniker 'Wiggles Larool' as the first family dog I knew was a lovely, lumbering old mongrel that had been christened Wiggles because she was constantly wagging her tail. Hardly in Baz's 'Tiger' category. Wiggles died when I was about ten and her replacement was a bit more Baz's style, a kelpie-border collie cross named April. April was a great dog for two boys to have growing up because there were two strains of working dog in her: there was no way she would tire out before we did. Baz soon came to rue teaching April to fetch a tennis ball as she spent the rest of her life driving us mad dropping a ball at our feet and then insisting that we throw it. And if a ball wasn't to hand she would drop a stick, a bone, a rock, even the cap off one of Baz's stubbies.

But as cool and rugged as April was, her fatal flaw was that she was absolutely terrified of thunder. Not long after Baz and Di had moved from Seaford to Patterson Lakes, a severe summer thunderstorm sent April over the six foot fence at the new house and into the night in a frenzied panic. Baz found her body a few days later by the side of the freeway. April had just kept running and running until an anonymous vehicle hit her some two kilometres from home. That was it for dogs, Baz decreed; the yard at Patterson Lakes was too small for a 'real' dog, so no more dogs.

Then along came Holly. As far as dogs go in Baz's universe, Holly was a cat. A silky Maltese terrier cross, Holly was small, as cute as a muppet, and full of personality. But she was yappy and a mollycoddled, indoors dog – the antithesis of what Baz thought a dog should be. Baz had been scornful when Di first bought her. She treated Holly with such indulgence that it made him fume. Coming home from the races armed with a belly full of beer and a plastic bag of Chinese takeaway, Baz would find Di cooking up a chicken fillet to serve to Holly. 'That dog eats bloody better than I do!' he would grizzle.

In a way, Holly was symbolic of how far they had drifted apart. Di lavished far more affection and attention on Holly than she did on Baz and though slightly contemptuous of the dog, Baz wasn't too put out as it meant his absences from the house weren't remarked upon nearly as much. In fact Di had bought Holly to keep her company while Baz and Tony Wilson headed off on their overseas jaunt.

But Baz's attitude to Holly had shifted markedly over the years. He had seen what a comfort she was to Di throughout her illness and once Di had gone, wouldn't countenance the many offers to adopt her. Though he was still as gruff as ever with Holly in public ('How about we take you down the vet for the big needle?' was one of the more common things he said to her as she looked up at him all cutesy) he had clearly become extremely attached to 'the mutt'. I guess she was one of his most tangible (and living) links with Di.

In her last weeks, when Di was confined to a hospital room, Baz had no alternative but to take care of Holly. Whenever I came home to visit, he would quickly press-gang me into feeding or walking her, but I reckon it was all for show. Always an outrageous flirt, Holly would make a fuss over me, rubbing her paw coquettishly over her face in order to entice a tummy rub, but by the end of the night she would have settled at Baz's feet or, when his guard was down, on his lap. When it became clear that Di was never going to return home, Baz suggested we try and smuggle Holly into the hospital so that Di could have one last hold. We couldn't work out the logistics of successfully sneaking Holly past the medical staff, so had to settle for Wok holding her up to the window so that Di could have one last look.

I have never been good at goodbyes (many's the dud party at which I have ended up being the last guest because I wasn't able to find a suitable, subtle exit strategy) so it absolutely killed me knowing that Di would never again see this companion who had been with her through the entire ordeal, offering unconditional love when the rest of the universe may have seemed indifferent. This little dog had ceaselessly been by Mum's side, sleeping at the foot of her bed in even the darkest chemo days. Di knew deep down that she would never see Holly again yet she didn't seem too upset, just smiled with serenity at her through the window as she struggled in Wok's arms. I couldn't bear it. I had to look away and as I did I noticed Baz, too, was looking up at the ceiling, blinking back the tears. Baz never growled again when Holly jumped up on his lap of an evening.

So you can imagine that Baz was understandably pretty keen to hang on to Holly. And when Wok walked into the kitchen the morning after his eventful arrival as if nothing had happened at the airport, expecting to be treated as some kind of returning hero, it wasn't surprising that Baz's smile turned ashen when, bounding in behind him, was Cody. Holly was one of those little dogs that are full of bravado when it comes to bigger dogs, especially when they are at a safe distance. Holly would strain on the leash, snarling and growling, but if let off her leash the pretence would end and she would be cowering behind your legs. Cody, a kelpie cross who looked for all the world like a wild dingo, had spent the previous couple of years rough-housing it with the pig dogs owned by Wok's mates up north. Holly started yapping at Cody and Cody, expecting a bit of fun, chased after her playfully, sending Holly retreating behind the couch from where she couldn't be coaxed. To be honest, Cody lost interest pretty quickly but within a day, Holly had become a quivering mess.

'Why'd you bring Cody for?' groaned Baz at the club later.

'She's me dog, Dad, I'm not going to abandon her,' Wok shot back defiantly.

'Couldn't one of your mates have looked after her?' Baz continued, though he already sounded defeated.

'Couldn't trust those idiots to feed her. You should see the way they treat their own dogs, Dad!'

So it was settled: Cody was to stay and hopefully Holly would chill out. We arrived home from the club to find that Cody had torn up half the garden and Holly, though locked inside, had turned into a freaked-out little fluff ball of neuroses. Even after a week she still hadn't settled down. Cody, who with Wok out visiting his mates all the time wasn't getting the regular walks and exercise she was used to, had energy to burn and when she wasn't digging up the fernery, took delight in chasing Holly around the house every chance she got. Baz couldn't take it any longer and on one of the mornings when Wok had actually slept the night at home and was having breakfast, Baz confronted him with the situation.

Baz, while generally a straightshooter, had never actually been very confrontational with Wok. That sort of parenting was often left up to Di, and since her passing, Baz had been at something of a loss in terms of knowing how to deal with my headstrong brother, but by now the situation had become intolerable. Rather than bringing comfort to Baz as was Wok's stated intention, the house was now descending into chaos. Baz was resolute. He was going to tell Wok it would be best for all concerned if he returned to Tully. Baz would let him know when the time was right for Wok to return. And if he wanted to stay, then Cody would have to go, and he would have to get a job, or at least do something more than come home at four in the morning after a night out at some mate's place. And so, Baz took Wok aside to have their talk.

The next thing I knew was that Wok was staying on indefinitely and Baz was going to send Holly to an artist friend of Di's who lived in the country. She had a similar yappy terrier and had looked after Holly occasionally when Di had been in hospital. Baz reasoned that this was the best solution but I knew that Baz was upset with the situation. Losing Holly, even temporarily, was crushing for him, particularly because Baz thought that Mum's artist friend was a flaky nut job. Baz and bohemia didn't mix well, and he had always been wary of Di's free-spirited friend. For a brief while she had gone out with one of Baz's drinking mates, during which time her penchant for always sitting on his lap in any social situation had led Baz to call her 'the Pole Sitter'. Di never did work out why he called her that. Baz knew that she treated Holly well, but with her New Age attitudes and her baby talk and coddling of the dogs, Baz claimed she spoiled Holly rotten. ('I feel like I've toughened Holly up a bit, Rupe.' He hadn't in the slightest – Holly had softened him – but he liked to think so.)

To compound matters, a week after giving Holly over, Di's friend came to town to stay a few nights at her daughter's house in Seaford. They went out for dinner together, leaving the dogs locked up in the backyard. Perhaps Holly could sense that she was close to home, or perhaps something spooked her – like April, she was afraid of thunder. Although, unlike her, Holly was also afraid of any loud noise, other dogs, cats, birds … though not people – except for Ace. Ace was as good-natured as you could get and generally small children and animals flocked to him, but one time when Holly was a puppy, Ace had jokingly held a wine bottle over Di's head as if he was going to smash it on her. Everybody laughed – except for Holly, who then and there committed herself to a lifelong vendetta against Ace, who was quite distressed at his pariah status.

Perhaps Holly thought Ace was in the vicinity, for in the brief hours she was left alone, she managed to squeeze under the gate and run away. The Pole Sitter was beside herself when she broke the news to us. Baz and I drove around the streets looking for her until I realised that the chemo really was starting to kick in and I had to get Baz home to rest. I spent days walking the streets of Seaford, hoping she would turn up, but no luck: Holly was gone. Baz was pessimistic. She had a tag, and an identifying tattoo so if anyone found her they would have been in touch.

I'd never seen Baz so down. The cancer treatment was beginning to have an effect, and for a day or two after his chemo Baz would be hard pressed to have the energy to make it out of bed. Losing Holly just compounded his misery. Even when he had recovered from the bout of chemo he didn't seem to approach things – like going down to the club for a few beers – with the same zest he had previously.

But then one day about two weeks later, when I went to pick him up from the club, a spark had returned. He was drinking with Donny, who still firmly believed that Baz had got his lung cancer from car exhaust fumes, mobile phones, passive consumption of lentils – anything but the cigarettes that had caused it. Donny was grinning from ear to ear, and Baz had a glint in his eyes I hadn't seen for weeks.

Barely containing himself, Donny burst out with pride, 'I found your dog. I found Holly!'

My heart rose and I looked around for her. 'Where is she?'

'I couldn't catch her, but I saw her.'

The heart that had been in my mouth with joy now slid down to somewhere below the pit of my stomach as I listened to Donny's tale. He had been down at the Patterson Lakes shopping centre when he noticed a scruffy looking dog going through a rubbish bin. He adamantly claimed that though the dog was filthy, he was absolutely sure it was Holly – same size, same colour. Donny had called out to it, and the dog had stopped and looked but as he approached it ran away. He was absolutely convinced it was Holly.

It sounded suss to me, but maybe Holly had made her way back from Seaford. Why it had taken her two weeks to walk five kilometres, and why she would have headed for the shopping centre and not home, was beyond me but I could see the hope in Baz's eyes so I told him to finish up his pot and we would go look. Interestingly, Donny didn't offer to come along; he'd done his bit, and sat there looking incredibly self-satisfied.

We spent an hour looking all around the shopping centre, car park, and nearby surrounds. Nothing. I took Baz back to the club and went searching again by myself, doing the same circuit and checking along the nearby canals for any sign of Holly. After a couple of hours I was about to give up when a movement caught my eye in the refuse bins at the side of the shops. It was a dog rummaging through the waste. I approached hopefully, calling Holly's name.

The dog looked up. She was, as Donny had said, quite scruffy and in need of a good bath. But this dog was more of a short-haired schnauzer than a fluffy terrier. And it was predominantly white with rufous markings, as opposed to Holly who was greyish overall. Aside from being a dog, this thing looked about as much like Holly as Donny did. I went back to the club, where Donny was adamant that he had seen Holly despite my news.

'I'm telling ya, Baz, it was Holly for sure.'

'Did it have short hair and was it white with a reddish patch on its back?' I interrogated Donny like a prosecutor from a TV law show leading a dopey criminal into a trap of their own making.

'Yeah, that's it! That's what I saw!' Donny sputtered triumphantly. 'See, I told ya, Baz!'

Baz shook his head and as he took another swig of his beer, muttered, 'You idiot, Donny. I've got more red hair on my arse than Holly has on her entire body.'

For once Donny was stumped for words. After a moment, he raised his glass to his lips and mumbled, 'Well it looked like Holly to me.'

Wok announced a couple of days later that he was heading back to Tully. Clearly his jaunt south had not been the triumphant homecoming he'd expected it to be. Baz was, as he had tried to explain, not about to cark it any time in the near future. As the chemo started to take effect, Baz was hardly in the mood for playing pool or going fishing, but rather, was spending much of his time lying down. I was probably even less fun to be around given how difficult I found it to engage with Wok – at that stage nearly everything I would have said to him would have been critical. Not wanting to start a fight, I found myself holding my tongue most of the time. Wok, who had never been much of a verbal communicator anyway, didn't really seem to notice at all, but it certainly wasn't much fun to be hanging around, hence his decision to head home, courtesy of another airfare paid for by Baz. Wok flew Qantas – I had got a follow-up call from the airline a couple of days later but seemed to have smoothed things over, at least to the extent that they didn't veto his flight when we booked it for him, though they did refuse to serve him alcohol. I made sure I booked him on a morning flight, before the pub opened, and timed my driving so that we could only have one beer at the airport before the boarding call.

As he left, Wok gave me such a big hug that I couldn't help but feel guilty that I had been so resentful of him and his attitude. Sure he had been a royal pain and had blithely turned Baz's world upside down without the slightest awareness of the strife he was causing but, after all, I reminded myself, he had as much right to be with Baz at that time as I did, so I would just have to suck any negative feelings I had in, and be damned sure I didn't become a problem for Baz myself.

I seemed to be feeling guilty about a lot of things. Perhaps it was transference of my impotence at not being able to do anything to fight Baz's cancer, but I really questioned whether I was deluding myself that I was doing any good looking after him. Perhaps after even just a couple weeks of taking on the role of Baz's carer I was already becoming too protective. Just because he was crook didn't mean he was mentally incapacitated and should be shielded from every potentially stressful situation. Does focusing on recovery necessarily mean a withdrawal from the life you are fighting to rejoin? Maybe I was already succumbing to martyr's syndrome: because I was the one making the sacrifice (although at this early stage this had only involved driving Baz to a couple of appointments, keeping an eye on him when he was bedridden after the chemo, picking him up from the club and feigning more interest than usual in his drunken stories), I believed only I could possibly know what (and who) was good for the one I was looking after. Maybe I had just overreacted to Wok's presence because I felt he was, in his own cack-handed way, muscling in on my turf as dutiful son. Maybe I was the problem.

When I got home from dropping Wok off at the airport Baz was sitting in his chair looking out contemplatively over the water. I asked him if he wanted a beer. He was just coming out of another round of chemo and hadn't had one for a couple of days – and when Baz turned down a beer, you knew he really was crook. He said that perhaps he was getting the taste back for it, so we cracked a stubbie each and sat in silence watching a pair of pelicans glide across the still waters of the lake. The yard had a track worn through it where Cody had torn up and down. The ferns looked traumatised. Holly's basket sat by the window unoccupied. The house had never felt this lonely, nor had Di's absence ever been so strong.

17   THE WORST BOOKIE IN THE WORLD

For a while, things seemed to be looking up for Baz on the health front. After cyclone Wok had left town, home life began to settle down to a fairly regular routine of chemo treatments, a few days of recuperation time, and then, once strength was regained, Baz's daily visits to the club would be resumed almost as if nothing had happened. Another visit to Dr Nick brought some good news: further x-rays revealed that the tumours in the lungs had reduced both in number and size. Not one to make wild claims, Dr Nick was cautiously optimistic that Baz was responding well to the treatment.

As we left Dr Nick's office, Baz commented, 'He's not really my sort of bloke, but I like Dr Nick – he's a straightshooter.'

'You just like him because he didn't tell you to keep off the piss this time,' I corrected.

'That might have something to do with it,' Baz chuckled, and then as an afterthought that was probably more of a forethought: 'What do you reckon we get down the club to celebrate?'

Not my sort of bloke. From Baz, this was usually a condemnation. Not being Baz's kind of bloke was, to his way of thinking, not being what a bloke should be – a decent, down to earth kind of guy with no pretensions; a bloke who looked out for his mates; someone you could rely on. But even if you were all of these things but weren't someone who loved a laugh, a beer and a punt, then I doubt you would have qualified as one of Baz's sort of blokes. You would then fall into the second category of those who weren't Baz's type of blokes: the ones, like Dr Nick, about whom Baz was able to add a caveat that even though he wasn't his sort of bloke, he liked him nonetheless. Other addendums that Baz used to deem a man's worthiness included 'but I like the cut of his jib' and 'but there's no bullshit about him'.

It made me wonder, was I Baz's sort of bloke? If I wasn't his son, would I have qualified in this most rarefied of categories? Probably not. I was hardly the sort of bloke that would walk into a pub and be able to talk unselfconsciously with a bloke like Baz. After having already spent several weeks with Baz on a daily basis, I was surrounded by Baz's types of blokes and seemed to be gaining some sort of acceptance, which in some ways was giving me cause for concern. After all, since an early age I had been moving away from Baz's blokey world. I found it too narrow, too stifling, too lacking in imagination. Did being accepted here mean I was compromising who I really was? It wasn't going to be the boys who would make the cultural shift here: if I wanted to connect with them on their turf, it would be up to me to come to them. I could get a conversation going when I talked about the best West Indian pace bowlers, or what was wrong with the Collingwood forward line, and I could even improvise in a discussion of Ford versus Holden without looking like too much of a fraud, but if I were to bring up the work of Helen Garner or the migratory patterns of the Double-banded Plover, I would be met with a blank if not downright suspicious stare.

The odd thing, though, was that the more time I spent among these blokes, the more opportunity I had to find hidden depths that were not immediately apparent. As individuals, many of these blokes were surprisingly interesting and complex people. I was beginning to genuinely like some of them. Damn it. It made it harder and harder to just drop Baz off and get the hell out of there as quickly as possible, which was always my plan. Baz would take mortal offence if I declined the offer to go in for 'just one quiet one', particularly if I couldn't concoct some specific excuse. When he began to add, 'The boys would like to see you,' and I started to feel like I wouldn't mind seeing some of the boys, I knew I was in trouble. I hadn't planned on the majority of my social life in my early thirties being centred around boozing on with a bunch of middle-aged grog monsters; I had steeled myself to endure it, but certainly hadn't expected to find myself enjoying it.

Sometimes, God help me, I was even looking forward to going down the club. As Baz and I entered that day, I have to admit that seeing Stinky there greeting us with his usual bullock's roar of a welcome – 'Baaaazz!' – did put a smile on my face. Stink was as rough as guts but of all Dad's mates at the club I would have to say he was becoming my favourite. As soon as he saw me behind Baz he bellowed, 'Seany! Seen any birdies lately?' Stinky probably gave me more grief about being a birdwatcher than any of Baz's other mates, but despite his obvious efforts at embarrassing me, I didn't take offence and never found it malicious.

It seemed to me that most of the relationships in that place were based on men putting up a front as they tried to chip away at everyone else's weaknesses. But with Stinky, there also seemed to be a genuine interest in what the other person was doing and his amusement at other's foibles was so incredibly infectious that he would draw laughter even out of his current target. And when it came to birdwatching, I knew Stinky's secret – he was actually something of a closet bird lover himself. He had tamed an injured Rainbow Lorikeet and would tell me with great pride of its latest escapades. Stinky was quite fascinated with my ornithological pursuits and would drill me with questions about birds and endlessly regale me with tales of the birds he had seen when he was working in the mining camps of the Northern Territory.

I had indeed been out birding since the last time I'd seen him and had a story that I had been saving up for him. The previous week I had been doing my regular bird survey of the local wetland, Seaford Swamp, when I had startled a Copperhead hidden in the grass. Not being a huge fan of snakes, especially venomous ones, I jumped backwards in alarm. The snake got just as big a shock and launched itself to escape, but in the same direction I had jumped. So as I came down to earth I had to do the splits in order to avoid landing on it, hoping like hell it would keep going and not strike up at my exposed parts. Stinky roared with laughter and began repeating the story to whoever would listen, announcing, 'Hey, fellas, did you know we've got our very own Crocodile Hunter in our midst?' It made his night, and gave me just that little bit more of an in with these men who I didn't really have much in common with. Stinky taking delight in one of the very things that set me apart from the others (most would rather shoot a bird than watch it) actually further entrenched their acceptance of me without me having to compromise my identity too much. How could I not love the bloke?

Stinky was actually closer to my age than he was to Baz's. He'd originally been best mates with my cousin Snail (and no, I have no idea why they called him that). Though my Aunty Joyce and Uncle Bernie were two of the most respectable people you could meet (Uncle Bernie getting drunk at a church function on a hot summer's day and turning the garden hose on the nuns notwithstanding), for some reason the genetics had blown a fuse in Snail and he was a bit of a mad bastard when he was a teenager. He seemed to have a knack for getting into trouble and the story goes that when he took on a train carriage worth of hoods on the platform at Mordialloc station, as well as a couple of the local coppers who came to break up the fight, it was suggested that it might be advantageous for all concerned if he spent a bit of time away from Chelsea. Faced with the prospect of incarceration or the open road, Snail chose the latter and took a job in one of the remotest mining camps in the country, where Stinky decided to join him.

One shudders to think what those two young blokes got up to in those Outback camps, but of the stories that are fit to print, my favourite was of Stinky's grog run. By this stage he was working on a road crew somewhere in the deserts of the Northern Territory. They had run out of their ration of beer and with the nearest pub a couple of hundred kilometres away, it looked like being a very dry week. Stinky took matters into his own hands and commandeered one of the graders, in which he set off to get them some more grog. The grader only did about fifteen clicks an hour so it was a long journey to the pub, and an even longer one back. When Stinky hadn't returned by sundown the boys started to get worried and sent out a search party. They found Stinky the next morning, passed out behind the wheel of the grader which had driven off the track and into the scrub before coming to a stop. The drive back had been hot so naturally he cracked open a couple of 'travellers' to quench his thirst. But it was a very hot day and geez those beers went down well … By the time he passed out, he had not only drunk his own slab of beer but most of the other blokes' too.

It's no surprise, then, that years down the track Baz and Stinky had hit it off, so much so that in his last year as a bookie, Baz took Stinky on as a clerk. Baz had actually retired from the rails in the last year of Di's life, but kept his bookie's license active so that he could still work the really big meetings such as the Melbourne Cup. Whispering Jack had been quickly snapped up by another bookie, his dulcet tones clearly irresistible, so Baz drafted Stinky into the baggie's role despite the fact that he had absolutely no experience. Stinky was every bit as loud as Whispering Jack but he was most certainly not what you would call a natural at the caper. For starters he seemed to be effectively illiterate. The major part of his job was to take people's money and yell out to the penciller the name of the horse they were betting on. Not a problem when the punter said, 'Twenty dollars on Phar Lap,' not so great when they said, 'Twenty dollars on number four.' Then Stinky was in real strife. I suspect he was innumerate too because it seemed to take him an age to even find number four.

Luckily we weren't overly busy as the stand we had been given was in the furthest corner of the betting ring away from the main action, but even there things got frantic at times, even more so with a bagman who had to stop and squint at the board while phonetically puzzling out the names of the horses. Normally this would have driven Baz, who on the track was all bustle, to sheer exasperation, but for the most part Baz wasn't even on the stand.

It had only been six months since he had retired from full time bookmaking but already Baz had lost his appetite for the battle with the punters. Di was fading fast at this point, and though he didn't outwardly show it, the cold, unavoidable fact that he would soon lose her was making everything else in his life pall. As soon as we arrived at the track and set everything up, Baz turned to me and said, 'You scrub up better than I do, Seany, you get up on the stand. We'll only get a bunch of young sheilas betting with us here, so they may as well have a good looking young bloke up there rather than an old fart like me.' And with that Baz spent most of his last days as a bookmaker drinking with mates at the bar and watching things from afar, an almost disinterested observer in what had been his previous life.

It wasn't the first time I'd taken over for Baz. The year before he'd taken Di on a holiday and I took out a temporary bookie's licence to run the stand for him. It was certainly an eye-opener and gave me an insight into his world. On the stand, facing a sea of punters all trying to find an advantage, you suddenly feel very exposed and vulnerable. The only thing for it is to put on a façade of bravado and not let the seething throng know that inwardly you are absolutely pooping yourself. So I would start yelling out the odds in that nasal intonation with a volume that would have done Whispering Jack proud. Playing such a role was actually quite exhilarating as I let my fantasies run away with me that I was a sharply dressed player, mixing it with the big money and gangsters and operators.

But then the reality that I was playing with real money hit home in a big way. On one of the first races we took bets on, there was a plunge and I had to turn the favourite down from 3 to 1 to about 6 to 4 to try and stem the flow of cash pouring in for it. As the horses entered the straight the favourite was neck and neck with a rank outsider that nobody had backed with us. They charged down the straight, switching lead with every stride. The difference to us was $12 000: if the favourite bobbed up we lost six grand, if the outsider saluted we won $6000. They were inseparable all the way down the straight and with the roar of the crowd building to a crescendo they hit the line. In the very last stride, the long-shot poked its nose in front and $6000 stayed in our bag.

The shot of adrenaline that coursed through my body at that moment was unlike anything I had ever felt. But as I was up on the stand, I knew that the eyes of hundreds of punters would be on me, and as a bookie is supposed to give nothing away (for there is nothing more annoying to a punter than a gloating bookie), I had to pretend that it was no big deal and continue on with the next race as if nothing had happened, when inside I was dancing like James Brown. No wonder Baz drank at the races.

But on Melbourne Cup day 1997 we didn't have to contend with anything quite so dramatic. As predicted by Baz, business was not overwhelmingly busy. He was also correct in predicting that having me on the stand would 'attract the young sheilas'. In particular I became the target of the attention of a very statuesque, but very drunk, redhead. She had Stinky going out of his mind with lust. ('She's bloody Nicole Kidman, mate!') As the day wore on, she became increasingly drunk and more flirtatious and at one point was literally rubbing her cleavage against me as she sidled up to coquettishly ask me which horse she should bet on.

To be honest, she was actually a bit of a pest as I was trying to keep the stand running and not lose Baz any more money. (This was the year Kerry Packer had sent the betting ring into conniptions with a multimillion dollar plunge on the cup winner Might and Power, and even we were not immune: Packer's money rippled through the ring as desperate bookies tried to lay off with other bookies. Luckily Baz was at the bottom of the food chain and only did about five thousand as opposed to the tens of thousands he would have lost if he had still been on the rails.) No matter how good looking this woman was, she was getting in the way of business and by the end of the day any sense of being flattered by her attentions had dissipated and been replaced with irritation. As we were settling up after the last race she stumbled back to the stand and vampishly (and slurringly) asked me what I was doing after the races. She said she would be at the casino and I should meet her there.

Baz and the boys were gobsmacked at her brazenness. They asked whether I intended to go and meet her. I had an ideological objection (political rather than moral) to the casino at the time and had refused ever to go there. I told them I wouldn't be meeting her. They were amazed. Stinky was apoplectic.

'She's Nicole Kidman! You're turning down Nicole Fucking Kidman! Are you fucking mad?'

'You saw her, Stink, she's pissed out of her brain.'

Stinky stopped his protestations for a moment, and then responded. 'And? Nicole Fucking Kidman! Pissed! You imbecile.'

Working the stand that day did make me wonder whether I could have taken over as a bookie from Baz. I believe the rules of succession in the bookie caper have changed now and it is easier to pass on a licence. But back in 1997 there was only talk of such changes. Being only two years out of uni, I certainly didn't have the funds behind me to get a licence in my own right, and wasn't going to hit on any 'colourful racing identities' to spot me a loan. I could have got Baz to back me, or even just continued running his licence for a while. We even tentatively spoke about it. He would have loved me to continue the family tradition but in the end advised against it as the nature of bookmaking was changing. With the introduction of phone betting and casinos and modern technology, it wasn't simply a case of setting the board and taking on the punters. With the speed of modern communications, a new breed of punter now had the edge over the bookie. The syndicates could have men on the ground in, say, Adelaide where they would report instantly on any changes to the betting to a major punter who could be on the phone in seconds placing massive bets with a bookie on that horse. The whole market was distorted, and it was becoming almost impossible for a lone bookie to survive. In the year before he retired, Baz had knocked off half the money it had taken him 25 years to accumulate. He didn't want to pass on the baton in that sort of climate.

And I think deep down both of us knew that I didn't really have the temperament to match it with the big players. With the Melbourne Cup coming up Baz suggested that he and I get out the bookie board and bag and run a book on the race at the Sports Club. Totally illegal, but the money involved would have been so miniscule that I don't think the gaming squad would have been making any raids. But I had already booked the betting gear for a friend's Melbourne Cup party. I had set up with Baz's old gear the previous year for the entertainment of the forty or so party-goers. It saved them from having to go down to the TAB to put their once-a-year bets on the Cup. I think I'd held roughly a hundred bucks and won about thirteen. It was all good fun so I thought I'd do it again.

As I left that morning Baz, who would be spending the day at the club, gave me a bit of parting advice: 'Now I know they're your mates, but it is your money you're dealing with. Remember, on the Cup you can work to a different percentage than normal and the mug punters won't care. They get their bet, you don't risk anything, everyone's happy.' I thanked him for the advice and happily headed off.

When I returned Baz was already in bed after a big day at the club. The next morning he asked me how I'd gone and I sheepishly had to admit I had lost over two hundred bucks. Baz was astonished.

'How'd you manage that?' he spluttered. 'You'd have to be the worst bookie in the world to lose on the Cup. What percentage were you working to?'

When a bookie sets the odds, he does so in order to guarantee (theoretically, anyway) that he will always win at least ten per cent of what is bet with him. This is in an ideal world where everyone bets on every horse so that the risk is spread. In reality this doesn't ever happen and in any given race there are always one or two horses that will lose you money. You just have to hope this doesn't happen too regularly. The trouble with betting on the one race only is that if the favourite gets up in that race you are screwed. Not that the winner, Rogan Josh, was the favourite, but it was all the punters wanted to back, so even though I was working to a whopping 140 per cent, the only two decent bets I laid at the party were both for Rogan Josh. Though I had shaved the odds and they got 4 to 1 instead of the 5 to 1 being offered at the track, there were no other bets to counter it and my day had gone down the gurgler.

Baz looked at me with pity and shook his head. 'Losing on the Melbourne Cup. It's hard to believe you're my son. Thank God we didn't set you up with a proper licence – I'd have to sell the house.'

So the Dooley bookmaking dynasty was to end with Baz, though truth be known it really ended with the death of Di. A lot of things in our family ended with her, but then again many things also began. Once Di was gone, the centre could not hold and we all began drifting ever further apart, with only the memory of her keeping us together in any way. With Baz falling ill, however, we were faced with a choice. Di was not there to rally us around Baz as she undoubtedly would have done. If we were going to come together this time it had to be of our own volition. Paradoxically, if Di had been alive when Baz was ill, I am sure that I wouldn't have spent the time with him that I did, or have had the opportunity to really get to know my father before it was too late.

18   HAVE YOURSELF A LONELY LITTLE CHRISTMAS

I had never been a massive fan of Christmas. I didn't mind it, but from an early age it didn't seem to hold the same magic for me as it did for seemingly everyone else. Wok was right into it when we were kids and would wake several hours before dawn and almost have to be physically restrained from ripping into his presents. By the age of ten the excitement had largely worn off for me, and even though I suspected that year I was finally going to get my long awaited first proper bike, I still mustn't have been that keyed up because during the night on Christmas Eve, a gum tree crashed through my bedroom window without disturbing me in the slightest. I woke in the morning surrounded by eucalyptus foliage. Amazingly the branches that had smashed through the window formed a frame around my sleeping body with the leaves dangling harmlessly above my face. Now that I think about it, I was probably bloody lucky to survive but at the time, apart from thinking it was pretty funny, it barely registered.

And the older I got, the less excited I became. In the end, in my later teenage years, the family would have to come and drag me out of bed so that we could get the present opening ritual over before we laid the table for Christmas lunch. Once I had moved out of home I would happily come down to see everybody for Christmas, but really I could take it or leave it. So I was taken aback at how desperately sad the first Christmas without Di was. She died three weeks before Christmas, so naturally it felt very raw, but it was also blatantly apparent how much we would miss her. Di had been the glue that kept the Dooley family Christmases together. Although Baz would traditionally cook the roast (aside from the disaster of the last Christmas before Mum died, when Baz had lined up some 'fresh' crayfish from a mate at the airport which turned out to be anything but), Christmas was really owned by Di. She was the real reason we would front up each year and, without her, every festive gesture seemed achingly hollow. The following Christmas was not quite so unbearable, but it had still lost its lustre. And now, as the third Christmas without Di approached, all seemed grim again.

Whereas November had held out quite a bit of hope, it proved to be a false dawn, and December brought not much in the way of good news. In late November Baz had come home from the club feeling very weak and had gone straight to bed. During the night he was cold despite sleeping under thick blankets, and he was suffering from stomach pains. In the morning he was terribly pale and after going to the toilet he came out even paler. His knotted stomach had produced a coal black beauty and as he knew from his bowel cancer days, that was a sure sign that trouble was a-brewin'.

As I drove him to the hospital, Baz pondered aloud whether Dr Nick had got it wrong and the lung cancer had spread to his bowel. As it turned out, it was nothing of the sort although it was related indirectly to the treatment. There was indeed blood in Baz's stools but this had come from the bleeding of his stomach ulcers.

With the correct medication, Baz's ulcers had been under control for almost fifteen years. Dr Nick felt that the chemotherapy had irritated the stomach lining and fired up the ulcers again. Baz was given a blood transfusion. It seemed to do the trick and the bleeding stopped.

Dr Nick kept Baz in hospital for a few days of observation, and while he was in there, he got up to his old tricks, trying to set me up with another of the nurses. Apparently his way of ascertaining whether someone was available was to ask her as she was changing his bedpan, 'So, love, are you married?'

Jo, the nurse he had in mind this time, replied, puzzled, 'Are you trying to pick me up, Barry?'

'No, not me, but you saw my boy. He's pretty good looking, don't you reckon?'

She was a bit stunned and tried to deflect him with, 'I'm 33, with an eight year old!'

'Yeah but are ya married?' Baz pressed on.

She wasn't, so Baz continued, claiming that I loved kids and was single which meant that every time I went to visit him and Jo was there, it was highly embarrassing for all involved. All but Baz.

I was astonished, not merely at his boldness but at his presumption that he would have any idea of what type of woman I would be interested in. Baz had had more than thirty years to get to know me and yet here was more evidence that he clearly had no idea of what I was really like, who I really was. He made the same sort of presumptions about almost every aspect of my life, especially my professional career. Though for the previous three years I had been working as a television writer, it still hadn't sunk in for him that this was the career I wanted to pursue. Whereas Di had been quite thrilled at any writing work I got, Baz continued to see it as a diversion in my path to becoming a lawyer (that is, now that any chance of me being a bookie had been snuffed out).

Baz was not one of those high pressure fathers who make their kids' life hell if they don't achieve; he merely lacked the imaginative capacity to understand that, having got the marks to get into law, I could ever seriously turn my back on that career path. I had no real desire to practise law and had only finished my degree because I didn't want to abandon something I had started (and because the most interesting subjects weren't offered until the final years of the course) but I had, since Baz's diagnosis, spent two weeks doing my first law job. I took the work as a paralegal because I needed some income. At this stage the only TV work I was getting was sending scripts on spec to a satirical program on the ABC – I think in fourteen weeks I only ever got two scripts to air (and hence two pay cheques).

The paralegal gig was welcomingly mind numbing. I was

required to proofread thousands of pages of statements in a dispute over a bridge maintenance contract for an insurance law firm. I didn't have to think about anything else, and could just go into the office and churn through the pages looking for transcription errors, and filling up my six-minute billable unit forms. (9.00 to 9.06 am: proofreading document; 9.06 to 9.12 am: proofreading document; 9.12 to 9.18 am: filled out this form.) I could see the attraction of such a job. While in there I had no time to fret over turning the latest political news into a zippy one-liner, or to worry whether Baz had taken his medication; there was just the blissful oblivion of paperwork.

But after two weeks the gloss wore off and I just became screamingly bored. I began to think too much and queried my superior about whether the other side might have had a case. That didn't go down too well and the phrase 'the banality of evil' began to swirl around and around in my head. Not that what was going on in that office was necessarily evil in any way (though they were representing a big insurance company), it was more that everybody there was so focused on getting their part of the job done right that the capacity to think beyond the immediate task at hand seemed to be lost. With thoughts like this after just a fortnight, I certainly wasn't cut out to be a lawyer.

Not that Baz could ever be convinced of that. Having cracked open one of the stubbies I snuck into the hospital for him, he expounded upon my future life as Sean Dooley, barrister at law. I protested how my brief taste had turned me even further off the idea. Baz would not be swayed.

'I know you don't like the city, corporate stuff. So why don't you go put your shingle up in a small country town, be the local solicitor? You like the country, and birds and all that sort of stuff. That way you'd make a good quid and have a nice life, with plenty of time to go and do your birdwatching, or even your acting at the local musical theatre group. Sounds a pretty good life to me.'

And he was right, it did sound like a nice dream. Just not my dream. You'd think he would have known that by this stage, but his next statement clearly showed he had no idea: 'And I'm sure that cute nurse could be convinced to move. Probably love her kid to grow up in the country.'

'Jesus, Dad, I'm not going to ask her out, OK!'

God he could be exasperating. But the most disturbing aspect of all this was that I did kind of fancy the nurse. She was actually quite lovely and reminded me of the nurse who had been on duty when Di had died. After I had found her body in the hospital room, I went out to tell the nurse and she burst into tears because she had grown very fond of Di in the weeks she had been looking after her. She said sometimes there are patients that really make an impression. We embraced and cried together and I remember feeling an overwhelming surge of . . . well, it was almost desire. In the midst of the horrible finality of death, holding her warm body to me represented life and I just didn't want to let her go. Jo not only looked similar to that nurse, but she radiated the same grace, I guess you'd call it. I actually did like her. Not that I would have let Baz know that. There is no way I would have let him have the satisfaction, so I told him if he kept on like that I wouldn't bring in any more stubbies. That shut him up.

Aside from being hospitalised, things were looking up for Baz. On the day he was discharged, Dr Nick popped in to see him to reiterate that all the signs indicated that the treatment seemed to be working. This may have been the case but it was taking its toll and starting to hit Baz quite hard. Even in the days after the worst effects of the chemo had worn off, he was still getting exhausted doing a minimal amount of movement. He kept complaining he was out of breath. I told him it must be the chemo, but he was convinced it was the lung cancer. I told him to just rest and began to do more around the house. By this stage I was doing most of the shopping and driving for Baz because he was just so buggered. Ever since he had taken over the food shopping when Di was crook he had got into the habit of only buying the ingredients for that day's meals. It was a habit he was loath to break as he could decide on a whim what he fancied that day, and it always meant he had the freshest ingredients.

It was a bugger for me though, but I began to pick up a few tips, both in the kitchen and in shopping around for ingredients. Baz sent me off to Reg's to pick up some prime porterhouse. I didn't identify myself as Baz's son and was given the normal steak that an ordinary customer would get. As soon as I served it up to Baz (cooked according to his instructions – medium rare so that you could still see a little blood in it) he put down his knife and fork after the first mouthful and said, 'Did you go to Reg's?'

'Yeah,' I replied, a little defensively.

'This isn't his good stuff. Did you ask Reg for the good stuff, the stuff he hangs in the back of the coolroom?'

I made sure I never made that mistake again.

I look back at those times and think I really didn't have to do all that much: a bit of shopping, cooking some meals and driving Baz to the club (sometimes he would walk over but I would inevitably have to drive him home), but when I look back at a diary entry I made around this time I see that I wasn't sleeping very well and was worried that I was going through my days on autopilot, not really feeling much of anything. I guess this was just a combination of having to deal with Dad's illness, not letting it get too overwhelming, and the fact that I felt I was stagnating a little down at Patterson Lakes. In more recent times I have read that carers have the highest incidence of depression of any group in society and I can see why. Not that I think I was depressed at the time, but I reckon the early signs might have been brewing.

Perhaps that was why I agreed to take a gratis gig on a film shoot as a stand-in when a friend rang asking for a favour. They were shooting just down the road at Seaford, about 500 metres from where Holly went missing, so I thought I would make sure I got there early and put in a quick hopeful scope of the neighbourhood in case she still happened to be around there somewhere ... well, it was worth a try.

I had just put down the phone when it rang again. It was Wok. He sounded pissed and I could hear trucks in the background. I asked him where he was, expecting him to be on the roadside near Tully.

'Parkes,' he told me triumphantly. That was in New South Wales, about a full day's drive from Patterson Lakes and about two days from Tully. He continued exultantly, 'Sean, I'm comin' home!'

My heart sank. Well, splattered on the floor, to be honest. I thought he had been bored witless last time. He'd only been back up there less than a month. The relief had been palpable when he had gone, and now he was on his way back. Why? And, more importantly, how?

He answered that by saying he and Cody had hitched a ride with one of his good mates, Andy, who was coming down to visit his folks in Gippsland for Christmas. He was coming home for Christmas, wasn't that great?! (Christmas was still four weeks away.) And then he added, 'Yeah, and we've had such a good time on our way down here, we've run out of dosh and haven't got any money to fill up the tank. Can you send us some?' When I reluctantly said I would put some money into his account, he replied with a phrase he had picked up in North Queensland: 'Too easy.'

Of course it was too easy. That was the whole problem. Everything was too easy when he had Baz to bail him out. There was never any expectation that, though he and his mate had blown all their money on grog and God knows what else, we wouldn't be there to get him out of whatever predicament he was in. And the most galling thing was that Wok was completely oblivious to any of the strife he caused. On the phone he sounded like it was a completely brilliant thing that he was returning, and that Baz would be dancing around the house for joy.

So I wired Wok the money but I didn't share his enthusiasm. And I didn't agree to his request that I leave his imminent arrival home as a surprise for Dad. We were struggling to keep him from dying of cancer; I didn't want him carking it of a heart attack when Wok and his mate walked in the door. If I had felt that I was becoming numb to everything, this call certainly got my emotional juices flowing. Cue another night's bad sleep. It was a seven am call for the film shoot, so I arrived with heavy black circles under my eyes and was relieved to see they had a plentiful supply of make-up on hand.

The film was an independent, low-budget job written and directed by a mother and daughter team. And good on them, I thought. They had no film board funding but they were out there, raising private finance, having a go. But as the day wore on and there was no sign of any progress I started to have my doubts. After waiting all morning with some extras dressed as prostitutes (the costumes looked like they had been borrowed from the local amateur light opera society's version of *Les Mis*) I was told that due to delays I wouldn't be needed until later in the day. I went home for lunch. Baz asked me to drop him down the club as he was catching up with some of his old work mates from his meter testing days at Port Melbourne.

After dropping Baz off I headed back to the location in a warehouse in an industrial zone. They were almost ready for the scene where I had to be a stand-in. I found out that the plot was about a young guy who one day finds a mysterious green spot on his body. It grows and grows until his entire body turns green. Even my diversions involved bloody cancer! It was a romantic comedy, they told me. The scene I was to be in was a dream sequence in which the main character meets his father, who died of the same condition. The lead actor played both roles. I was to be stand-in for him while he was dressed as his green father. This meant that I too had to be painted green.

I pointed out that I was about six inches taller than the lead actor, and my head was a different shape. They said it didn't matter and proceeded to spray-paint my face and various other parts green as I sat there and waited for my shot at celluloid glory. And waited. And waited. Eventually my time came, but they couldn't work out the logistics of the scene, particularly because I was six inches taller than the lead. After much dramatic whispering between the mother and daughter, it was decided to cancel the shoot for the day; they would shoot it again tomorrow using just the main actor. I wonder if Geoffrey Rush got started this way?

When I arrived home, still a light shade of green as the make-up hadn't come off properly, Baz was crashed out on the couch snoring his head off. It must have been a big day with the Port boys, who really knew how to drink. There was a message on the machine from Brucey at the club to say that Baz had left some raffle tickets over there and could I come and get them. Some of the Port boys were still there, including Mick Hogan. Of all his drinking partners from the old days, none quite possessed Mick's fixed determination to demolish as many pots as possible.

And so it was that afternoon as I walked into the club. Mick was still there and, to put it delicately, was very, very pissed. He seized hold of me and began a rant about what a beautiful man my father was. Despite his being four and a half sheets to the wind, he spoke with such impassioned eloquence about how much Baz was loved by those who knew him that I was almost moved to tears. And they would have spilled, too, had he then not moved on immediately to tell me just as fervently how much everybody loved me as well. As he stood there patting my cheeks, tears rolling down his own, repeating, 'You're a terrific kid, Sean, a terrific kid' I started to get the giggles. I'd never really been in one of those drunken Aussie bloke 'I love you, mate' moments before.

By the time we'd got Mick into a taxi and I'd had a couple of beers with Brucey, it was quite dark when I got home. I expected Baz to still be asleep but he was up and about, mainly because Wok and his mate Andy had just arrived. They had set off from Tully about a week earlier, and judging by their appearance and smell, they hadn't seen a shower in that entire time. Since his last visit Wok had started to grow a beard, but it paled in comparison to Andy's whiskered creation that would have put any of the Hatfields or the McCoys to shame. (He even had the missing teeth to match.) The two of them reeked – of campfires, of dogs, of a week-long binge – but at least they weren't actually drunk the night they arrived, and we all talked rather amiably before Andy decided to head off down the track to his folks' place and Wok decided he would defongerate around to a mate's place. (Defongerate was a word that Baz claimed he and his mates invented when they were younger to describe the act of getting the hell out of somewhere, but I believe it is also used to describe the act of removing a lingering smell, which in this case seemed rather appropriate.)

We actually didn't see as much of Wok this time. He ended up spending a lot of time down at Andy's in Gippsland, so his visit didn't create quite the same turmoil. Things seemed to be quietening down and Baz and I were developing a routine. There was still time for myself and as I realised that, with any luck, this situation would go on for another year, I needed to make sure I didn't entirely stagnate while I was looking after Baz. With no job offers likely to come in over the summer I decided I needed a project and so registered a show for the upcoming Melbourne Comedy Festival. Years before I had done a Nick Cave impersonation for a uni revue which had worked a treat, and I'd been threatening to turn it into a one-man show for years. Sure, a one-song repertoire was a pretty flimsy excuse for a show, but many a festival show had been based on less. It gave me something to focus on other than the spectre of watching Baz slowly die.

For by this point it had become pretty clear that he was not going to beat this cancer. On the second anniversary of Di's death we were back in Dr Nick's office for his next prognosis based on the latest scans of Baz's chest. The news was not great. The area of Baz's lungs that had been clear six weeks before was now peppered with little black dots. Dr Nick momentarily lost his professionally mild demeanour and furrowed his brow deeply. This was not good. The cancer had come back and with a vengeance. Baz asked whether this was why he was always short of breath. Dr Nick said that given the extensive spread he was surprised Baz wasn't out of breath all the time and recommended that he get an oxygen tank. Dr Nick still wanted Baz to continue with the treatment but would think about tweaking it, to see if he could stem the advance of those little black dots, trying to prevent them from becoming big black dots.

Afterwards at the club, I pointed out to Baz that it was the second anniversary of Di's death. He replied that it wasn't until the sixth. I corrected him that it was the fourth, and that he had got the date wrong on her tombstone as well.

'Oh well,' he said, raising the pot glass to his lips, 'no point getting it changed now. You'll just have to wait until I join her. You won't be waiting long.'

I protested that if I had anything to do with it, we would be sitting in the bar having a beer come next Christmas. Baz shrugged his shoulders doubtfully. He wasn't distressed but he did seem resigned. I wanted him to be railing against it in all fury, but he seemed to have a fatalistic acceptance. This wasn't like Baz, I thought. Just then some of the boys entered the club. Dave the Pom yelled out that Baz owed him a beer. Baz fired back with some comment about him being a tight Pommy bastard who would never shout in the first place so there was no way he could possibly owe him a beer. Fifty Bucks sidled over and proceeded to tell us how he had just come from drinks with Alan McAlister, the recent ex-president of the Collingwood Football

Club, and how he had the scoop that Nathan Buckley was going to be traded back to Brisbane in a direct swap for Michael Voss. Baz was telling him it wouldn't matter if they got Royce Hart, John Coleman and Jesus himself, the Pies would still be a shit team, and they all began their usual roared conversation. This was more like Baz.

And so Christmas rolled on. I am not sure where Wok was, but he certainly reneged on coming along to our cousins' places on Christmas Day. This was the third year Baz and I had followed this routine: the family of Aunty Jan for lunch, that of Aunty Joyce for dinner. Both had large, raucous families that it was always great to be among but behind all the cheer was the sad, inescapable fact that Di was not there, that this wasn't really our Christmas. And this Christmas, Baz brought along an extra guest – his oxygen tank. It was the first time he had taken it out in public and though it didn't get much of a workout, just having it there served to remind us of not only who was not at the table, but who might not be there come next Christmas.

19

BEATING THE FLOWER DRUM

I decided not to see in the new millennium with Baz, even though I knew it could very well be his last. Somehow the option of going down the club for a drink with the boys was not my idea of how I wanted to spend the last few hours of the twentieth century. No, I was determined to farewell the year, the decade, the century, in a much more exciting manner – I spent it spotlighting for owls. Baz couldn't understand it; I can't think why!

My partner in crime was my oldest birdwatching mate, Groober, he of the Cann River engine seizure on New Year's Eve fifteen years earlier. We hadn't been on a road trip like this for several years but he was the only one of my friends foolish enough to agree to spend New Year's Eve this way. My aim was twofold: to try and see one last new bird for my list in the twentieth century, and to have the first bird I saw in the new millennium be an interesting one. So we headed north up the Hume Highway to a little town called Chiltern, where the nocturnal action was far more exciting than anything the big city had to offer, as well as being free of hundreds of thousands of meatheads.

As we set off in Groober's car we joked that we hoped nothing would go wrong on this trip. Right from that East Gippsland trip our sojourns together seemed to strike disaster. Over the years in my company Groober had managed to: hit a kangaroo and virtually write off his car in Western Australia, get the car bogged in a thunderstorm in the Big Desert, and once when we were birding together in suburban Seaford he managed to get run over by a horse as we were crossing Nepean Highway, one of Melbourne's main arterials. But we figured that time had mellowed us, and hopefully our run of bad luck had played itself out so we cranked up the Midnight Oil tape louder and pretended we were eighteen again.

Our target bird was the White-throated Nightjar. I'd heard this secretive nocturnal bird many times but never managed to get the binoculars on it. Groober had seen them before coming in to hawk insects over the water of a dam in the middle of the forest at Chiltern. We arrived just before dark and made our way down to the edge of the dam. In the twilight we heard the maniacal cackle of the nightjar from up the ridge. The calls kept getting closer and Groober readied his spotlight. Then in the dim light I saw the silhouette of one against the evening sky.

'There!' I pointed it out to Groobs. He flicked the switch on the spotlight. Nothing happened. The bird made its one pass of the dam for the night as Groober fiddled about with the light – he had forgotten to connect the wires to the battery terminals. Later in the night a big wind blew up, drowning out any owl calls that we might have heard so we turned in early. When we awoke we discovered that our jinx wasn't broken. Groober's car had a flat battery and we spent the morning walking into town to wake up the local mechanic.

Baz was highly amused by all this when I finally got home and kept rubbing in what a good night I'd missed. There was quite a crowd at the club and after midnight Baz had left to have a nightcap at Ando's place and then eventually turned in around two. He was adamant it was a great night, for which I was happy, though a little regretful that I hadn't spent it with him. He did say that he had found it a little hard going, which he put down to the fact that he hadn't taken the oxygen tank with him. Speaking to Ando and his wife Barb later, they said the reason he had needed three attempts to scale the small rise from the lakeside beach to the edge of our back door had more to do with the amount of beer he had put away rather than with any lack of oxygen – at three metres above sea level, our backyard rarely required the use of extra oxygen. Apparently the entire party had come out to watch the spectacle of Baz staggering up the slope.

A few days later Baz was back in hospital – another episode with his ulcers. Again a transfusion and a few days' bed rest did the trick and he was back to what now passed for normal. The chemo (and the steroids he was taking to alleviate the chemo symptoms) had bloated Baz, so the rest of his body was catching up with his rotund beer gut that had taken decades to cultivate. And while he'd had very little hair to begin with, it had now all but disappeared. He was using his oxygen tank almost daily by this stage but he still seemed fairly hale and hearty. On visiting him in hospital a couple of days into his stay I smuggled in a six-pack. As it happened, Ace was there and the three of us sat around and chewed the fat. When we ran out of beer Baz sent me out to grab some more – luckily the hospital had conveniently been built next door to a pub with a TAB. When I returned with the beers and his winnings from the TAB Baz joked that he might never want to leave.

As we were laughing, Jo the nurse came in to tell us to keep it down. We all tried to hide our beers, like school kids caught out by the teacher. She smiled and shook her head and rolled her eyes. Baz offered her a beer. She seemed half tempted but said she'd get the sack if the other patients smelt beer on her breath. She reiterated we should keep it down but made sure she shut the door after her so that we wouldn't disturb the rest of the ward.

As soon as she was gone Baz was into me. 'I told you she's all right, Rupe. Why don't you ask her out?'

'Oh would you leave it alone. I'm not interested, okay?' I protested.

Baz turned to Ace. 'Can you believe him, Acey? I line him up with a good sort and he's not interested. You've got to worry about him.'

For a long time I suspected that Baz suspected I might be gay; the fact that I had brought a couple of girlfriends home over the years apparently not sufficient to allay his doubts. I was involved in too many things that in Baz's reckoning ticked the homosexual box: theatre, birdwatching, I was a bit of an intellectual, and sometimes I would refuse a beer and have a lime and soda instead. Baz was appalled.

'What are you drinking that rubbish for? You know they gave lime juice to sailors in the navy to stop them from getting randy out at sea. You know that, don't you?'

'They gave sailors lime juice to stop them getting scurvy, Dad,' I countered, but he was not convinced.

He'd only ever called me on it directly the once. It was when Di was still alive and I had come home for dinner and was telling them about my plans for the upcoming Twitchathon (a 24-hour birdwatching race that I entered with Groober and a couple of other mates each year to raise funds for conservation – well, that's what we say; we're really in it for the sheer thrill of the competition). Di, who was generally supportive of all my extracurricular activities, was obviously a little concerned I was spending so much time on a bird race and asked me, 'How come you don't bring any girls home for dinner?', to which Baz added, half jokingly, 'Yeah, are you a poofter or something?'

I replied, 'No, Dad, I'm a birdwatcher.'

Baz, taking a sip from his stubbie, muttered under his breath, 'I think I'd rather you were a poofter.'

The irony was that only the week before Baz was hospitalised, I had hooked up with someone over a few drinks at a pub in the city. But asking an inner city girl back to your pad in Patterson Lakes was guaranteed to get a reaction on a par with asking her back to look at your cloak made from human skin, so by the time we had ended up at her place and she'd asked me to stay the night, I had to turn her down as I had to get home to take Baz in to see Dr Nick first thing the next morning. I never told Baz, partly because I didn't want him to feel guilty about being a burden for me, but also partly because I didn't really want him to know about my personal life and I enjoyed keeping my sexuality a bit of a mystery for him.

After we had finished a couple more beers (I'd picked up some lights because I was driving – another nail in my manliness as far as Baz was concerned, until Ace had one as he also wanted to avoid a date with a booze bus) I headed home, telling Baz that he had to be fit and out of hospital by the end of the week so he didn't miss out on his belated Christmas present. Baz's eyes lit up: 'I wouldn't miss it for quids,' he smiled.

Shopping for presents for Baz was always tough. He simply never wanted anything, so he always tended to draw the short straw when Christmas came along. When we were kids it was things like hankies and socks. As we got older his default present tended to be bottles of whiskey. Not that he ever complained, but I had brought back his favourite Irish whiskey duty free when I returned from Europe so another bottle would have seemed like overkill. And I wanted to buy him something special this year. It might be his last Christmas, after all. But what do you buy for someone who probably won't be around for much longer? Even if I had found a good physical present, there was that thought gnawing at the back of my mind that it would only serve as a reminder that the object would outlast him.

My solution was to fork out for a meal in a restaurant that

Baz had always wanted to eat in – the Flower Drum – which for years had held the distinction of being Melbourne's, and possibly Australia's, finest Chinese dining establishment. Over the years Baz's taste for Asian cuisine had evolved from the 'chow' in a saucepan of the early days to something far more elaborate. Long before it became the stereotypical yuppie fare, Baz sought out new Japanese restaurants when they opened, and though he was extremely unadventurous when it came to Italian or Indian – or pretty much any other type of foreign cooking – he'd dive headlong into plates of sushi with abandoned gusto.

For years he had talked about eating at the Flower Drum, which held an odd place in the consciousness of Melburnians. While it was universally regarded as the pinnacle of Asian cooking by the fine dining cognoscenti, it was also frequented by the sort of cashed-up bogans of the sporting fraternity that Baz would listen to on the sports radio channels – the type that would think Cognoscenti was the captain of the Italian Davis Cup team in the sixties. So Baz kept hearing the Shane Warne and Sam Newman types banging on about the 'bewdiful chows' that they tucked into at the Flower Drum. But for all his expressed desire, Baz had never eaten there.

So for Christmas I booked him, me, Ace and Chris for a dinner there. It would cost the earth but I knew it would be worth it because it was one thing Baz really wanted that I could give him, the memory of which he could take with him always. It was extremely important for me that Ace and Chris were there to share it, as they had shared so many dinners with Baz and Di.

Theirs was a friendship for the ages, the sort that most people only dream of having. Paradoxically enough, when they first met, Chris and Di didn't get on. Chris thought Di was dull and Di suspected Chris was a bit ditzy. When Ace announced they were going to dinner together for the first time, Chris made him promise that he wouldn't allow her to get stuck with Diane when they had nothing to say to each other. Ace promised, but of course as soon as they were at dinner, Baz and Ace excused themselves to duck out to put a couple of bets on at the trots. Forced to have to talk to each other, Di and Chris did so, and basically they never stopped until Di passed away forty years later. It was funny, after Di's death I wouldn't get upset when I saw Baz or Wok, but as soon as I spoke to Chris we would both start tearing up at how much we missed her. Even writing this now has got me a little misty-eyed. Ah, the power of the Godmother.

The restaurant closed over the Christmas–New Year period and the earliest we could get in was toward the end of January so by the time the big night came, both Baz and I were so eager for it to be good that our nerves made us lose our appetite. Almost.

We were given the table closest to the entrance, which kind of exacerbated the feeling that we were interlopers, a feeling not helped by the fact that I was lugging Baz's portable oxygen tank in case he became short of breath. By this stage it wasn't like he was struggling for every breath – that was something we had to look forward to – but he would occasionally find himself coming up short in the oxygen department. So we tried to hide the tank in the corner and get on with the business at hand. We were immediately swamped by efficient staff placing napkins on our laps and filling up glasses with the requisite courtesy, but I got the distinct impression they were looking at us as if we were country rubes who had come wide-eyed to the big smoke for the first time.

But once the first dish came out, I think they were in for a surprise as Baz was right onto everything. I have only ever experienced such a transformation in staff attitude once before, when I went to buy a guitar when I was nineteen. I knew I didn't know the first thing about what sort of instrument to get so I took along my professional musician friend Barney. A pony-tailed wannabe rock star approached us cockily asking whether we were interested in the acoustic we were looking at, then took it down and for our benefit displayed his virtuosity on the instrument (a clunky rendition of 'Stairway to Heaven'). When he'd finished he looked at us smugly. Barney took the guitar off him and proceeded to let rip a series of complex riffs that would have put Jimmy Paige to shame. Then he simply handed the guitar over to the poor schmuck and said, 'He'll take it.' I reckon that guy went and enrolled in accountancy the next day, his dreams of being a rock god over. The same thing happened at the Flower Drum as Baz let rip with his appreciation of the subtleties of this style of Cantonese cooking, picking ingredients and naming flavours and asking questions of the staff as to what technique the chef had used. By the end of the evening, Gilbert Lau himself (the owner of the Flower Drum, who has since left to establish another, more low key restaurant) was hovering around the table, laughing and joking with Baz.

When we got home, and for days afterwards, Baz rhapsodised about the meal. It was exquisite. The san choi bao was the best I had ever eaten, the Peking duck was to die for and the other five courses were close to perfection. Interestingly, the one dish we were both slightly disappointed in was the crayfish stir-fry. It wasn't that it wasn't any good, it was just that as both of us were huge fans of crayfish, we had been looking forward to it enormously, so when it didn't live up to our high expectations we were slightly deflated. As I drained the glass of the last drop of Baz's Irish whiskey, I put my finger on it: 'You know what, Dad, you've cooked cray better than what we had tonight.'

Baz sipped his whiskey contemplatively and then nodded. 'I think you're right, Rupe.'

That Baz was capable of such quality culinary feats was directly attributable to the fact that he slogged his guts out in the kitchen at Patto trying to create that perfect, irresistible dish for Di. Her illness had been the most horrendous ordeal for Baz, yet I couldn't help feeling that it was the salvation of him.

He thought about the meal some more and then as I took his empty glass to put in the dishwasher, he said to me, 'I wish Di had been there tonight. She would have loved it, wouldn't she?'

'Absolutely, Dad, without a doubt.'

He looked towards the roof and said softly (Baz usually never said anything softly), 'Yep, Didy, you would have loved it, love.'

20

THE BREADMAKER

January came and went and though Baz's ulcers seemed to have settled down, there was a general decline in his overall condition. The chemo hadn't had much effect and Dr Nick was recommending that he start another round of treatment in a month or two that would aim to keep it at bay for as long as possible; it would be more of a palliative measure to lessen the effect of the disease rather than bring about any cure. Though he was always reluctant to make any predictions, we certainly got the sense from Dr Nick that we were looking at around six months.

Baz continued on, not changing his routine and determined to squeeze as much enjoyment out of life as he could. As I spent more and more time with him I realised with growing admiration that this really was his approach to life and that he was doing everything in his power to live according to his creed. Though we never like to confront it, everything ends and death is inevitable. So if you see the ending of something as what defines that thing, then every life ends badly and is ultimately futile. But

Baz implicitly embraced the notion that life is to be lived. It is how he'd always been, and he wasn't about to change now.

In this respect the boys at the club treated him just as they always had. If Baz was not going to wallow in self-pity, then they weren't going to indulge it. The banter remained the same. The shit-stirring and the alcohol consumption too, though occasionally Baz would have to pull up stumps early as he was getting too exhausted. Even after the chemo had stopped, such days were happening more frequently. At times like this when he couldn't make it to the club, I would occasionally go over there for a drink on my own. I could not have imagined doing this even a few months earlier. I now felt comfortable there and had even become a member and been given my own key.

It was when they could get me alone that (usually after a few) the boys would approach me and ask after Baz. They always framed the question in terms of, 'How's he doing … within himself?' This always seemed a strange expression to me, as he certainly wasn't going to be doing anything 'outside himself'. I knew they were asking how his spirit was, but it still sounded funny the way they all said the same thing. It is a remarkable testament to Baz that his best mates couldn't see a difference in him. But with Baz it was pretty much what you saw was what you got. There was very little subtext going on; Baz was writ large in bold characters with very few footnotes.

The answer that I gave them was one which seemed to be the truth: Baz was doing well within himself. Knowing that mortality was looming, Baz had not really undergone any great change in attitude or beliefs. He became neither more nor less religious, mainly because he felt comfortable with his faith and this latest turn of events had caused no great ructions in his belief system. His bad news didn't change the way he felt about life and he said to me the same things after his diagnosis that he had said before, that he believed in God and an afterlife. 'But,' he would add with a smile, 'if I'm wrong, what does it matter? I'm not going to be there to know about it.' You could say his faith was of great comfort to him, but it was no greater or lesser a comfort than it had been before he knew he had lung cancer.

If you took the question of how Baz was within himself literally, that is physically, then things weren't so crash hot. The oxygen tank was a regular companion and he would need to spend a couple of hours a day on the machine at home to really feel like he was getting enough of the precious stuff into his body. It was odd because he certainly didn't sound wheezy and was not prone to coughing fits as I would have expected. We figured these were to come. But Baz could feel that as the cancer spread within his lungs he just wasn't getting what he needed from them.

The effect of all the medication he had been on had bloated him out considerably and he was having real trouble with fluid retention. At night in bed his legs would swell up until the definition of his ankles was lost in elephantine puffiness. Every day I would have to roll some surgical stockings over them to redistribute the fluid. One night I forgot to take the stockings off and in the morning Baz had almost lost the feeling in his feet as all the fluid had been forced up over his ankles and pooled above them so that his legs looked like piano legs. It took a good half-hour of rubbing for them to return to something like normal and for him to get the feeling back in his toes. I apologised to Baz, adding that I was a pretty crap carer. He replied with a tenderness that surprised me: 'You're doing all right, mate. I don't know what I'd do without you.'

It hadn't dawned on me that I had been doing that much for him, and his statement set me to thinking. I guess it had got to the point where Baz would be seriously inconvenienced if I hadn't been around. He had trouble even bending by this stage and I was finding that every morning one of my chores was to hoist his underpants up over his legs as he lay back on the bed. And when you think about it, no child wants to cop an eyeful of his father's scrotum, let alone at such close range.

Dad's sister Judy arrived from Canada and we all went out to the club to celebrate her arrival. Aunty Jan had been the next closest in age to Baz and they had grown up very close. (After he died Jan told me that when they lived for a time in Sydney at the end of the war, she and Baz would sometimes go out having swapped their school uniforms with each other, pretending they were the opposite sex as they walked through the streets of Sydney. If only I'd known this when he was alive I would have been able to give him heaps of grief over his being a pioneer in the Sydney cross-dressing scene.) But as Jan had been a teetotaller all her life, she and Baz hadn't been quite as close as adults. Of all our relatives, Baz and Di had probably spent the most time as adults with Aunty Joyce and when he was alive, Uncle Bernie, but Baz seemed to hold a special place for Judy. I think when they were young and stupid, Baz and Jude had shared a similar partying spirit before she met her Canadian husband and moved across the ocean. So her arrival, her first visit in a few years, made for much celebration.

In fact it was a double celebration, as that day Baz was presented with honorary life membership of the Sports Club. For once in his life Baz seemed lost for words. He was genuinely touched that the boys had gone to the effort. He tried to give a thank you speech but choked up and I looked around and saw that nearly everyone there was holding back tears. There was a tight-throated silence that seemed to go on for an eternity, broken only when Big Terry shouted out, 'Enough of this blubbering. Let's all get a drink, for fuck's sake. Scuse my French, ladies,' he added, nodding to Baz's sisters as the whole room cracked up.

It was a joyous occasion and I was reminded again why Di was attracted to this family in the first place – they weren't backward in having a good time. Even Wok turned up. He had been something of a man of mystery during this stay and had rarely been home. He was certainly not one for turning up to family functions, but he soon relaxed and was getting into the swing of things.

Amid all this I was relaying how it had been with Baz to my cousin Gary, who was the manager at the local social security department. He said I was crazy not to have applied for a carer's benefit. I protested that I wasn't doing that much. Gary replied that given what I had just told him, I more than qualified and he would follow it up the next day. It wasn't all that much, he said, but it was recognition that I was now spending so much time with him that I wouldn't have been able to look for other employment. While having an income would be welcome, I felt a little reticent about it, not only because when I wasn't helping Baz I had been spending all my spare time writing my comedy festival show but because I guess in a way I didn't want to admit that Baz was in such a state that he needed a full time carer. In my mind I had thought that the point where I officially became Baz's carer would be a turning point – one of no return – in Baz's decline. Still, I guess one should be compensated for copping an eyeful of your old man's nuts.

I felt a little guilty as I realised I was actually starting to enjoy life down at 'Chateau Patto' with Baz. With the tranquillity of its lake view there were far more unpleasant places to spend your days. I was even developing a bit of a social life, and it wasn't based purely on the blokes at the club – it was also based on the women. I had struck up a friendship with one of Stinky's daughters-in-law, Tammy, who like Leslie would pull a few shifts pouring beers at the club. Tammy was a gorgeous girl who relatively late in life, after she had started a family with her husband Brett, had discovered a creative side. She had started writing and performing and was taking an acting course in the city. I wouldn't have expected a touch of the avant-garde in that corner of suburbia, but there you go.

One night Tammy had one of her drama school friends come down to the club. I suspect the two of them were doing a bit of undercover research for some character workshop but

Louise seemed to fit in with the rough-house atmosphere well enough and the three of us stayed until stumps. This was one of Baz's chemo days and he had remained at home. Baz was a favourite of Tam's and she had been talking him up to Louise all night, so in the end she laughingly proposed that she and Louise come back to our place and they would do a striptease for Baz to give the old man a bit of a thrill.

We all tiptoed giggling into Baz's room to find him sleeping peacefully. Tammy started to cry, any thought of her original plan falling by the wayside. So instead the three of us got stuck into Baz's whiskey and went wandering down to the shore of the lake. There was a brilliant phosphorescence to the water and every time we made a splash it would shimmer in the moonlight.

After the girls had stumbled back to Tammy's place in what might have been a first for the area – a wife staggering home at three in the morning after a night on the grog at the Sports Club – I went back down to the water, sitting on the jetty, dropping sand into the water to make it glisten. I had come down here in the middle of the night a lot since the days when Di was sick. Sometimes I would sob until I was worried my howls echoing across the water would have the neighbours calling the cops. Many nights I would just sit there with my melancholy thoughts as I watched the bream break the surface of the dark water. But this night, while the melancholy was still there, I felt thankful that I was here, that as shitty as it all was, I was blessed to have experienced all of this.

I felt even guiltier when the week I got my first carer's payment I headed off to Adelaide, leaving Baz to be checked on by a combination of his sisters and his next-door neighbours Janice and David, who had been incredibly supportive throughout both my parents' illnesses. Ostensibly I was going over to get my artwork done for my show poster as my designer friend was in Adelaide for the Arts Festival, but really I was abandoning my ailing father for a three-day twitch.

A twitch is not some euphemism for anything kinky; it is simply when a birdwatcher chases after a rare bird to add to their list. Such a birder is known as a twitcher or, in the US, a lister. The word twitcher comes from England. It derives from a nickname for two birders from the 1950s who would go chasing after rare birds in the English countryside on a motorbike with a pillion. Being England it was usually bloody freezing so when they arrived at their destination they would be shivering so hard that other birders joked that they were twitching. The name stuck, much to their mortification, and came to describe an entire tribe of whackos. It is a form of extreme birding in which the twitcher will drop everything when he (for it is usually a he – as if your average woman would be stupid enough to get involved) hears of a rare bird that he hasn't seen. Ever since I was a teenager and began hanging out with the likes of Groober, it has been my sport of choice; not that I got to go twitching too often back then as the birds tended to turn up in distant locations and I rarely had the time to chase after them. Or when I had the time I never had the funds. Or when I was earning good money, to rush off for a bird at a moment's notice would mean I was likely to lose that source of income.

So when Australia's first twitchable Short-billed Dowitcher turned up at a salt field a couple of hours north of Adelaide it was the perfect excuse to go over and kill two birds with one stone. Not literally, of course, for killing the dowitcher would be wrong – a dead bird doesn't count for your list. As usual, Baz thought I was crazy so I tended to play up the business side of the trip to him. He was happy for me to go, for he was conscious of not wanting my social life to suffer because of him. An odd tussle goes on between patient and carer, between dedicating yourself to helping somebody else and still maintaining a sense of an individual life, that I think both parties are acutely aware of. So once the roster of people to check in on Baz was sorted (Aunty Judy stepped up to the plate and offered to stay with her baby brother as it would be their last chance to spend any time together, for once Judy went back to Canada, she knew she wouldn't be able to get back to see him again before the end), I could head off with a relatively clear conscience.

I didn't see the bird, a wader from North America with long legs and a long, straight bill like a thick black knitting needle with which it would probe the muddy shores for tasty treats like crabs, worms and insect larvae. This individual was very lost, having taken a wrong turn on its migration to South America. It managed to stay hidden while I was looking for it. Once I had returned to Melbourne, there was little sympathy from Baz, who just shook his head and said, 'I'd understand it if you were going all that way for a sheila.'

Baz hadn't actually minded my birdwatching habit so much

when I was younger – it was a healthy hobby for a kid. It was grown men getting excited over a feathered bird that Baz had a problem with, especially when his young son was hanging around with them. Looking back I can see why Baz felt that way – here was his teenage son hanging out with a bunch of older men, often dressed in heavy coats like flashers, who favoured lurking in bushes carrying all this high-powered optical equipment. God knows what Baz made of it when they said things like, 'We went down to the Mud Islands and had a Fairy Tern.'

Di was always slightly uncomfortable with my dalliance with such characters too, particularly when one Saturday afternoon when I was eleven I ran into the house breathlessly exclaiming I had met two men down at the swamp and they said they'd take me out into it with them. She said later that she had never seen me, normally an unflappable, reserved child, so excited or move so quickly as I grabbed my binoculars and raced out the door. She was sure she would never see me alive again. Baz's problem was even more fundamental than looking out for my safety. He just couldn't fathom blokes who were too different. Difference was viewed with suspicion, particularly if it seemed to be a deliberate choice. In Baz's world a migrant, a homosexual, an intellectual, a Collingwood supporter, could be deemed a good bloke only if he accepted and embraced the cultural norms. For someone to turn his back on the blokey orthodoxy and embrace the unusual was almost treasonous. For the most part, I had been able to keep my birdwatching out of the direct scope of Baz's experience in a version of a 'don't ask, don't tell' policy. But the day I found a rare bird literally in Baz's backyard, my secret world came crashing into Baz's life.

It was the second Christmas without Di and I was staying a few days with Baz at Patterson Lakes. It was shocking weather, the year that storms decimated the Sydney to Hobart yacht race, killing six sailors. On the back of these howling gales a type of seabird called a Bridled Tern was blown across from Western Australia and sought refuge on, of all places, Baz's jetty outside the house in Patterson Lakes. It was the first and still the only record of this bird for the entire state, so when I discovered it I was honour bound to report it to the birdwatching community. Before any of them arrived to confirm my sighting I made sure Baz saw the bird and all its salient features so that I would have at least one witness to this extraordinary visitation.

As soon as Baz found out that birdwatchers were on their way he muttered in horror, 'Not those bloody freaks! I'm off to the club,' and scarpered out the side door as the twitchers made their way through the front door. The bird soon flew off and only three others got to see it, but that didn't stop a steady flow of twitchers lurking around the neighbourhood for the next couple of days. For years I had successfully hidden the exact nature of my birding addiction from Baz; now it was out there in front of him, naked and confronting. It made him think I was even weirder.

But what was truly weird – no, more appropriate to say would be what was truly interesting – was how over the previous few weeks as Baz had needed more and more time to recover from the ravages of the ever-expanding cancer and the daily grind of pumping enough oxygen into his lungs, he had a lot of time on his hands in which he had nothing to do but stare out at the lake and the birds that floated past. It actually brought him a great deal of peace. He had even befriended a couple of the local pelicans and if he didn't turn up at the appointed time with his handful of fish scraps or bacon pieces, they would waddle up to the back door and insistently tap their hook-tipped beaks on the glass.

One evening Baz wasn't up to feeding them and I took over, managing to coax one of these magnificent creatures to gingerly rip a piece of meat from my hand. Baz watched on from inside as the quiet droning of the tank pumped oxygen into him through the tube below his nose. When I came back in he was unusually quiet before he said, 'You know what, Sean, I'm one of the only people to have seen a Bridled Tern in Victoria. How many people can say that?' and he sat back smiling a satisfied smile.

I was somewhat taken aback. I said to him, 'I wouldn't go saying something like that around the boys – they might think you were turning into some kind of soft sheila,' to which he replied, 'Yeah, they must have put the wrong sort of gas in the tank.'

We both smiled again and I reached out for his hand and grabbed it tight for a good minute. There is no way either of us would have felt comfortable doing that six months earlier. This was dangerously close to girly behaviour.

The other girly thing that I had begun doing was the cooking.

As Baz got physically weaker I began to take over all the cooking. At first it had been minor league stuff like getting Baz breakfast. (Though for Baz, breakfast could be an elaborate affair involving every jet on the stove-top.) Then I progressed to more complex, more sacred cooking duties. Baz would sit on a stool leaning against the kitchen bench, a fresh coldie in his hand, and guide me through the arcane mystery of cooking a roast chook his way. I began to really enjoy these times and as he dispensed his tips, our conversations would meander around to all manner of topics and for the first time in our lives I had a sense that we were sharing parts of ourselves with some kind of deeper meaning. I kept thinking that I should be writing down all his tips and recipes, but figured that we still had months and months of this and that by the time Baz was gone I would have learned his secrets almost by osmosis.

The first real breakthrough had come with the bread-making. When Di became sick Baz had enrolled himself in a short bread-making course. Pretty soon he had become a master baker and the house was regularly filled with that fantastic aroma of freshly baking bread that real estate agents say you should try and replicate if you are selling your house and have potential buyers coming through. For years I would get slightly annoyed whenever I came home and Baz bailed me up with his latest proposed variation. While the bread was undoubtedly nice I'd just roll my eyes and couldn't see why he had to make such a bloody fuss about it. What I couldn't see at that stage was how this was Baz's expression of care for the family, particularly for Di, and it was more than just extra sesame or caraway seeds.

Making bread was the first thing to be totally beyond Baz. His method included severely pounding the dough to properly aerate it and distribute the yeast. Quite early on in his treatment he lost both strength and energy and so initially passed that part of the procedure on to me. After a month or two I had taken over the whole physical process and would make it under the strict supervision of Baz's watchful eye. Then came a day when Baz was unable to get out of bed and I was given his blessing to have a crack at it solo. The first few times I ran in and out of his bedroom to consult with him but the results never seemed to match up to his efforts. It seemed to be one of those immutable laws of nature – thou shalt not make better bread than thy old man.

Then one day I was bashing away at another loaf when I had one of those serendipitous breakthroughs. After giving the dough a particularly brutal pounding I covered the bowl in plastic wrap and placed it by the window in the sun. Baz had given me strict instructions to retrieve it after about 45 minutes. I got busy on other stuff, writing, messing about on the computer, watching the cricket … I can't remember what else exactly, and forgot all about it. When I remembered the mixture about two hours later it had expanded over the top of the mixing bowl like the head of a badly poured beer. Thinking I had probably ruined the batch I slung it in the oven and hoped for the best.

After it had cooled I was out somewhere and when I got

back Baz was tucking into a slice of the fresh bread with only a dab of butter. He asked me what I had done differently.

'Oh, you can taste it, can you?' I asked, about to apologise.

'Too right. It's beautiful, Rupe. You've got that fluffy consistency I've always aimed for but never got. Even if I get better, from now on you're chief bread-maker in this house.'

I couldn't have been prouder, but it was a pride tinged with sadness. This meant that Baz had made his last loaf. His physical degeneration was gathering apace and I wondered how many 'lasts' we would go through in the coming months. Usually I guess you never know it is the last time you will do something but with the inevitability of terminal cancer, these moments are brought into focus all too sharply. And while part of me was pleased to have impressed Baz with my baking, the title of bread-making champion was one that I so emphatically had not wanted to wrest from him. Sometimes there is no joy in a son succeeding his father.

21 THE FIELD GUIDE TO VICTORIAN PUBS

For as long as I can remember, going right back to when I was a kid tagging along with Baz and Ace and their mates on their trips around the state to various racetracks, Baz would talk about writing a book about the pubs of Victoria. He reckoned there were very few left that he hadn't at least had one drink in. A favourite game on those long drives would be for them to try and catch him out on a pub. Jeparit? Baz could not only quote the name of the pub and which side of the street it was on, but he could tell you the name of the publican who had served him a beer in 1971.

Baz got his grounding as a connoisseur of Victorian pubs when, as a young fella, he was a sales rep for tobacco company Philip Morris. One evening after I had cooked dinner and he lay struggling to get enough oxygen into his lungs, he mused about whether he should sue Philip Morris for encouraging him to smoke. It wasn't a good look for the rep not to be smoking the company's product so Baz said they would fill up a box on his desk with free cigarettes and would ply him with sample packs that he could smoke in the car on the long drives around Victoria.

'The bastards knew even back then that it was bad for you but they never told us,' railed Baz, before quietening down and adding reflectively, 'No point suing them, though. I was an idiot smoker before I worked there and I was an idiot smoker after I left there – it took me till I was fifty-five to wake up to myself.'

Those days on the road kindled not only the cancer that was to kill him, but his encyclopaedic knowledge of the state's pubs. He reckoned there might have been only a handful whose doors he had never darkened. And to my great surprise I was about to introduce him to one more.

As we headed into March I became increasingly preoccupied with getting my Comedy Festival show into shape. With most of the script and songs written, it was the thousand little things that a self-producing performer has to deal with that were taking up much of my time: the poster, trying to get publicity with another 150 shows competing for attention, finding decent musicians who weren't booked up with gigs that would clash with a month-long season, and getting the venue organised.

Baz was doing all right, but he did need a bit of supervision so I was palming him off on our next-door neighbours and my aunties far more than I should have. But one day when I had to go to the venue to finalise things, everyone else was busy so Baz came along with me. As the venue was a pub, this was no great inconvenience to Baz. Rather than drink at the club, he could knock a few back at the John Curtin Hotel.

After I had been given a tour of the upstairs venue that I was to perform in, Baz and I sat down and had a beer with the publican, who coincidentally was called Warwick. On being introduced, Baz commented that his other son was also called Warwick. Publican Warwick expressed surprise that I had a brother, as I hadn't mentioned it before – in fact until I had brought Baz into the pub I hadn't mentioned anything about having a family. I must have done this often, for I remember that when I told a friend at uni about Di getting sick, he said to me, 'You know, Dooley, I never actually imagined you as having a family for some reason.' I was quite taken aback but I guess I almost felt a little pleased with myself to think that I came across as a bit of an autonomous, self-sufficient package.

Perhaps this 'Man with No Name' fantasy was due to being adopted. Maybe at some early stage when I looked around at the people surrounding me and realised they weren't anything much like me, I turned inward somehow. Although I was always a dutiful son and loved my family deeply, I seemed to have spent most of my life slowly moving away from them emotionally. Indeed by my early twenties I probably had, at least in my head, become totally independent of my family, so that what happened with them felt like it was happening on the periphery of my actual life. I would forever be that kid sitting quietly at the table with one eye on the external world, while being slightly absent from the fury of the world going on around me – watching *The Flintstones* as my brother stabbed my mother with a fork.

I think all I really longed for was the peace that comes with solitude, but losing Di had shown me what an illusion that idea was. And, having committed to looking after Baz, I was right in the middle of the turmoil of this all too real family situation whether I liked it or not. I think initially I was kidding myself that I could somehow deal with it all and remain above the emotion of the fray, be able to impose some sense of peace on it all, that I could somehow have a degree of control over things. But as Baz's illness progressed and the realisation that I would soon have lost both my parents in a short space of time grew ever more visceral, the crazy reality of it all seemed to be crashing down around me. At times I felt like Charlton Heston in *Planet of the Apes*, screaming 'It's a madhouse, a madhouse!' as everything around me went ape. There was Baz's determination to stick to his mad social routine at the club. There was the rapid advance of the disease. And then there was Wok.

He had been drifting in and out of the scene at Patto for the previous three months, a phantom presence in the house. He would disappear for days or weeks, sometimes down to his mate Andy's place in Gippsland, sometimes to – we didn't know where. In some ways it was probably better that we didn't know exactly what was going on. During one of his absences I came home to find a death threat directed against Wok on the answering machine. I didn't ever play the message to Wok or Baz, because I didn't want to unduly worry Dad and I didn't want to unduly inflame Wok's temper, but I did try to subtly grill Wok about what was going on his life. Wok, as usual, was fairly evasive but he did confess that he had been sleeping with a machete under his mattress for protection when he stayed with us at Patto. All very well for Wok who was hardly ever there. I am not sure what Baz and I were supposed to do should this maniac come calling. It was so nice and relaxing having Wok at home; a real tonic for Baz's recuperation.

Wok had an energy at that time that just seemed to cause tension in the space around him. He seemed to me to be displaying clear symptoms of unresolved grief. Or unresolved something. He was barely sleeping and would go wandering the streets and foreshores of Patterson Lakes at two in the morning taking Cody for a walk. He was self-medicating more than usual. He would be out drinking with his mates till late then be up at six leaving an acrid waft of medicinal herb mingling with the steam of his early morning shower. I approached him a couple of times and suggested that maybe he needed to talk to someone about how he was feeling: first Mum, now Dad dying. It didn't have to be with me or Baz or anyone he knew, it could be a professional that I could arrange for him to see. He wouldn't have a bar of it and stonewalled me every time, saying he didn't have a problem.

Rational self-awareness was not one of Wok's strong suits; he still seemed to think his presence was having a beneficial effect on Baz, that he was being supportive. And I know he genuinely and passionately wanted to help, to be there for Baz, but in order to be a rock for someone, you have to have anchored yourself in the first place. At this point, Wok was a piece of flotsam in his own life, a rubber thong that had washed overboard, floating haphazardly around the ocean.

For a while during this period he focused his energies on arcing up over the fate of Baz's boat. Since the death of his fishing buddy, Uncle Bernie, Baz hadn't used the boat very much and after his diagnosis it had just sat at its mooring gathering barnacles. In the past I would occasionally accompany Baz out onto the bay but he found it too frustrating as I would not throw a line in myself. 'You eat the bloody things, why don't you want to catch 'em?' he would ask, exasperated. I'd reply that he was catching enough for both of us and I was happy just to be out on the bay enjoying the tranquillity of the water, the birds, and spending time with my father. Baz would respond with a shake of the head as he baited his hook, 'You're a bloody freak.'

While Wok was up north, Baz had given the boat away to my cousin Michael, the son of Baz's brother Ken. Michael lived down on the coast and Baz figured he could make better use of it. Wok was livid when he found out. He gave Baz all sorts of grief over it, saying it should have gone to him as it would come in very handy up in the mangrove creeks around Tully. Baz finally relented and said he would tell Michael it was only a loan until Wok came and collected it. I later asked Baz why he had caved in to Wok yet again. Baz said he did it for some peace and quiet and besides, he added, 'As if Wok will ever get his act together to tow it all the way to North Queensland.' Yes Baz, as if . . . In the end I just had to let these things go. If Baz wasn't going to deal with them, why should I be the one pointing out the obvious tensions that were hanging in the air unresolved? I had other things to deal with.

Like trying to get a Comedy Festival show together. As we sat in the bar of the John Curtin, with this other Warwick, Baz recalled the last occasion he had been there. It was some time in the early seventies when the pub was still the main watering hole for the unionists who worked across the road in Trades Hall. Baz had just been in there for an after-work drink when Bob Hawke, then union leader of the ACTU, had waltzed in and, in honour of some industrial relations victory or other, shouted the entire bar. Warwick shouted us the beers this time, I think as impressed by Baz's yarn-spinning ability as he was motivated by sympathy for the oxygen tank Baz was dragging around.

After we had finished our beers, I asked Baz if it was OK for us to visit one more pub. I had to go to the Standard in Fitzroy. It had been my local before I had moved back in with him, and I wanted to register for that year's footy tipping competition – even if I couldn't be physically living my inner city life, I could at least have this one tenuous connection to it. To my astonishment, Baz admitted it was a pub he had never been in before, possibly the only pub left in Victoria not on his list. There was hardly a soul in there when we entered. I hadn't been in for a while and Andy, the owner, greeted me cheerfully. He came and had a drink with us, and even though it wasn't anything particularly special, just three blokes having a quiet beer on a slow Monday afternoon, I was brimming with pride. Not only had I introduced Baz to a pub he hadn't been in, but it was one where the publican knew my name and where, this time, I was one of the boys. For possibly the first time in my life I felt I was on the same level as Baz in an environment that was traditionally his home turf. It was a milestone in our relationship.

And a week later, Baz would be dead. While sitting at the bar at the Standard, Baz had needed to use his oxygen tank but aside from this his health had generally been good. Only the week before Dr Nick had been saying that the shadows that had also appeared on his liver – the dreaded metastatic growth – had actually shrunk with the latest round of treatment and he was still confident that Baz had at least six months left in him. So none of us was prepared for what happened next.

It started on St Patrick's Day, a day that Baz had been looking forward to for months. His plan had been to put on a St Pat's feast for the boys at the club. Essentially this involved truckloads of Guinness and a couple of hundred oysters. The Guinness was not a problem – all Baz had to do as secretary of the club was to order in some extra cases from the supplier – but the oysters were more problematic. Baz was dead keen on making sure the boys got the best quality oysters, which was pretty funny really as for most of the boys the idea of haute cuisine was having barbecue sauce on their party pies. They were, in Baz's lingo, 'total Afghans'.

Baz had gone off his usual seafood supplier after the 'Christmas Crayfish Incident' in which, despite assurances that they were fresh off the plane from King Island, he had been given frozen crays which when cooked for Christmas lunch had all the flavour of a crab stick and the texture of soggy chalk. So, in the weeks preceding the big day, we had been searching for a new supplier of quality oysters. While I am as mad for seafood as Baz ever was, oysters were never my favourite but I had to admit some of what we sampled were out of this world.

With the supplier settled, the type of oyster selected ('Tasmanian, of course, you can taste the ocean in 'em, Rupe') and the menu worked out (a mixture of raw oysters with lemon juice as well as Kilpatrick, Baz style) I was surprised to find that on St Patrick's Day morning, Baz was not keen on going to collect them.

'I'm not feeling too great, Rupe,' Baz said. 'Can you go get them by yourself?'

He was still not crash hot when I left him a couple of hours later to head into the city for some business to do with my show ('I suppose I'll have to go along to this one too, hey, Rupe?') and when I returned home around eight o'clock, the house was quiet. No surprise there, I thought, as I imagined Baz would have come good and would be down at the club celebrating his Irish heritage by getting blind drunk. I settled down to wait for the phone call to come and pick him up.

Not ten minutes later the phone rang, but it wasn't Baz, it was Aunty Jan: 'Hi, love, we've just got back from the hospital. We had to take Baz down there. He's not good.'

I raced down to the hospital to find Baz deathly pale, his hands like ice to touch. He still managed a half-smile and said, 'Bloody ulcer again.'

For some reason, the usual blood transfusion hadn't managed to restore the balance and stop the bleeding. When

I arrived, they were organising a second transfusion. Baz, however, had more pressing matters on his mind.

'How'd the oysters go?'

I promised to check the club on my way home to assure him they had gone down a treat. By the time I got there, all but a few of the hardest drinking blokes had gone home. Those that were left were absolutely smashed. There were no oysters, and very little Guinness left, and I couldn't get much sense out of anyone so I assumed Baz's catering had been a great success. I told him so the next day. The second transfusion seemed to have done the trick and the colour had returned to his face. He looked pleased and smiled.

'So, the boys had a good time then? Brucey, Ando, Terry, the Pom?'

'Yes, Dad.'

'What about Stinky? Did he like it?'

'The last I saw of Stinky, he was claiming that the oysters and stout had kicked in and was staggering across the oval yelling out to Leslie to get ready for him.'

'He probably didn't make it past the cricket pitch,' Baz snickered.

'Wouldn't be surprised if he was still there. The under 12s are probably using him as the wickets at the non-striker's end,' I added.

Baz laughed out loud, and gave me the 'stop making me laugh' routine. He assured me he would be OK and as he certainly looked better than the night before, I felt comfortable about going away for the weekend to a friend's wedding in the country. In fact I barely gave him a second thought for the rest of the weekend. It was only as I turned into our street on the Sunday night and my mobile phone rang that I had any sense of foreboding.

Again it was my Aunty Jan. Where her phone call on Friday had been merely serious, this was far more edged with sadness: 'You'd better get down to the hospital now. They don't know if Barry will last much longer.'

May you never get a phone call like this. There is nothing so devastating. It is a simultaneous, dull, awful blow to both the head and the gut. It had only been a little over two years since I had received a similar call about Di. It felt all too achingly familiar, that sensation where everything seems to be in slow motion but your mind is racing with myriad thoughts, ranging from the practical (I better get Baz's address book to let people know) to the absurdly pointless (I wonder when Baz would have last had sex, and did he know at the time that it would be the last time?) and all of them leading to that one, inevitable, brutal conclusion – this person is about to die.

Baz was holding on when I arrived at the hospital, much to my relief on several fronts, not least because I had missed Mum's passing. It is said that sometimes a dying person will hold on until their loved ones leave the room, as they don't want to burden them with their going. Maybe this is what happened with Di. I was glad I found her before anyone else did, but I wished I had been there to bear witness to her last moments. I was going to make damn sure I did that with Baz. It was more fitting too.

Whereas Di had been quite private, Baz was as gregarious as they came and I am sure there was a part of him that wanted an audience.

He lasted through the night but the bleeding continued unabated despite the regular transfusions. The next morning Dr Nick and a surgeon met with Wok and me, my Uncle Tarz and my aunties Jan, Joyce and Judy ('Dr Nick, have you met the ugly sisters?' Baz piped up from the bed.) They said they would do exploratory surgery to see if they could staunch the bleeding and if that didn't work, they said there was nothing they could do; the transfusions were doing little but wasting precious resources and delaying the inevitable.

By this time Baz was in a lot of discomfort. He felt deathly cold and every so often his body would be wracked with spasms of pain. It ripped my guts out to watch on, essentially helpless. All I could do was be there and try to reassure him that it would be all right and help wipe his brow and rub his hands for warmth. I felt so absolutely bloody useless. The nurse Baz had been trying to set me up with came on duty and as soon as she walked in I could see a glimpse of the old Baz as he still attempted to lay on the charm. With her on one side mopping his sweat-soaked body and me on the other feeling pretty useless, he tried to keep up the banter and even tried to introduce us for the twentieth time: 'Jo, have you met my son Sean?'

We both rolled our eyes but this time Jo showed no embarrassment as she clearly had a job to do and not even Baz's ham-fisted matchmaking attempts could deter her. I watched her work away on Baz, at first thinking how useless we are at comforting others. I wanted her hands to bring magic to Baz, to end his suffering, to fix him. But they didn't. I could feel anger rising in me. We had lost Di only two years before and that had seemed tragically unfair. To lose Baz so soon just seemed cruel. Why couldn't Jo or Dr Nick or the surgeon fix my father? A pair of caring hands was not nearly enough. He needed a miracle, and there were none on offer.

But as I stood at the side of the bed holding one of his hands, I watched Jo work at soothing Baz and she seemed to be succeeding. He relaxed slightly and his spasms weren't so intense as before. Maybe this was the best we could hope for in life – just the mere fact of reaching out to somebody else, as inadequate a gesture as it seemed, was all that we really had. And maybe allowing somebody in was the only solace we would ever get; but at least it was some form of solace and it was better than facing the world alone.

As these thoughts soaked in, a strange feeling came over me and I realised I was having strong feelings of desire for Jo. I've never heard of anyone having such thoughts in that type of situation before but maybe that's because they aren't stupid enough to confess to something so inappropriate. But at that moment, as death seemed to be cloaking the room, she represented life – she was a mother, a nurse, a carer, and I had to agree with Baz, she was a pretty good sort. I managed to suppress any carnal thoughts and get back to the task at hand, but afterwards I did wonder, with a smile, how Baz would have reacted if I had tried to jump her bones over his deathbed. I reckon he might just have given me the thumbs-up.

As it was, even on that grim day, there were still glimpses of that cheeky, irreverent Baz. He was mortified that throughout the day he would evacuate his bowels with the blood that was flowing through his stomach. It was particularly unpleasant and Baz would be terribly apologetic. When he could feel another attack coming on he would call out for a bedpan, but the nurse said they were out of bedpans. A frantic search of the ward ensued and the bad news came back that they were all in use. Baz, who was writhing in pain at this point, was not impressed, but looked up at me and said, deadpan, 'Can't they just knock some old sheila off hers and give it to me?'

The nurses couldn't see what was so funny but I started cacking myself. It was that sort of day.

Around midday they whisked Baz off for the exploratory surgery. It didn't work. There was no one bleed that they could locate – his stomach was awash with blood. There was nothing they could do to staunch the flow. It was up to us – up to me – to say no to the transfusions, in which case he would die. They told me he would die if we continued with them, but it would be delayed by a few hours at best. Baz recovered from the sedative and said he didn't want any more transfusions. He accepted that his time had come, and felt ready. But then he asked if it was all right by me. My father was asking my permission to be excused from the room. It was his call really; I couldn't stop him for although slipping in and out of consciousness, he was still compos. He just wanted to know if it was OK by me.

Even now, almost eight years to the day after the event,

I have to stop writing this to pull myself together. For one moment, there are no jokes I can use to hold back the bursting of the emotional dam. My dad would have kept fighting a painful and inevitably futile battle to stay alive if I had wanted him to. One of the last things I ever got to do for my old man was to let him know it was OK for him to die.

Baz also wanted me to organise a priest. As we all stood there around the bed, holding hands as the priest intoned the equivalent of what I guess were the last rites, Baz, turned to me and whispered, 'I know you don't believe in this shit, Sean, but can you just play along?'

Holding back tears, I had to whisper, 'But you believe, that's what's important.'

Baz closed his eyes and let the blessing flow over him. It wasn't like the last rites as said by Father Mulcahy on *M*A*S*H** (another dinnertime favourite from childhood), but I remember there was a sense of solidarity, of everyone being there for Baz. The priest got us all to say our own blessing, one by one, to let Baz know just what he meant to us, how much we loved him. It really was a blessing indeed. Afterwards Baz seemed very happy and at peace and again turned to me and said, 'See, my mob's not that bad after all, are they?'

'No, Dad, not too bad,' I tearily replied with a smile.

So we all sat and waited for what was to come. Ace and Chris came in and Baz got to say goodbye to his two dearest friends. I think seeing them upset was about the most unbearable moment of the entire day. He was slipping fast, drifting in and out of consciousness. Every now and then he would have a spasm of pain and would cry out for his sister Judy. She'd look embarrassed as there was no particular reason why he should be calling on her when the other sisters were in the room. Jude had only been in the country for a couple of weeks. She'd probably seen him for about four weeks in total over almost forty years and Joyce and Jan had been there for Baz the whole time through both his and Di's illnesses. Maybe it was because Judy was at the foot of the bed and she was the only person he could see in the room. Joyce and Jan didn't seem too put out, but it added yet another level of strangeness to the whole business.

After a while even these spasms subsided and Baz remained quiet. There was no death rattle this time so the room was generally very quiet as we all sat by him in our misery. After a particularly long pause, Aunty Joyce said, 'Did you go to the bank, Sean?'

It may have seemed an odd thing to say but earlier in the morning Baz had said to me that he wanted to make sure we had enough money to cover expenses over the funeral period and that I should go and get some money out of his account. If I did it after he died, he said, the authorities might claim it was stealing. All of us were concentrating on how to get Baz fixed, but he was already thinking beyond that. He knew.

I hadn't got around to it and by the time Joyce mentioned it, Baz had pretty much slipped into unconsciousness, so I couldn't ask him where his card was. We searched the hospital room without luck and it was decided I should dash home as he must have left it in his bedside drawer. Home was at least twenty minutes from the hospital. As I rushed into the house, the phone rang. It was Aunty Joyce, saying to forget the card – I had to get back immediately. By the time I did, Baz was already gone. I missed him by five minutes. Just like I'd missed Di.

When I arrived back a nurse was solemnly filling out the final details on Baz's medical chart. She left the room and I was hoping that the others would do likewise as I wanted time to say goodbye alone. But nobody made to move. I felt I didn't have the right to ask them to so I said goodbye with everyone looking uncomfortably on as I let out aching sob after aching sob.

After a strained minute, in an attempt to alleviate the awkwardness, one of the aunties said, 'There's nothing wrong with a man showing his emotions. It's healthy to let it out.'

And they all nodded and cooed in agreement. At a time of such intense emotion here we all were trying to be terribly polite to each other. I would have laughed if I hadn't been keening in pain. After another agonising pause, one of the other aunties finally proclaimed, 'I think we might let you and Warwick be alone with your dad for a while.'

I couldn't have been more grateful but I was unable to meet their eyes as they all filed out. Wok left the room shortly after, as I think seeing me cry made it all the more difficult for him. Alone, I could really unleash. It had been a very intense six months, but still it was a shock. Baz should not have gone so quickly. It meant he didn't have to go through the horror of advanced-stage lung cancer where every breath would be a struggle, but even so,

I didn't want him to go. Not this soon. The floodgates had opened and there was no stopping them. I sobbed uncontrollably.

Once I was spent, I just stood there looking at the finally peaceful physical form that had been my father. After a while, my Aunty Joyce popped her head in and, seeing I'd stopped wailing, told me, 'We found Baz's card. It was in the drawer.'

She handed me his bankcard and his phone-betting card for the TAB. I looked at the latter and smiled. I knew there was still fifty bucks on the TAB card but I had forgotten to ask Baz for the password.

Much later, I headed back home, where I had been looking after Baz for the past six months. I went to the fridge and saw the plate of oysters he had kept so we could share his Kilpatrick recipe. It was a recipe I would never get to learn now. I noticed that there was only half a loaf of the last batch of bread we had baked together. I don't think I've ever made bread since. I've now forgotten that and most of Baz's kitchen secrets. He was meant to be around long enough for me to learn them all by heart.

The oysters were most probably on the turn. I took them from the fridge, scraped them from their shells and walked down to the lake and onto the jetty. I sat there and tipped them into the water, knowing they would feed the bream that Baz would no longer catch for me to cook up for breakfast.

22 WHO'S GOING TO MAKE THE GRAVY?

Seven years after Baz died, I pulled his roasting pans out from the back of the kitchen cupboard. I'd moved house four times since he died and they'd always made the journey with me. Every time I shifted house I had culled more of Baz and Di's stuff. It was always painful, letting go of those physical connections. The absolute worst was removing Baz's message from the answering machine. It was a bad, stilted recording as Baz was never at ease with technology, but it was freaking people out when they rang and heard my father answer the phone. Wiping off his voice was like losing him again. As time wore on, though, I realised that unless there was a specific reason to keep something, my life would remain cluttered with the past, unable to move forward. When we grieve for a loved one, there is the danger that we won't let go of the grief for fear of letting go of the memory of that person. The grief becomes a connection to them and to let go is to somehow reject the loved one, reject the validity of their memory. But which do you think your loved one would really want for you? To go forward in life and be happy, or to cling to that ugly bedside lamp that you never really liked anyway because it reminds you of your mother?

Having said that, I still couldn't bear to part with those metal dishes because I thought that one day I would cook a roast again. After seven years of stir-fries and curries, pasta and risotto, kangaroo steaks and noodle dishes – some of which followed what I could remember of Baz's recipes, many of which didn't – I finally bit the pullet and got those roasting pans out. When, finally, I came to cook a roast again, I decided on using Baz's favourite pan: an almost ovoid shallow metal dish with five spikes sticking up in the middle to hold the roast in place while you carved it. It looked like a medieval torture implement and the spikes made it ridiculously hard to stir the gravy adequately. But it was Baz's favourite. I think he had inherited this stainless steel beauty from his mother, Alma – maybe it was the one pan she held back from donating to the war effort to make fighter planes out of. The superstitious side of me felt that as so many magnificent roasts had rolled off that pan, maybe the magic would hold and mine could match its predecessors.

By this stage I was a few months married and we were having some friends over for dinner. I had, for some reason, volunteered to cook a roast chicken. I hadn't used those pans since those last weeks with Baz. As I fired up the oven and began preparing the chook, the heat from the oven, the clang the pan made as it hit the oven rack, the smell of the roasting bird, all conspired to make the memory of Baz and Di more palpable than it had been for years. I was suddenly transported.

St Joseph's Church in Chelsea had been packed to the rafters at Baz's funeral. The Dooley family alone could have filled half the space, but there were people from the races – bookies and more than a few punters – the Port boys, those he had worked with at other jobs, neighbours and friends and, of course, the blokes from the Sports Club. I gave the eulogy at both my parents' funerals. Public speaking was never a big thing in the Dooley family – they were most likely to be heckling loudly from up the back in true Baz style – so as it was something I didn't mind doing, the older I became the more family functions I spoke at. But it was more than that. This was the last thing I could do for my parents. During their life I hadn't been able to build them things or make enough money for them not to worry about my future (or provide for theirs) or bring them grandchildren. But I could use words and so there was never any question I wouldn't see them off with as good as I could muster. It was my parting gift to them.

During Baz's eulogy I mentioned that there would be a wake at the Sports Club and that all were welcome. One of the last things Baz said to me as he lay dying on that hospital bed was, 'Make sure you look after the boys – give them a good time at the wake.' How could I say no to such a request? I also laid it on the line that because Baz had died as a result of what he called 'those filthy, rotten, mongrel cigarettes', out of respect for him there was to be no smoking inside the club for the duration of the wake. It was my way of having a dig at the Donnys of this world, and it also meant that I and any other non-smokers could enjoy the day as the extractor fans in the club were absolutely useless and I would always come home from an evening there with Baz smelling like a smoked ham. I didn't really expect anyone to comply but amazingly, to a man, they did. Even Donny. I liked to think it was out of respect for Baz that they didn't light up, but it may even have been out of respect for me. At about six o'clock as the wake entered its fifth hour with no sign of abating, a delegation of the blokes – including Jimmy, Donny and even big scary Terry – approached me and asked respectfully whether it was OK for them to start smoking inside now that it was getting dark. I could have kissed them.

Wok, my fellow orphan, had left all of the funeral preparations to me. When the funeral director came around Wok's only request was that Baz be buried in his best suit. 'Dad was always such a good dresser,' he explained. 'He really took pride in his appearance and I know he would want to look his best.'

To me it actually seemed a waste for Baz to be dressed in a quality suit. I was convinced that he would much rather it go to somebody else. In the end I had a word to Wok and convinced him to change his mind. Wok seemed fine with this but to this day I really regret having overridden him on that issue, particularly as it was the only thing he specifically asked for. I feel now that I denied Wok his input and his chance to express something of how he felt towards Baz.

It was interesting, though, as it showed the different views Baz's sons had of their old man. To Wok, he was the classiest man he knew, certainly the best dresser. He was the exemplar of how to live a good life. To me he was a man of the people and would have abhorred the pomp as much as the waste. And though undoubtedly neat, I never thought he was a particularly sharp dresser, his style indistinguishable from many late middle-aged men of his generation: a lot of polo shirts and a little too much polyester.

I guess, being adopted, I would be perfectly placed to have an opinion in the age-old nature–nurture debate. Given that I am so totally different from both my parents and particularly my brother, you would think I would come down on the side of the argument that says your genetic heritage dictates who you are rather than your cultural heritage. But I don't think it is as easy a call as that, and I believe that what happened with Wok after Baz's death illustrates this.

At first there was no discernible change in Wok. If anything he was even more lost and angry and seemed to be heading down the same disaffected path. Before he died, Baz had said to me, 'Look after your brother when I'm gone, will you, Rupe? I don't want to see him piss his inheritance up against a wall.'

It might have seemed a harsh thing for Baz to say but, once the estate had been settled and our inheritance came through, Wok said to me, 'Sean, can you look after my inheritance for me? I reckon I'll just piss it up against a wall.'

I thought about it for a minute and then told Wok that, no,

I wouldn't look after his money for him. I said that this was Baz and Di's last gift to him and it was up to him to do with it what he wanted, whatever he felt was a testament to their lives. It was not for me to deal with. As much as I loved him, I wasn't going to jump into the role of parent, abrogating any responsibility on Wok's part. I knew that Wok would say he wanted me to look after it but the first time he rang pissed asking for a chunk of money for some hare-brained scheme or other, I didn't want to cop the abuse for saying no. It was up to him to decide what he was going to do with it. He could piss it up a wall if he liked, but it didn't have to be that way.

I wasn't hopeful, as the signs had not been good. There had been the matter of the boat. Contrary to Baz's prediction, Wok had decided to get the boat up to Tully. Unfortunately our cousin Michael wasn't coming to the party. He claimed no knowledge of Baz's intention to give the boat to Wok. As far as he was concerned it was his – he had already transferred the rego and had put a new engine in.

Wok was ropable. He was threatening to drive down to Gippsland and 'punch the living shit' out of our cousin. Thanks to Baz not being able to stand up to Wok, he left a fine mess.

I knew what Baz had said to Wok, but I had no idea what he had told Michael. Wok claimed one thing, Michael another. I was in an impossible position. I'd asked Michael to be one of the pallbearers at the funeral as his old man and mine had been such good mates. Calling him not long after on Wok's behalf was very awkward but I managed, for the sake of peace within the family, to convince him to hand over the boat if we paid him for all the expense and inconvenience he had been through.

I went back to Wok and told him of the deal I had brokered. Wok erupted; it was his boat by rights and he wasn't making any deal. I realised that Wok was more attached to his sense of injustice than he was to Baz's boat so I told him that I was finished, I wouldn't do anything more, and he better not mention the stinking boat again because I wanted nothing to do with it. Wok headed off to Queensland still not satisfied. About three months later I got a call from a very drunk and belligerent Wok demanding his boat back and if I was too gutless to do something about it he would come down and sort the prick out himself. I yelled back down the line that he had blown his chance and that I would not talk to him when he was in a state like that.

I really thought that would be the end between my brother and me, but something changed in Wok up in Tully. He suddenly realised that most of his supposed mates were just a bunch of no-hopers who were going to bleed him dry because he had some money. After a few months Wok returned to Melbourne and he actually turned his life around. When the estate was finally settled and we sold the house at Patterson Lakes, rather than piss it all up against a wall, Wok bought himself a house and, for the first time in his life, a new car that didn't require major surgery on the blocks to get it going. And most surprising of all, he bought one that only had six cylinders! Through his new neighbours he met a girl and the next thing I knew, Wok was married with two children and a steady job that he has now been in for a number of years. He stopped self-medicating and when his wife lost both her parents in under a year, he was an absolute rock. And best of all, for the past few years he has actually seemed happy.

The redemption was complete in my eyes when he rang one year to ask me if I was going to the Dooley family Christmas party. Wok had always recoiled in horror at family things, and when he did go would sullenly lurk in a corner. Now he was harassing me to come along. This was all the more amazing as the person hosting the party was our cousin Michael. I was dreading the confrontation over the boat, so I was gobsmacked when Wok walked over to Michael, shook his hand, thanked him for the party and asked how he'd been. For the first time in his life Wok had let go of a personal hurt in consideration of others, that is, his family. As he said to me afterwards, 'I still reckon that boat should have been mine, but I don't want my girls growing up not knowing their cousins.'

It was a staggering moment, one that Baz and Di would have been exceptionally proud of. It was clearly the example they had set in the way they had dealt with people all their lives that had been the deciding factor here. Wok may have been born with a set of genes that predisposed him to certain behaviour, but it was undoubtedly the environment in which he was raised that ultimately dictated how he chose to act upon those character traits. Who knows, in any other family Wok may have fallen off the rails, but there was something in the way he was raised that always just saved him from his worst excesses. It is just an enormous pity that Baz and Di weren't around to see it bear fruit. I am totally convinced that having Baz and Di as parents made Wok a far more tolerant and generous person than he otherwise would have been, whereas I believe that if I had not had them as my parents I could quite easily have become far more introspective, withdrawn and disengaged. Baz and Di gave Wok a touch of class and me a bit of the common touch.

It was a good thing that the kitchen in our flat was separated from the dining room, as the more these memories burst into my consciousness the more I needed the excuse that my eyes were red-rimmed because I had just been hit with a blast of hot air from the oven when people checked in to see how the roast was going. As I progressed with the meal, those times in the kitchen at Patterson Lakes flooded into my mind. Baz would be sitting at the bench opposite me, stubbie in hand, keeping an eye on proceedings as I went about cooking, telling me to make sure I gave the chook an initial blast for twenty minutes to crisp it up, and then as I turned the temperature down, to cover the chook in foil to stop the skin drying out completely. Then, as he was assessing whether I had skewered the bird with his special set of prongs in the correct position so that it would cook evenly all over, he would tell me some story from his past such as eating watermelon by the banks of the Murray. For probably the first time in my life I didn't find those stories annoying or tedious. Perhaps because I knew there was so little time left, I made damn sure I enjoyed the time we had. And Baz even occasionally listened to my stories.

As I took out the chicken and wrapped it in foil while I turned the oven up again to crisp the potatoes ('give 'em one last blast, Rupe') and began battling those damn spikes to start stirring the gravy, I wondered what I would have told Baz about the seven years he'd been gone.

Firstly I'd have to fess up that I had actually taken his advice and asked that nurse out. A couple of weeks after Baz's death when I was down at the hospital paying off the last of Dr Nick's bills, I made a detour to the ward Baz had been in and managed to track Jo down.

'I know that you cared a lot for Baz while he was here, and I want to say how appreciative we all are,' I began. 'And I know that Baz kept trying to set us up together, so I think it is only fair to him that we have at least one date, don't you think?'

She was stunned but agreed, probably breaking all sorts of ethical codes, but technically I wasn't her patient, so where was the harm?

Unfortunately I had no happy ending to relay to Baz. Jo and I saw each other for about a year, and it was a very happy one. She was a truly lovely person and her son was a terrific kid. As much as it pained me to admit, maybe Baz had been right about his choice of woman for me. Maybe there is something to the idea that parents do innately know what is best for their children. But the very reason Jo and I got together was, ultimately, the same reason it didn't work out for me. There was much regret in ending it, but I realised that after being there throughout Di's illness and then spending that time as Baz's primary carer, I had lost myself a bit and wasn't ready or most probably able to take on the responsibility of looking after anybody else for a while. I should have gone off and been by myself afterwards. I needed to look around and work out just where the hell I was in this world, not immediately attach myself to somebody else emotionally. The pain of losing both Mum and Dad was still so raw that it was hard to orient myself in any one direction. Under any other circumstances it might have worked out with Jo, the irony being that we wouldn't have met under any other circumstances than the one that made our relationship ultimately impossible for me.

I would then have to add a further confession to Baz, that in the aftermath of his death, it wasn't Wok that pissed his inheritance up against a wall, it was me. Sure, I could have put a substantial deposit on an inner city terrace house, which is where I had always thought I would want to live, but the thing was, I was no longer sure where I wanted to be. I was quite lost. So I bought a four-wheel drive and set off for a year's birdwatching around Australia. I was trying to break the record for seeing the most birds in a year, something I'd secretly dreamed of doing ever since I was a kid. I doubt on the one hand that Baz and Di would have understood it, but in the end I know that they ultimately wanted me to be happy. And to be honest, spending that year essentially being selfish was the best thing that I could have done. I not only broke the record but I was able to come to terms with everything that had happened in the previous few years. I had to spend an enormous amount of time by myself on long Outback drives which gave me the chance to process everything that had gone on in the previous decade. Before that year the grief was still raw. After it I was able to think of my parents without feeling as if at any moment I could double over in pain, though there are occasional moments when I am caught unawares and I will be struck by those overwhelming feelings, even ten years on.

The 'Big Twitch', as I called my project, had other unintended consequences. As I travelled I sent email reports to a birding website for other birders to share. I started sending them to my non-birding friends too, as a way of letting them know where the hell I was. They seemed to enjoy the reports even more than the birdwatchers and the seeds were sewn for a book. *The Big Twitch* was published in 2005 and what I thought was financial suicide at the time I first put the binoculars around my neck and headed out the door turned out to open up an entire new career. What I thought was the most stupid thing I had ever done turned out to be the making of me.

And once I had become quite used to the idea of being alone, (and was enjoying it) along came someone who completely knocked my socks off. From the moment I met Eleanor I thought to myself, 'Now that's the type of woman I should go out with.' It didn't actually occur to me at the time that if that was the way I felt then I should ask her out as there was a fair chance another one like her would never come along. It took a mutual friend, who suggested I call her, to make me realise there might actually only be one like El. If I had not gone through the whole Big Twitch experience, and everything that had led up to it, I would probably never have pursued her. But because I finally felt comfortable with who I was, I wasn't afraid of rejection: I knew that I was fine by myself, so I was finally in a position to take a punt on a long shot. Baz would have been proud – he'd always told me never to back an odds-on favourite. As a bookie, he would say that because he would usually lose a motza when the short-priced favourite would win. But I took it to mean more than that – Baz was telling me that if you played it safe in life, ran with the herd taking minimal risks, you might get a return on your investment but it would never be worth terribly much. Much better to take a punt, as long as you are prepared to cop the losses, because when you win, the rewards are so much sweeter. Thankfully I was in luck when it came to Eleanor, who seemed to like who I was and a couple of years on we found ourselves married and expecting our first child.

And here I was, back in the kitchen, roasting another chook. But this time I was not cooking because someone was sick; far from it, for as El wandered into the kitchen to check on my progress, she looked a picture of radiant pregnancy. With her hand resting on her belly (the baby was already overdue), she asked if there was anything she could do to help with dinner. I was stirring the gravy in Baz's pan, trying to get the right consistency. (Another of Baz's legacies – keep stirring the gravy. It may seem like it will never come together but if you persist and don't take short-cuts, you'll get there in the end and the results will be so much better than anything you can buy off the shelf.) I turned to El and said all was under control. She went to leave, nicking a piece of the roast I had just carved. Her eyes widened and she nodded appreciatively. 'That's amazing. So juicy.'

'I was taught by the master,' I said, stirring like fury. The grating of the fork on those spikes was a sound that had always annoyed the hell out of me growing up but now I found it strangely soothing. With one last vigorous stir the bubbling gravy had, as if by magic, coalesced into just the right thickness, meaning it would move across the meat like magma across a lava field. Just as Baz would have done it.

I looked about the kitchen. It really was as if I was still cooking with Baz. And I don't just mean the smells and the tastes, or even the fact that the kitchen looked like a bombsite with dirty utensils strewn over all available bench space. It was more that I was not just cooking a meal, but giving something of myself to those I loved. As she headed back to the lounge room, El gave me a broad smile as she pinched another piece of chicken and absent-mindedly touched my cheek.

You wouldn't be dead for quids.

BAZ'S TEA-BAG CHICKEN

Baz died before I could really commit any of his dishes to memory. The following recipe is how I remember him making tea-bag chicken. You don't have to use tea bags at all – tea from any source will do – but I think Baz liked the name of this dish. It appealed to his creative side without any risk of being called a tosser because tea bags are such a prosaic ingredient. It was actually the use of tahini that was exotic for Baz. Before making this, he had never even heard of it. When I told him that tahini was the main ingredient of hummus, Baz made sure that he always referred to it in the future as 'homos'. And would inevitably add, 'Homos – that's the stuff you like isn't it, Rupe?" Baz probably didn't use chilli the first time he cooked it because he didn't want to upset Di's delicate stomach, but I'm pretty sure he used it on subsequent occasions.

Ingredients
1 chicken breast per person
½ cup tahini
¼ cup plain tea
2 tablespoons soy sauce (the darker the better)
2 cloves garlic (finely chopped or crushed)
1 tablespoon sesame oil
1 tablespoon red wine vinegar
1 tablespoon caster sugar
⅓ cup spring onion or shallots.
1 seeded red chilli, chopped (optional)

Method

Combine all the ingredients (except for the chicken) in a bowl and whisk together. Pour over the chicken in a bowl or sealable container, cover, and pop in the fridge for at least a couple of hours.

When ready to cook, take out of the fridge and allow to reach room temperature. Preheat the oven to a medium heat. Take chicken from marinade and place in a roasting dish or on an oven rack lined with foil. You can put the fillets under a griller but try not to have them too close to the element or else the marinade will burn and bugger the whole thing up. If you are grilling, it might pay to cover the top with foil before it reaches this stage.

Try to turn once only as the coating can easily come off and it will look like a bloody mess when you serve it. If you like, you can baste with some of the excess mixture but my effort to emulate Baz's method has ended up looking quite ugly. (Tasted good but.) Cook for about ten minutes each side if baking (slightly less if grilling). Let it rest for a few minutes. Slice the breasts and serve on noodles or cucumber salad.

Serves 4

ACKNOWLEDGEMENTS

Although this book is based on my memories of events within my family, there were instances where I was unsure about my recall of exactly what happened when, where and to whom. To Warwick and Narelle Dooley, Janice and Arthur Mildenhall, Joyce Diamond, and John and Chris Kent, I am deeply indebted for your graciousness in providing information when requested, and for reading early drafts and pointing out where I had got things totally wrong. You never asked that I write about you yet you were always encouraging and supportive, and for that I am eternally grateful.

To the other members of my family, all the boys from the club and the races and anybody else who appears in these pages who I had neither the time nor capacity to consult, I thank you for the friendship you gave to Baz, Di and myself over the years.

To all the staff at the Peter MacCallum Cancer Centre, Beleura Private Hospital, Peninsula Private Hospital, Como Private Hospital and the various clinics that Baz and Di attended over the years, your compassion and dedication to my parents was overwhelming and I thank you all. Particularly the nurses: I was constantly amazed at how you all kept going that extra yard and were always there with a cheery smile in what must have been incredibly emotionally draining circumstances.

And to those who were with me along the way, bringing this book to fruition, I am deeply indebted. The origin of this book was a short story I wrote for the Daffodil Day Art Awards run by The Cancer Council of Victoria. It was the indomitable Andrea McNamara at Allen and Unwin who saw the potential in the idea and was willing to back it and plunge into the madness of working with me for the third time to see 'Baz' come to fruition.

This book was written with the aid of the Readings Glenfern Fellowship which provided me with a space to write for a year at Glenfern, the National Trust building which is run by the Victorian Writers' Centre. In particular, I thank Mark Rubbo, Joel Becker and Iola Matthews for making it a wonderful residency. I would also like to thank the gorgeous Janet Tait for offering up her lounge room as a temporary office space once the Glenfern Fellowship ran out.

To my beautiful wife, Eleanor, and amazing daughter, Edie, I cannot adequately thank you both for the support you gave me, the faith you've shown and the untold joy you have brought into my life.

And finally I would like to thank the nameless bureaucrat from the adoption agency for allocating me to Diane and Barry Dooley. I couldn't have asked for better parents. They not only provided the fodder for this book but inspired me in so many ways, not the least of which was the dignity and grace with which they faced their impending deaths.

ABOUT THE AUTHOR

Sean Dooley is a Melbourne author who has worked as a
television comedy writer. He is a contributor to *The Age*,
ABC radio and 3RRR, writing and talking about birds, environmental
issues, sport and, well, anything, really. But his greatest claim to
fame is that in 2002 he broke the Australian birdwatching record
for seeing the most species in the one year. He then wrote
about it in *The Big Twitch*, thereby publicly outing himself
as a bird-nerd. *Anoraks to Zitting Cisticola: A whole lot of
stuff about birdwatching* was published in 2007.

Printed in Dunstable, United Kingdom

85050397R00194